BEYOND LEANING IN
A New Kind of Novel to Spark Discussion and Change

"Melanie Ho's book makes you stop and think. It is unique—a workplace novel with characters who feel real, authentic and genuine and who are confronting hard and difficult situations. As a reader, I was constantly stopping and thinking about new concepts, all of which are grounded in research, and asking myself how can I as a leader create a better work environment for women, but also for men."
—SCOTT SCHIRMEIER, President, Technology and Partner Development, EAB Global

"In *Beyond Leaning In*, Ho creates unforgettable characters and a compelling plot that takes us beyond *Lean In* to surface the systemic obstacles working women face. This important book helps women see the real structural challenges they face. It also challenges employers to be partners in bringing about meaningful change."
—MARY PAPAZIAN, President, San Jose State University

"Melanie Ho has brought the challenging nuances of advancing gender leadership while running a highly effective organization into focus. We can relate to, commiserate with, and learn from her characters—in a way that is more accessible and, frankly, more human, than from a traditional leadership book or corporate equity and inclusion training."
—CHRIS PROULX, Global Director, Humentum

"A timely, readable, and powerfully important book for all leaders, especially now, when so many women are feeling pressure to re-evaluate their place in the corporate world, and even the workforce. If we can't find a way to create more inclusive workplaces to retain talented young women, we will all feel the consequences."
—MELANIE BOWEN, Chief Operating Officer, Mindoula

"I went into reading *Beyond Leaning In* skeptical of how different a novel would really be than an advice book. I was so wrong. I found myself unable to put *Beyond Leaning In* down, engrossed in the nuance, humanity, and depth of the characters and of its exploration of systemic inequity in the workplace. This book is both urgent and empathetic—I learned so much about work culture and about myself from reading it. I'm recommending it to everyone I know (and work with!)."
—SAMANTHA PINTO, Associate Professor of English at the University of Texas at Austin

"*Beyond Leaning In* is a page-turning novel with compelling characters and storylines. It also seamlessly weaves in authentic and timely examples of how much further we have to go when it comes to achieving true gender equity in the workplace. It's a must-read for anyone who aspires to be a leader, an ally, or simply wants a clearer sense of the hidden dynamics of professional life today."
—JOHN HSU, Founder and Principal, NLN Solutions

"*Beyond Leaning In* is a business book for the future. By weaving essential equity research and concepts into a page-turning novel, Melanie Ho gives us the perspective and understanding we need to be true champions for intersectional equity in our workplaces and beyond."
—VERONICA LaFEMINA, Managing Director, Strategy and Planning, American Diabetes Association

"*Beyond Leaning In* is one of the best books I have come across addressing the challenging and complex issues of gender equity in workplaces. Each and every character brings to life issues that all of us can relate to in one form or another. The book can be used in college classrooms, HR departments, as well as boardrooms."
—JEET JOSHEE, Associate Vice President and Dean, California State University-Long Beach.

"*Beyond Leaning In* is a cautionary tale, a mystery story, and a practical fable for our times. By turning the fictional setting of a company in trouble into a laboratory for nimbler, more equitable models of corporate culture, Melanie Ho delights and instructs, and what she teaches will make organizations stronger."
—DAVID SCHABERG, Dean of Humanities, UCLA

"*Beyond Leaning In* does an incredible job of showing the importance of intent vs. impact when it comes to workplace interactions and is an easily digestible way to comprehend some of the more nuanced issues around gender discrimination. It highlights well-intentioned but ultimately harmful choices that those in leadership can make. This book could easily be used in teams and among leadership to foster discussion on how to mitigate bias at work."
—RACHEL MURRAY, Co-CEO and Head of Community,
　She+ Geeks Out

"Dr. Ho tells a story that's both captivating and mindset-shifting. Her book's brisk plot meant that I couldn't wait to pick up the characters' threads every morning. And as I read along, I found myself thinking differently about my work, my colleagues, and the role of gender in the office."
—JEFF MARTIN, Senior Director, EAB Global

"*Beyond Leaning In* truly goes beyond equity statistics and related annual reports—it paints a picture of real-life workplace dynamics, including gender equity, microaggressions and diversities you cannot see. From Board member to intern, it's a necessary read."
—SYDNEY BROWN, Executive Coach and Corporate Consultant,
　S.E.B. Consulting

"Melanie Ho's use of a fictional workplace and all of the different perspectives of those who work there helps us to grasp the complexities of diversity, equity and inclusion. Competing interests, cultural forces, lack of awareness are all aspects that make changing attitudes and behavior such hard work. The story is so engaging and fascinating, I had a hard time putting it down."
—Lynne Schaefer, Vice President, Administration and Finance, University of Maryland, Baltimore County

"There's writing that is fun to read and writing that teaches you real, tactical things. The two types usually aren't found on the same shelf, let alone in the same book. But this book is the rare exception. It helps you see the everyday ways in which inequity is alive and well in our workplaces (and, really, everywhere). Beyond making you aware of these patterns and practices that we're all a part of, it also shares how to break out of them. And it does all of this by showing, not telling. You get rich, engaging (if infuriating) characters that feel all too real. To make any real, intentional progress on issues of inequity, we need to be willing to grapple with them. This book makes that tussle a little bit less daunting and a lot more enjoyable."
—Karishma Furtrado, Founding Staff, Director of Data and Research, Forward through Ferguson

"In *Beyond Leaning In*, we see Ho's cast of characters emerge from a cloud of unconscious programming to humility and a desire to learn. Ho takes readers on a journey and asks us to flex our empathic muscles as we inevitably see parts of ourselves in each character. It beckons the question of not only 'Where did they learn this belief?' but rather, 'When and where did *I* learn this?'"
—Huong Diep, PsyD, ABPP, Board Certified Psychologist and International Consultant

Beyond Leaning In

Gender Equity and What Organizations are Up Against

A NEW KIND OF NOVEL TO
SPARK DISCUSSION AND CHANGE

MELANIE HO

Publisher's Cataloging-in-Publication data

Names: Ho, Melanie, author.
Title: Beyond leaning in : gender equity and what organizations are up against / Melanie Ho.
Description: "A new kind of novel to spark discussion and change" — from cover. | Includes bibliographical references. | Washington, D.C.: Strategic Imagination, 2021.
Identifiers: LCCN: 2020925874 | ISBN: 978-1-954106-00-0 (pbk.) | 978-1-954106-01-7 (ebook) | 978-1-954106-02-4 (audio)
Subjects: LCSH Leadership in women. | Women executives. | Leadership. | Sex role in the work environment. | Women executives—Psychology. | Business women—Psychology. | Organizational change. | Diversity in the workplace. | Corporate culture. | BISAC BUSINESS & ECONOMICS / Women in Business | BUSINESS & ECONOMICS / Workplace Culture | SOCIAL SCIENCE / Women's Studies
Classification: LCC HD6060.6 .H6 2021 | DDC 658.30081—dc23

Cover design by: Laura Duffy
Interior design and production by: Domini Dragoone
Author photo © Ginny Filer Photography
Comics by: Melanie Ho

Published by
Strategic Imagination
6218 Georgia Avenue NW Suite 1-598
Washington DC 20011-5125
www.strategic-imagination.com

This book is dedicated to the memory of my father, Kie Ho, who explained the word feminism to me when I was a little girl, modeled his dedication to leadership and to the written word, and always encouraged me to do things differently.

Additional comics by the author are included in the back of this book.
The full collection can be found on www.melanieho.com
or by following @melanieho13 on Instagram

Want to get the most out of this book?

Download a free guide, designed to help you:

1. Reflect on key concepts and your own next steps

2. Discuss what you've learned with friends and colleagues

3. Go deeper by accessing my free multi-media content (comics, short videos, podcast episodes)

Go to https://www.melanieho.com/readers or scan the QR code to subscribe to my newsletter and download the guide.

Let's Chat!

Each month, I randomly select one new subscriber from the link above to receive a free 30-minute virtual session with me. This can be used as a coaching or consultation session or an informal coffee chat, and it can also be gifted to a friend.

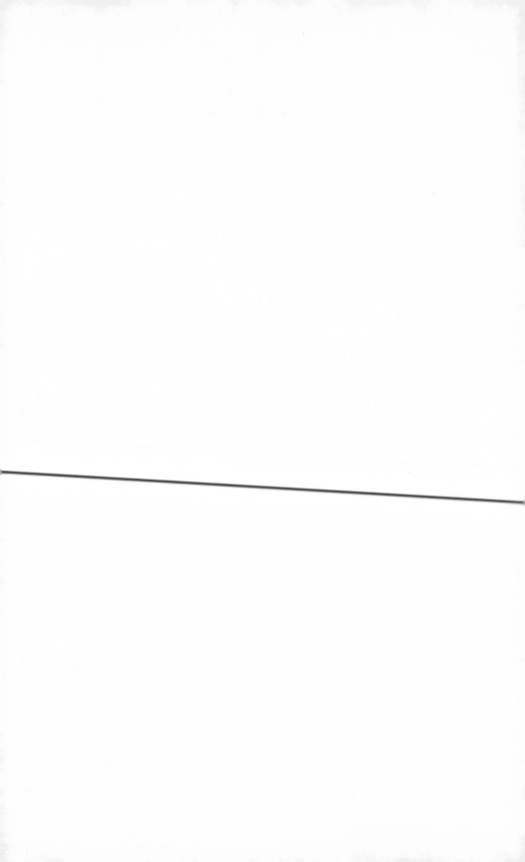

Contents

Partial Staff Roster

George, Chair, Board of Directors

Debra, CEO and co-founder

Jack, CFO and co-founder

Terry, Chief HR Officer

Leland, Chief Product Officer (replacing Natalie after she departs)

Dan, VP, Partnerships

Tom, VP, Marketing

Bart, AVP, Human Resources

Amber, Senior Director, Product Development

Meg, Senior Director, Product Development

Calvin, Senior Director, Product Development

Cassandra, Director, Learning and Development, HR

Haley, Director, Marketing

Chad, Director, Marketing

Kyle, Director, Product Development

Shannon, Director, Product Development

Rita, Director, Finance

Jessica, Intern

Paige, Intern

Ethan, Intern

Preface

The characters you're about to meet are fictional, but I hope they seem true to life. This book was inspired by hundreds of conversations with women across industries, in-depth research on gender in the workplace, and my own observations from my path to becoming a corporate executive in my thirties.

While our main character, Debra, is the CEO of a technology company, the challenges that she and her employees face in this book are universal. Over the last decade, I've talked to professionals from companies large and small, non-profits, government, healthcare, law, and education. Most women wonder if their experience is unique to their industry, or even to their specific employer. Some might find solace in the fact that many of the barriers to gender equity are the same wherever you go. That fact can be comforting, but it should also be unsettling and infuriating.

The title of this book, *Beyond Leaning In*, is not meant to diminish Sheryl Sandberg's work, which has inspired countless women, including myself. When *Lean In* came out, I was excited by the national dialogue it fostered. But I was also frustrated. Sandberg is nuanced about the many different challenges women face, but the phrase "lean in" has become shorthand for the idea that the main barrier to gender equity is women not raising their hands often enough due to a lack of confidence and/or the difficulties of balancing work and family. In truth, as women advance in their careers, they find so many other obstacles in their way.

Gender equity is not a neutral topic. Reading about or discussing the inequities around us—gender or otherwise—can naturally lead to discomfort and emotional reactions. One unfortunate by-product is that diversity discussions often lead to an unintentional sidestepping of the issues. A prominent example of this is how often workplace diversity trainings on topics like unconscious bias get wrapped up in defense of the well-intentioned. If one theme becomes clear by the end of this book, I hope it's the difference between intent and impact. Good intent does not lessen or excuse bad impact.

To that end, you won't find any villains in this book—no male bosses propounding the inferiority of women, no females determined to keep other women down, no obvious sexual predators. Our setting is a company that's doing a lot of things right, with characters who mean well. Part of what makes gender inequities feel so intractable is that they exist despite our best intentions.

We are a society that looks for simple solutions. We want there to be one root cause problem that we can weed out to make everything better. Yet it's that desire for simplicity that has stymied our progress to date. Truly confronting inequities, gender and otherwise, requires us to understand—and have meaningful conversations around—the complexity of the problem.

The good news is that getting a handle on that complexity doesn't require us all to spend years on study and analysis. What it does require is that we put ourselves in the shoes of those around us and then understand how we're all interconnected. Sometimes it's harder to gain that kind of perspective when we're too close to a situation. Without even realizing it, we fail to see crucial elements that would help us make sense of our own experience or better support those around us. Stories have a unique superpower for confronting these gaps in our understanding. They give us the opportunity to empathize with characters in a different world while providing sufficient distance to objectively examine what's getting in the way of these characters.

Beyond Leaning In is focused specifically on one component of equity—gender gaps, largely as they occur in business and in what are often referred to as white-collar professions. Throughout the book, you'll find concepts related to how inequities persist at individual, systemic, and cultural levels that likewise apply to other types of diversity (i.e., race, ethnicity, sexuality, gender identity, disability, neurodiversity, socioeconomic status, geography, and more) and a wide range of occupations. These other forms of diversity are not explored in depth in this book, not because they lack importance, but because I believe that diversity, equity, and inclusion (DEI) efforts fall short when "diversity" is collapsed into one umbrella that cannot give sufficient voice, nuance, and context to the multi-faceted barriers facing any single group or intersection of identities. If you enjoy reading this book and would like to join me in a broader conversation about equity, identity, and the workplace, please visit my website.

As you enter the fictional company in the pages that follow, you may feel angry, sad, frustrated, irritated, overwhelmed, and/or even defensive on our characters' behalf. But we cannot confront gender inequities effectively without looking at situations that ignite these types of difficult emotions. At the same time, my goal is for the glimpse into these characters' lives at work to ultimately lead to reasons for hope. At most organizations, the good intentions are there, waiting to be more effectively channeled. By understanding the world of these characters, we see our own anew—and can focus on the right solutions as a result.

Find the podcast and webcomics based on this book:
www.beyondleaningin.com

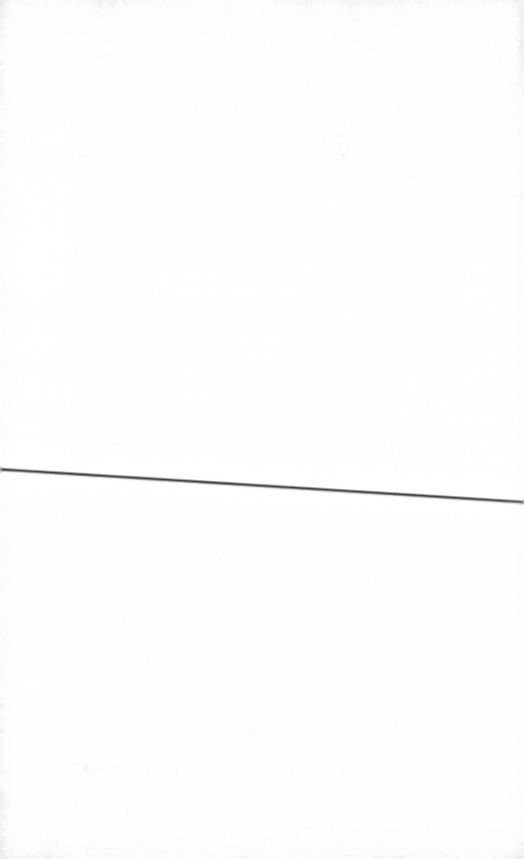

PART ONE

The Gender Engagement Gap

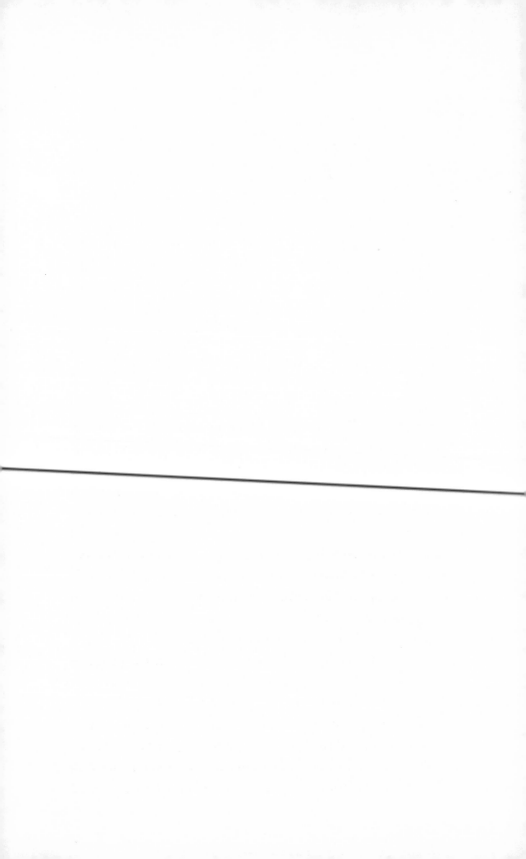

CHAPTER ONE

Natalie

"**T**his job just isn't the right fit for me anymore," Natalie said, her voice full of guilt. She was speaking at a slow, halting pace. Slow for anyone, but especially for Natalie, the company's Chief Product Officer. Her team often laughed fondly at the pace at which she talked, accompanying her words with soft, quick hand gestures, moving to the lilt of her phrases.

Today though, Natalie was facing Debra, her CEO and mentor, and she paused several times during her rehearsed speech. Her hands stayed in her lap. She felt terrified that, if she spoke at her normal pace, she would unconsciously let out an inappropriate laugh or forget everything she had entered Debra's office to say.

"I can't tell you how grateful I am to you for the amazing opportunities; how much I've loved working here."

"We love working with you too, Natalie," said Debra.

It didn't escape Natalie's attention that Debra had emphasized the present tense, as if she knew what was coming next. But Natalie couldn't let her mentor's response derail her. "I've been thinking a lot about other kinds of work I might be interested in and decided I need to devote myself to job-hunting full-time. My last day will be four weeks from now."

Debra's face remained composed, but Natalie saw the CEO's shoulders stiffen as she took a short, quick breath. When faced with slightly bad news, Debra responded immediately, with the usual verbal fluency that made her a compelling leader. When there was really bad news, *mission-critical,* Debra reminded Natalie of how she had once felt during a boat ride in Brazil she had taken as a college student, when the boat had gone straight under a waterfall.

"Can I ask what led you to this decision?" Debra was clearly trying to keep an even tone. "Do you have another position lined up?"

"I've been feeling burnt out," Natalie said. "I think it's just time for me to explore other opportunities, and that's hard to do in a job as demanding as this one." She paused. "But, again, I want to thank you for everything you've done for me, and I want to help ensure the transition is as smooth as possible for the team."

As CPO, Natalie managed almost a hundred people. Even at the age of thirty-nine, she had been on the receiving end of countless moments like this one. She knew that, for any manager, an employee resigning to focus on job-hunting—with no job lined up, no educational plans, and no personal commitments—was a special kind of slap.

She felt the guilt in her shoulders. She knew sales were down. She had seen the quarterly financial projections. None of it was a surprise—a few new competitors had entered their market, seemingly out of nowhere. The economy wasn't great. Natalie had also noticed George, their Board Chair, around a lot more lately. It was hard not to feel sympathy for Debra's predicament.

Be strong, Natalie reminded herself. Stick to your talking points.

She had rehearsed the spiel dozens of times. While cooking dinner. While on the elliptical at the gym (the person on the machine next to her had glanced over curiously before quickly looking away). She had even rehearsed it aloud to her sister over brunch last weekend.

"I don't see why this is causing you so much anxiety," her sister had said. "Aren't you feeling confident about your decision?"

"No, that's not it," Natalie had said. She'd done all the due diligence: pro/con lists on several pages of yellow legal paper, hundreds of dollars of sessions with a career counselor. The decision felt right.

Her sister had looked puzzled. "Then what's the problem? It's just a job. People leave jobs all the time."

But it felt like more than just a job to Natalie. Twelve years ago, she had arrived fresh from business school to work in sales at a small start-up. Her friends had been busy trading business cards from the kinds of places that make alumni placement offices salivate and parents namedrop to their friends. For Natalie's first six months, she had questioned her choice of going to a small, unknown enterprise.

Then she had been assigned a project where she worked closely with Debra. From those earliest years, Natalie had realized Debra had a rare gift as a leader. She could find the perfect Venn diagram intersection between your best self (which Debra saw long before you did) and the company's most pressing needs. Under Debra's thoughtful direction, Natalie had rotated through departments, been promoted early and often, and, three years ago, had advanced to CPO. In the past year, Debra had given Natalie increasing responsibilities beyond her job scope, which had been large to start with, and she was loving how much she'd been learning.

Her hand was only shaking a little as she handed Debra a manila folder. Debra looked surprised, as if she hadn't seen Natalie holding it when she entered the room. "I've drawn up a transition plan for the next four weeks to ensure my off-boarding is as successful as possible," said Natalie.

CHAPTER TWO

Debra

Debra swore to herself. The formal language. The clipped tone. All so different from Natalie's usual nature. The five-page, double-sided transition plan.

Debra had managed people for over three decades. How many resignations had she personally received in that time? Dozens…no, at least a hundred…maybe more. She had become good at pattern recognition. Sometimes, despite the person's insistence they were leaving, Debra felt a light inside. Hope. There was something about the way an individual gave notice that made it clear the situation could be turned around. In those cases, the resignation was a cry for help. Redemption was in sight.

Other times, all she felt was dread. Shortness of breath. Heat rising from her chest up into her face. Uncertainty as to whether her heart was beating faster, or slower, or somehow, impossibly, both at the same time. It was in these worst moments when she was truly centered in her body—when she knew that employee could not be saved.

But she had to try. Every tool in the toolbox.

What you do in the next twenty minutes could make or break the company's financial success this year, Debra told herself. Everyone in a corporation might be a cog, but some people were more indispensable than others.

Natalie was a lynchpin. Especially now, with sales down and Debra receiving urgent daily messages from her Board Chair, George, asking how they planned to turn things around.

"I know you've been burning the candle at both ends," said Debra. "You've mentioned before that you and your team are pretty stretched with all the new demands. What if we moved someone like Haley over from another department? Or, are there any other senior staff—in any department—where it would help if we moved them to your team?"

Debra knew that Natalie considered Haley a rock star: the kind of employee who made your life as a manager a hundred times better.

"Haley is fantastic," said Natalie.

The right words, the wrong tone. Debra could hear the "but" coming.

"And I'm sure she'd make the job a lot easier, though I don't think she'd want to leave marketing," Natalie continued. "But, even if she did, it wouldn't change my decision. This just isn't the right fit."

Clearly a talking point Natalie was determined to repeat.

"You're so good at what you do," Debra tried next, "But I know you have so many talents and interests. As you know, we're planning to open an office in Europe next year. I've really appreciated your early advice on that project. What if we moved that up, allowed you to focus all your time on that? You've mentioned before that international business was an area where you wanted more experience."

For a second, Debra thought Natalie looked tempted. Was she imagining herself living in Zurich, London, or Milan? Debra almost wished she could hand her a travel brochure right then. Or maybe a travel brochure was too old-fashioned for someone Natalie's age. What would Debra's daughter, only a few years younger than Natalie, find compelling? If only Debra could pull up the perfect photograph on her phone.

"Thanks for remembering," said Natalie. It was clear from her tone that she'd be holding her ground. "Maybe call me in a few years after the international presence has been built. I know the company will do really well abroad, and you know I've always wanted to live overseas. It's just not the right time."

Debra rotated to the next tool in her head. Salary wasn't Natalie's primary driver. If anything, she'd worried for years that Natalie would get sick of the tech sector and find a non-profit or foundation job— less money, more meaning. But still worth trying.

"Your annual performance review is coming up in a few months," she said. "Given all your responsibilities and accomplishments, I'd been planning to raise your salary 15%. We could accelerate that to occur even faster."

It wasn't an entirely true statement—they hadn't planned to raise anyone's salaries by much at all, given the current budgetary situation. But Natalie didn't need to know that.

Debra hated not consulting with Jack, her CFO and co-founder, on a financial matter when things were so tight, but she knew he'd understand and agree. He took pride in having personally recruited Natalie as one of their MVPs—most valuable players—at a networking event years ago.

"That's very generous," said Natalie, "And thank you, really. That means a lot to me. But my mind is made up."

"What if you shifted to 50% time? That would give you time to job-hunt." Not ideal. But half of Natalie would be better than nothing. "We could be as flexible as you need with your schedule; you could have your pick of assignments."

Natalie politely declined, again.

"Is there anything else you can say to elaborate on your decision?" Debra asked before adding, "It feels like you're biting your tongue."

It was a phrase they often used among the executive team when they discussed anyone—whether themselves or their staff—having beliefs, worries, or frustrations that they weren't expressing. Usually, when Debra asked Natalie if she was biting her tongue, Natalie would either say that Debra was mistaken (and she was just distracted by something else going on at work or in life), or admit that yes, she'd been withholding.

This time though, Natalie only repeated, "It's just not the right fit."

Debra took the hint and sighed, longing for a glass of the Pinot Noir that was stashed in her desk drawer. She took pride in her skills as CEO—God knows, it hadn't been an easy journey to the top—but how had she been so out of touch not to see this coming? True, Debra had been feeling for some time that there was a generational gap; that she didn't understand the concerns raised by some of the rising senior women. It wasn't unusual for someone like Debra, having recently celebrated her sixtieth birthday, to feel distant from her daughter's generation. But now Natalie was the fourth senior woman in the past year to depart. The other three had also been on the younger side of the leadership team: in their thirties or early forties, those that could probably be categorized as older millennials or the end of Generation X.[1]

Debra knew she wouldn't get any more details from Natalie today. She promised to look over Natalie's transition plan. She knew it would be impeccable.

CHAPTER THREE

Jack

Heads up—we're discussing engagement survey results at the
ELT meeting today. Big gender gap—women 20% less engaged
at senior levels.

Fuck, Jack thought as he looked at the text message he'd received from his CEO Debra while standing in line at the gourmet coffee bar that they had installed on the third floor of their office building.

As CFO, Jack didn't typically allocate mental space to things like the employee engagement survey. Such matters resided squarely in the fuzzy domain of Terry, their Chief Human Resources Officer. But a gender gap wasn't good—especially now, with all the national attention on challenges women faced in the workforce. And especially the day after Natalie had given notice. He, Debra, and Terry hadn't yet figured out how to communicate Natalie's impending departure to the staff.

Even more troublesome for Jack: there was no way the engagement survey results wouldn't be stinging for Debra. She had fought her entire career for issues related to women's leadership. Jack took pride in the fact that, in the three firms where they'd worked together at varying points across their careers, he had helped her do so. At the management consulting firm where they'd both started working right after college, Jack had been a few years ahead of Debra. She often credited him with helping her navigate the hostile culture for women that had been the norm then. He considered himself enlightened. Neither of them wanted the technology company they founded together to be one where women were less engaged than men.

But sales were down 10%. For Jack to do his job as CFO, he couldn't have Debra being distracted by anything that wasn't directly connected to the bottom line. So he mentally swore twice as he read Debra's text.

Fuck #1: the survey results themselves.

Fuck #2: now he'd have to contend with a distracted CEO. This was the kind of thing that would keep Debra awake at night, exactly when she needed to either be obsessing over their sales numbers or *maybe* sleeping so she'd be refreshed to do so in the morning.

"Are you sure you don't want to try one of our gourmet syrups?" the young barista asked Jack, as he did every day. "Or perhaps a latte—we've got almond, coconut, and oat milk." The barista had no idea that every day, Jack bristled inside at this question. How much did all those milk alternatives cost? Did they even finish one container before having to throw it out?

Outwardly, he smiled, put on his reading glasses, and peered curiously at the tabletop chalkboard where someone wrote the flavor of the day each morning.

"Pistachio! What's that like?"

Jack liked to think of himself as a young sixty-two, but his coffee-drinking habits were set. It was black and scalding or nothing. However, he knew that even meaningless banter with an executive like himself carried a larger symbolism for the front-line staff. *"The executives are really friendly and approachable"* was a comment that had been posted on Glassdoor, the website where employees reviewed their employers. Terry had forwarded it to the Executive Leadership Team, or ELT. She frequently told them that such things mattered when trying to recruit the best talent—millennials in particular apparently looked for "social proof" on potential employers online the same way they did for restaurants and pop-up bars.

After retrieving his coffee, Jack entered the elevator and pushed the button for the eighth floor, where the twelve members of the ELT met every other Tuesday morning. Jack was the last one to arrive at the large conference room adjoining Debra's suite.

For the most part, their Santa Monica office building was decorated as you'd expect of a technology firm: modern furniture, funky accent chairs, mini fridges stocked with no fewer than three flavors of sparkling water and two types of coconut water.

Debra's suite was the lone exception. The centerpiece of the room was a U-shaped mahogany table, which she polished herself every Friday evening before leaving for the weekend. Fifteen high-backed black leather chairs surrounded the table, with a row of smaller chairs along the side of the room. A navy accent wall boasted framed photos and articles about the company along with a shelf holding various plaques and trophies. At the other end of the room, there was a pull-down projection screen above a narrow mahogany console that always held a pitcher of ice water, several glasses, and two stacks of marble coasters.

As Jack sat down, he did what he always did when he entered a meeting. He looked around the room at the attendees who had arrived before him and calculated the cost of all the coffee they'd brought with them. If he squinted, he could make out the Sharpie writing that revealed what was inside each cup: PKS for pumpkin syrup, AM for almond milk, MCH for matcha. Jack knew, down to a cent, how much each drink cost. These were not details worth the space in the CFO's brain. But Jack couldn't help it. Once he knew a set of numbers, they wouldn't leave his head.

He tried to excise this train of thought from his mind so that he could listen.

Terry, the Chief Human Resources Officer, was holding forth before the group, fiddling with a laptop while projecting slides on a screen. "As you all know, this year, we decided to contract with an outside firm that specializes in employee engagement surveys. The survey provides a pulse check on how employees feel about their jobs, whether they're likely to stay at the firm, areas where we're strong, and where we need to improve. Based on how staff answer a series of questions, our vendor provides an engagement score for our employee base as a whole as well as individual departments or segments. We can also benchmark against similar organizations. In the future, we'll be able to see where we've improved or worsened compared to previous times."

Terry then clicked quickly through a bunch of slides.

After Debra's text message, Jack felt relieved that Terry had a lot of good news to report. Especially when their performance was compared to the national averages. Their employees, on average, were happier, liked their managers better, and felt more confident about their career paths than at similar firms. They were more likely to recommend the job to a friend. Even the negatives—they needed to upgrade their sustainability policy, better training for entry-level staff—were areas where the ELT had been spending a lot of time lately. They hadn't been caught completely off guard.

The next few slides included qualitative comments. *"I'm always inspired by my co-workers to do my best." "We have a great mission." "I've learned and accomplished more here than I thought possible." "Our team environment feels like a wonderful family."*

Even if he hadn't received Debra's text, he would have known that Terry was building toward bad news. You wouldn't waste the time of the executive team with half a dozen slides of positive comments unless the other shoe was about to drop.

A title slide came on the screen, announcing that other shoe: GENDER GAP.

"There's a slight gender difference in the results for junior- and mid-level employees," said Terry as she flipped to the next slide. "But across almost every department, women at the director level and above are about 20% less engaged than men."

Terry's eyes drifted to the framed articles and plaques on the far wall of the room. Jack followed her gaze.

Was she looking at the framed business magazine articles about the mentoring program that Debra had created for high-potential women? That program had helped increase the percentage of women in senior positions from 30% to 45% over five years.

The awards for being a great company for working parents? They'd sent company-wide announcements each time and featured the accomplishments on their recruiting website. Many of their most talented recruits, both men and women, had reported that these awards had positively influenced their decision to apply.

There were also profiles of Debra herself as a CEO who had shattered glass ceilings and gained a reputation for helping women across the tech industry and beyond. The women on Jack's team often mentioned to him how meaningful they found it to see a strong woman at the helm, especially in tech.

Jack turned his attention back to Terry. Usually, HR people had a talent for hiding their emotions. On most days, Terry seemed almost robotic to Jack, albeit in a vaguely pleasant way. Today, despite herself, she sighed audibly before clicking to the next slide.

"After seeing this data, I had our team run some of the numbers on departures," said Terry, fiddling with the clicker. "80% of senior departures over the past three years have been by women, even though women are only 45% of the senior team."

Fuck. He and Debra had speculated that the retention data was pretty bad, but this was the first time he'd seen the numbers. He looked around the room at the rest of the ELT. Most of the group looked as appalled as him. Surprised, too. They were staring at the data on the screen and couldn't look away. But the youngest members of the executive team? Unhappy, but not nonplussed. Half of them were exchanging knowing glances with one other—as if to say, *"Why is everyone so surprised?"* The other half were staring down at the glass conference table as if they were afraid they'd unintentionally exchange a knowing glance.

"We just got these results yesterday," said Debra. "For me, it was a bit of a shock, thinking about how much work we've done to support women leaders. But obviously there's more to be done. Let me assure this group that we'll be doing everything we can to better understand what's driving this data."

Jack worried about the "everything." We won't have time, he thought to himself.

PART TWO

Denial

CHAPTER FOUR

Debra

Later, Debra would reflect on two mistakes she made in the following weeks.

The first mistake occurred during a meeting Debra had with Jack and George about the ELT's goals for the year.

They met at Thai Pantry, a hole-in-the-wall restaurant that might have seemed like an odd place for three high-powered executives to meet. While the venue had a few windows facing the outside world, they were oddly tinted in a dark gray that let no light in. Moreover, the dim lighting did nothing to disguise the fact that the rice noodles tasted as if they had been smeared in ketchup, and the chicken satay was unforgivingly dry.

However, the restaurant was located exactly four blocks from their office: the perfect radius to ensure a leadership lunch at peace. The lunch patterns of their staff were fairly predictable. Within three blocks of their building, mediocrity in food was excusable for convenience. Four blocks or more, the food had to be memorable. Thai Pantry was the perfect example of neither A nor B, not memorable or convenient. In other words, Debra could dine there without concern that her staff would interrupt or overhear.

Any CEO worthy of the role had the sense to know that ears literally were everywhere. But Debra's worry about eavesdroppers had grown tenfold over the last few years after George retired younger than planned and became dedicated, to say the least, to his role as Board Chair. It felt like she and Jack were constantly trying to get ahead of his next demand. Some of his ideas were smart; others so foolhardy that she feared any staff overhearing George's musings would totally lose confidence in who was steering the ship. (Thank God she had talked him out of acquiring his nephew's failing start-up.)

As they waited at their usual Thai Pantry corner table for him, she wondered how the lunch would go and realized she'd forgotten to breathe.

George walked in a few minutes later. "Just flew in from Chicago this morning, and I brought you your favorite popcorn from the airport," he said, handing her a bag of the familiar caramel-and-cheese popcorn mix. For Jack, he had brought a stuffed hedgehog. "I remember you said your granddaughter Juliet collects these. Happened to see one in the hotel gift shop."

This was the good change in George now as opposed to the George she'd first met a decade earlier. Before, he probably hadn't even known Jack had a granddaughter, much less her name or favorite animal.

He set his briefcase down on one chair and sat down on another. "I had a good call with some of your engineers this morning," he said. "They helped explain a few of the bugs I'd noticed in one of the apps I was on last week."

This was the bad change.

Discussing bugs in a single app was the kind of micro-managerial, "in the weeds" behavior she'd worry about if anyone on her executive team engaged in, much less their Board Chair. As she considered how to reply, her gaze went to his green paisley tie and gray blazer. George still always wore a suit every day, even though he'd left his wealth-management job four years earlier to care for his wife when she was first diagnosed with cancer. After she passed a few years after that, he had decided to stay retired. That meant all his energy now went into this company.

How do you tell someone who is using work as therapy that they need to stop? She and Terry had discussed the need for her to say something six months earlier; Debra had even reread her well-worn copy of *Difficult Conversations* in anticipation. And then, just as she had been ready to broach the subject, they had suddenly been hit by a new competitor. The economy had taken a turn. And the sales problem had become a serious one. At that point, she'd lost the opportunity to say he needed to get out of the way.

Debra felt her jaw clench and was reminded of her dentist telling her that she needed to stop grinding her teeth at night. "We're definitely on the bugs issue," she said.

An empty sentence—after all, when were there not bugs? But she really didn't have a more elegant way to change the subject. She took the mahogany padfolio out of her handbag. "I've brought a one-pager outlining our annual ELT goals," she said, pulling out three copies of the document. Pale blue paper with a crisp Arial font outlining the company's financial goals and the ELT's top priorities for the year. Two new mobile app launches. Four relaunches. A big IT systems implementation. Redesigning their sales processes. All while selling one of their apps that no longer fit with their portfolio to another firm.

A list like that might typically take the company two or three years to complete—and not without most of the staff working frequent nights and weekends. But George had made it clear that this wasn't the time for a "normal" pace—they'd be expected to complete these goals by the end of the year.

"This looks good and more or less like what we discussed via phone last week," said George. "But the last goal here is new to me: Investigate and resolve senior gender engagement and retention gap. What exactly does that mean?"

Debra had added the item to the end of the list just that morning. She'd typed the line, deleted it, typed it again, hit delete. Cycle, rinse, repeat. At least four or five times. It had stayed on the list, less out of conviction but because she'd just retyped it when she looked at the clock and realized it was time to hit print before lunch. Reality check? She wasn't sure how they would get the rest of the list done, much less an ambiguous item about engagement. But then she thought about Natalie, the engagement survey results, the data that Terry had shared about the retention of senior women leaders. Could she just let all that go?

"There's a pretty big engagement and retention gap when it comes to senior women," she said to George.

She saw the puzzled expression on his face and wished she'd contemplated the right messaging earlier. Decades of experience had taught her that, even while executives liked to tout old-school management aphorisms like "culture eats strategy for breakfast," mentioning "people issues" would get women leaders associated with a softness that inhibited their effectiveness. The higher she climbed the ladder, the more she realized the way to survive was to keep her thoughts about squishy topics like engagement to herself—compartmentalized somewhere in her brain to worry about later until those thoughts eventually faded from her consciousness.

George leaned back in his chair. "You know that gender equity is really important to me," he said.

The statement sounded canned, but she knew it wasn't just an empty phrase. She remembered him calling her after he'd read *Lean In* with his daughters and had been eager to discuss it.

"Look at how many awards we've won for family-friendly policies, how much the women admire you, Debra, as their leader," George continued. "But I worry about your time and the executive team's time. Everything else on this piece of paper is going to be hard to get done on its own."

When Debra didn't answer him right away, he added more directly, "If we don't get all the business objectives on this piece of paper done, there's no way we'll improve our sales fast enough to satisfy our investors. We might even need to resort to layoffs."

She let that hit her. Layoffs wouldn't be good for anyone—men or women. Before she could say anything, George softened his message slightly, though his tone—the verbal equivalent of a cement wall— did not change. "A 10% sales decline isn't the end of the world—I know you were all caught off guard by new competitors, and I've seen this company bounce back before. But the market's tougher now. Knowing that, do you think there is any executive bandwidth to do anything else?"

She'd had to preside over massive layoffs a few times during her career. Each had been dreadful, especially having to decide who stayed or went. Debra looked at Jack and registered his concerned expression. It wasn't just the employees' jobs that would be on the line, but theirs too if they didn't improve the numbers. They could be forced to leave this company they'd built together and had expected to be their last big hurrah before retirement.

"I'm not saying do nothing about the gender gap," said George. "I think you need to have Terry revisit the policies: maybe there's more you can do with that women's leadership program you started a few years back. I just wouldn't spend a lot of time worrying about this. You're doing all the right things—more so than most companies. Think of all the awards you've won. The numbers are probably a fluke."

Weren't numbers always a fluke when someone didn't agree with them? But she also knew that George had a lot of good points. They *were* doing the right things. She looked again at the goals sheet in front of her. There *was* so much to get done.

Jack was always careful not to disagree with her too strongly in front of George—a united front was important for smooth Board/management relations—but he spoke tentatively at this point. "I am pretty worried about how we're going to get everything done as is, Debra," he said. "That doesn't mean we should do nothing. I'm concerned too. But remember that idea you had a few weeks ago for holding a guest speaker series with female executives from other companies? Let's have Terry's team start planning that. Seems like a good quick win."

"Yeah, I guess that makes sense," Debra said slowly. A guest speaker series seemed hollow compared to the problem. Could that really make a dent in the engagement results? It was hard to imagine what kind of magical guest speaker could have kept Natalie from quitting.

But it wasn't like she had a better idea. How could she know what to do next when the younger women were all biting their tongues?

Her mind flashed to images of watching people having to leave with their boxes. The sum of years at the company thrown into a 2x2x2 cardboard void after being told their roles would no longer exist.

Perhaps Jack and George were right. They couldn't afford the distraction. She scratched the last item off the list in front of her.

That was her first big mistake.

The second big mistake was hiring Leland.

In her final weeks, Natalie had tried advocating for Amber, a senior director on her team and her clear number two, to be her replacement. "You know Amber has been stepping up to so much of my job already as you've asked me to focus on other company-wide initiatives," Natalie said. "She's completely ready, and you and I have both told her in the past that she has a future as a CPO. As I've mentioned in her performance reviews, there are a lot of parts of the jobs where she'll be much stronger than I ever was—she's really the perfect fit."

Debra asked Jack what he thought as the two co-founders found themselves back at Thai Pantry only a few days after their lunch with George.

"I think Amber's great," Jack mused. "But she's moved really quickly up the organization—is she ready? She's just really young. I wouldn't want to overwhelm her."

"I've been really impressed by Amber," said Debra, "And I trust Natalie's judgment." She paused. "But I don't know how we'd make it work. Both the two new product launches we've promised George and the Board are in areas where Amber has the greatest expertise. Even though she'd still theoretically oversee those projects as CPO, she won't have as much day-to-day impact on them if she's busy doing everything else. Can we afford to divide her attention like that?"

"I was thinking that too," said Jack. "In a lot of ways, Amber is more valuable continuing in her current job rather than being promoted to CPO. I think it'd be easier to find another person to do the CPO job than to replicate the kind of expertise Amber has doing her current work. Do you remember Leland? Maybe we should give him a call."

"Would he really be interested in a change?" Debra asked. She remembered meeting Leland over mini-quiches at one of Jack's holiday parties. He had been half a decade behind her as a UCSD undergraduate, so they had mostly bonded over a few professors they both remembered before talking briefly about work. He wasn't a CPO yet, but he was in charge of a large team at his company. From what she recalled, he loved his job.

"I saw him at the racquetball club last week," said Jack. "He doesn't really have any opportunities to advance in his current gig. I bet he'd be interested."

Debra paused and rubbed her right index finger against her temple. "Amber will be pretty upset. Do you remember last year when we asked Natalie to start doing more outside of her job purview and Natalie started delegating more to Amber?"

"I remember," said Jack. "We were in a tight budget time, and we didn't give her the raise she asked for. We figured we could try to keep her dissatisfaction over salary down by reassuring her that we were grooming her for Natalie's position—that the extra work compared to her peers wasn't for nothing, especially as Natalie would continue to take on other responsibilities, maybe eventually lead our international expansion."

"Yes," said Debra. "We told her we couldn't imagine anyone but Amber becoming the CPO after Natalie."

"Well, she can still be CPO someday," said Jack. "She's young. What, in her mid-thirties? It's amazing she has so much responsibility already at that age—a lot more than I did at that point in my career. She'll have plenty of time to advance. We just need to help Amber see that she has plenty of time to get where she wants to go." He paused. "Anyway, Leland's a good guy. She'll think so too, I'm sure."

Debra worried it wouldn't be quite as easy as Jack hoped. But she didn't see any other options. They'd have to interview Leland, of course, but that felt like a formality, especially as Debra looked at his LinkedIn profile on her phone while she and Jack waited for the check. His resume was impressive. They knew a lot of people in common.

As she and Jack exited the restaurant, she felt lighter than she had in while.

Most of Leland's interview went well. That was all that mattered, right? For the first thirty minutes of their conversation in her office, he elaborated on the accomplishments on his resume with the right blend of specificity (so you knew he wasn't just B.S.-ing), confidence (he took pride in his work), and humility (he wouldn't be a jerk).

The last thirty minutes left her feeling uncertain though. She shifted her attention from questions about his resume to the "behavioral questions" that Terry had given her.

"Tell me about a time when you had to make a decision with imperfect information," Debra said, flipping to a clean sheet in her steno pad to jot down his responses.

"Well, a lot of decisions are marked by imperfect information, so I don't know if I can pick one," he said, suddenly losing the confidence of his earlier answers. It almost sounded like he was talking to himself, not to her. "I think of decisions a little bit like I think about hiking. Sometimes you reach a fork in the path and need to decide where to go."

He wasn't about to cite Robert Frost, was he? Debra noticed that he was speaking in the rising declarative, ending each of his sentences as if they were a question. He'd been doing that the whole time, she realized, but now it had become particularly acute. That manner of speaking was a pet peeve of hers—it made her doubt whether the person had conviction in their statements or was truly questioning what they were saying.

But she didn't want to judge him on speaking style—what mattered was the substance.

"You really have to take in all the information around you," Leland said. He scratched at his beard for a few seconds before continuing. "Footprints on the ground. The breeze. Is there water nearby? Have you been here before? How long are you going to walk down one path before deciding if it's right or if you need to turn around? Are you optimizing for the path that's quickest, or most scenic?"

Not helpful. The point of behavioral interview questions was that, in asking someone to tell you about how they faced a situation in the past, you'd be able to extrapolate how they might deal with something similar in the future. All she knew about Leland from his answer was that he'd probably drive a lot of people crazy while on a hiking trip—standing in one place philosophizing while the rest of the party made it to the campsite without him.

She tried a few other similar questions—all in the hopes of gaining an understanding of Leland's decision-making style, and especially how he'd do in their fast-moving enterprise. What they needed from him would be greater agility than in his current, larger, and more established company.

For each question, his answers were similarly amoebic.

"I just worry he'll be passive when it comes to the decisions we need him to make," she told Jack and Terry that day. The three of them were sitting at the small table near the window in her office to compare notes on their interviews with Leland and make a decision. Under normal circumstances, for such a senior position, they would have done a lot more interviews, brought him in over several days. They would have seen multiple candidates for comparison.

However, desperate times called for less-than-ideal shortcuts. Those products they'd promised George they would grow wouldn't relaunch themselves.

"Yeah, I wish he'd have gotten to the point faster," said Jack. "But he reminds me of Mac." It took her a while to place the name. Then she recalled a quiet and mild-mannered vice president at one of the firms they'd worked together at decades ago. "People thought Mac was passive because he was just so nice and quiet like Leland, but he was very entrepreneurial, a real go-getter. You know, not one to bluster."

She looked at Terry. "Some of his answers are a bit of a red flag," Terry said. "But you mentioned the first thirty minutes of the interview went really well, right? His references check out. My team could do some more intensive recruiting, but it'll probably take three to four months minimum to find someone—and there's no guarantee we'll find a better candidate."

They could consider Amber, Debra thought to herself. Of course, that would just create another hole—they'd have to find a replacement for Amber. Besides, Leland had almost two decades more work experience than Amber. Perhaps he wasn't good at the interview, but with his extra years, he would likely be even better than she was when it came down to the job.

"You're right," she said. "Those first thirty minutes did go well. There's just too much to get done without having a CPO—not without putting an unreasonable amount of extra work on the team, and that's the last thing I want to do."

"No hiring decision is ever perfect," said Terry.

"Exactly. This is just how business works," agreed Jack.

"Okay," said Debra, "Let's make the offer."

CHAPTER FIVE

Leland

L eland had been CPO for six months since joining in January. Two months earlier, he'd stopped trying to sit at the head of the table when he convened his departmental leadership team. What did it matter; they didn't respect him. He knew that his suit fit—it was tailored, and expensively—but whenever he sat in front of them, he felt like the sleeves were too short. He wondered if a rip had appeared in the elbow since that morning. Sometimes he even found himself checking, even though he knew it wasn't there.

Also, he had gained weight since he'd started the job. Many days were too busy to eat a real lunch, and he found himself snacking on potato chips and Twix bars all day. And workout routine—ha! Come to think of it, maybe it wasn't his imagination.

Maybe the suit was too small and about to rip at the seams.

As if he would have time to buy a new suit. Double ha. If he weren't running this meeting right now, he'd probably collapse in delirious laughter under his desk at the thought.

When he'd arrived at the firm at the beginning of the year, Debra and Jack had told him that sales were down 10%. This morning, the ELT had learned from Jack that sales were down *another* 10%. If it weren't for the success of the new products—which, in all honestly, were mostly Amber's doing, not his, even if she did technically report to him—they'd be down even more. The existing products, a good chunk of which he was expected to relaunch, were all tanking.

His team couldn't be held entirely accountable—sales and marketing were obviously culpable too. At least that's what he told himself when he wanted to feel better. He'd inherited the problem, and there were others who, one could argue, should have been even more accountable for fixing it.

But could he point to anything concrete he'd accomplished to help?

Sure, Debra had praised Leland for rewriting an inter-office memo template, something that he'd hoped would improve product, sales, and marketing team collaboration during these high-pressure times. He'd done something similar at his previous company, and that meant he could adapt his old template, finding a way to add value right away. But he knew this accomplishment was small potatoes, something they could have hired a junior manager to do at one fifth the salary cost. Not the kind of accomplishment any self-respecting CPO would ever put on their resume.

Leland had considered himself highly adept at his previous job, even though he had worked for a bullying CPO named Rick—Leland's female friends at the office liked to say that Rick was "the embodiment of toxic masculinity." Rick's toxicity wasn't just psychological: he even forced his direct reports to hold managerial check-ins on his cigarette breaks. Leland wondered how much secondhand smoke he'd inhaled sitting on that wooden bench in the courtyard behind their office building.

It was bad enough when Rick smoked while sitting on the bench next to him. When Rick was really angry, he tended to stand up and tower over Leland, smoking and shouting at the same time.

He had managed to put up with all that. He knew that Rick's

interactions with him—alternating between indifference and fury—
said more about Rick than they did about him.

He'd been looking forward to working for Debra. But every time
she bestowed her damningly faint praise on him, it felt even worse
than Rick's ire. It felt almost like she was trying to convince herself,
through his occasional glimmers of value, that she hadn't made a terrible decision.

Now, as he sat at the conference table with the leadership team
that reported to him, he looked down at the stack of twenty 5x7 index
cards he'd neatly arranged in front of him. He'd spent several hours
at 2:00 am carefully writing down what he would say at the meeting.
Admittedly, it was a mishmash of different topics. What they needed
to do to increase efficiencies so that cost savings could make up for
the shortfall in revenues. His philosophy of product innovation. How
they could do a better job supporting the marketing team.

It was a good thing Debra wasn't there. He knew she'd see the
index cards as representative of many of his larger problems. He was
unfocused, trying to do too many things at once, and then doing
nothing as a result.

But no matter. What he needed was to get through the bullet points
on the twenty cards as quickly as possible. Then they'd all stop staring at him, waiting to see what he was going to say next. Judging him.
He could move to the next item on the agenda; let someone else talk.
He read the first card. He didn't look up, didn't want to see their reaction.

He read the second card. What's wrong with you Leland, he
scolded himself. You can't run a meeting staring down at index cards.
Make eye contact. Look around.

But then, out of the corner of his eye, he thought he glimpsed a
few glances exchanged. Better to not look up and know for sure. He
couldn't afford to think about how much they disliked him.

He read the third card. He told himself that the best way to get
them to respect him was to make sure he said the right thing; got the
message right. He wouldn't remember what to say without reading

the cards. Some days he barely remembered what each of his direct reports did. Ironically, he'd probably feel better if they were just honest and told him he was an idiot, but instead they almost looked sorry for him.

The weekend before, in-between doing work emails at home, he had met up for a beer with a friend from his old job and tried to find the right words to describe how his new team seemed to view him. "It's like...sympathetic disdain," he had finally said.

"Man, that's rough," the friend said. "But you finally got the corner office. You're big time. Who cares if they don't like you. You're in charge."

The friend had given him a fist bump. This felt wrong and a bit juvenile for two men in their fifties, but Leland had done it anyway. It would have been rude or awkward not to return the gesture. He had tried to see himself in his friend's eyes. He had always wanted to be a CPO, and he'd finally achieved that. Debra had been busy for the last few months selling one of their less aligned apps to another company. As a result, she'd given him a lot of independence—or a long rope.

He read the fourth card. It wasn't his fault that the company had been in such a bad spot when he arrived. He was trying to help. Who cares if they didn't like him?

He read the fifth card. But he did care. He'd always gotten along so well with his teams in the past. He'd been successful at every job he'd had. He'd never experienced anything like this before. Was this what happened when you got to the corner office—or was it him?

Sixth card. Maybe they were right. He had no idea what he was doing.

Seventh card. Had he ever seen an executive staring down at cards to remember what to say? No. What was wrong with him? But he couldn't stop. It was easier to pretend he didn't know what they thought of him as long as he kept looking down.

Ninth card. He cursed Jack for that day on the racquetball court, when Jack had told Leland that this job would be an easy transition for him. He cursed his own hubris for believing it. He cursed his new team for not appreciating him, not helping him.

Tenth card. He looked up briefly. A few of them nodded politely, but others looked completely distracted. Texting. Staring out the window. He felt even more self-conscious and accidentally flipped too many cards and fumbled until he found the right one.

Eleventh card.

Twelfth card. They seemed like nice people. He saw that they cared about each other.

Thirteenth card. Most of them had worked together for a long time, but not all of them.

Fourteenth card. So that meant they weren't categorically against outsiders. Just him.

Fifteenth card.

Sixteenth card. But it wasn't his fault. Could anyone succeed in this job? He wanted the business to succeed. For God's sake, he had made these index cards at 2:00 am.

Seventeenth card. Almost there.

Eighteenth card. God, he was bad at this. It was a small comfort that neither Debra nor Jack had attended this meeting. When he'd first started at the company, they told him that he needed to establish himself with his team independently. He suspected they'd soon decide it had been too much rope. He'd felt like this ever since the financial results came in for the half.

Nineteenth card. Not his fault.

Twentieth card.

Done.

CHAPTER SIX

Debra

As Debra left the office to drive to George's, her assistant gave her a sympathetic smile and handed her a dark chocolate bar, even though it was only 10:00 am. Debra slipped the candy into her handbag, aware she'd need it later and grateful that her assistant had known without being asked. There was only a small number of staff at the company—mainly the most senior executives and those who supported them—who understood that when George called you to meet him at his home office, it couldn't be good.

As Board Chair, it was certainly George's prerogative to meet on his own turf. However, he rarely asked them to do so. Instead, he loved driving to their offices near the beach or finding an interesting new venue for a working breakfast or lunch. He only held meetings at his penthouse condo downtown when he wanted to make it clear that he was in charge.

When she got to his home office, he didn't bother to offer her a cup of coffee or a glass of water, even when his housekeeper brought him both on a marbled tray as soon as Debra sat down. Another power play. Usually, he went out of his way to be hospitable—or at least to ensure that "the help" was demonstrating the hosting prowess for which he paid them handsomely.

At least she'd anticipated this, Debra thought as she took the water bottle out from her handbag. She noted his eyes flash toward it, but he didn't say anything.

It was a silly victory. He had every reason to be furious with her.

And it was about to get worse.

"The Maximilian Group is pulling their investment," he said.

She felt the churn in her stomach.

The Maximilian Group was one of their largest investors.

She wished she had vodka instead of water in her hand.

George continued, using what Debra would have called one's outside voice if there were any humor in the situation. "Six months ago, when sales were only down 10%, we discussed the plan that would get us back on track." He pulled that light blue piece of paper they'd discussed at Thai Pantry out of his desk drawer with a flourish that made her suspect he'd specifically placed it there for the drama of retrieving it. "How have we done at these?"

Might as well remind him first that there was some good news. "We've been able to market the new product launches faster than expected, and the sale of one of our apps to another company is almost complete," she said, though without any celebration in her voice, as she knew what was next. She also knew that this wasn't the time for spin. George had been at their offices a lot lately, asking questions. "As you know, the relaunches have stalled. We were supposed to get half of the sales processes redesigned by last month and have only completed about a quarter. And the IT systems implementation is about two months behind."

"Well, at least you're aware of what's going on," he said.

Ouch. Even more painful: she wasn't even sure if the backhanded compliment were true. Did she really know what was going on?

Things were moving incredibly slowly with the product relaunches, and the truth was she wasn't sure why. Leland kept explaining to her that it was due to uncontrollable circumstances. Even worse: she had no idea if he was right or not. Her intel wasn't any better with the IT systems implementation or the sales process redesign: the leaders of both were blaming Leland, and she couldn't tell if he was a convenient scapegoat or truly at fault.

As far as she could tell, the only real thing that Leland had accomplished in six months was redoing the template they used for inter-office memos. Debra had planned to spend more time with Leland in his first six months, but the sale of one of their apps had come with a number of CEO-worthy fires. Also, since Natalie had been at the company from the very beginning and had worn so many different hats during that time, it turned out there were a lot of investors, clients, and corporate partners who were alarmed by her departure. Debra had been spending a lot of time one-on-one with them.

She was working more hours than ever, but it felt like she was going the wrong direction on a treadmill.

Worse yet, she had no idea how to get a handle on the problem fast enough.

Jack had always had the strongest relationship with the Maximilian Group, so they were ironically the one investor that she hadn't personally decided to worry about. She vaguely remembered Jack saying that Maximilian wanted to talk to the CPO as they had detailed questions about the roadmap. Had Jack dropped the ball here or had Leland?

Probably both. But did it matter which of the two was most to blame? Either way, the responsibility ultimately fell on Debra. It was Debra who hadn't paid much attention to one of their most important investors.

She tried to think what to say to reassure George, but it didn't matter. He stood up from his chair.

"We're going to need to see real progress at the Board meeting six months from now in January," he said before he started walking toward the door. "Otherwise you might not be the right person to steer this ship."

Six months to save her job.

When Debra got back to the office, she was relieved to see her next appointment was with Amber. At least she was one person who was helping Debra keep her job.

Even though Amber smiled as she walked in the room, Debra had to confront the fact that their interactions had felt different since Leland had been hired. The smile—it was partly sad, partly accusatory. Lately, it seemed to come with the hint—just a hint—of a sigh.

Three months into Leland's tenure, Debra had started to check in weekly with Amber one-on-one. It was partly an insurance policy for their bottom line: if Leland's relaunches failed, at least Amber's new launches would compensate for it. Debra had pushed Amber to go even faster than had been the original plan. This had required a lot of creativity on the part of Amber's team, launching slimmer products and putting in more extra hours than Debra wanted to admit.

The meetings were also Debra's way of making it up to Amber: a silent acknowledgment that she knew the younger woman could run circles around the new CPO.

Whenever she felt bad, Debra tried to remind herself that Amber was still relatively young—she'd have plenty of time to become a CPO. She'd get over the disappointment.

Today, they spent a productive half hour discussing a few additional new launches that Amber's team was evaluating. Debra didn't tell her about the Maximilian news—she'd have to speak with Terry and figure out the right way to communicate that to senior management—but she did note that there was some urgency to getting the new launches done faster.

"You know that revenue from our existing products has been declining," said Debra. "As a result, we need to get two additional new launches identified pretty quickly—say in the next six months. I know that's a bit of a change in what you were expecting."

"Okay," said Amber slowly, obviously absorbing the information. "I think I can figure out how to rearrange the team. Will I be able to hire any additional help given the accelerated timeframe?"

Debra didn't even know if Amber would be able to keep all her existing staff given the layoffs they'd probably need to do soon. But she couldn't say that. "Unfortunately, no, but I'm happy to help you re-prioritize items on your team's plate."

"Okay," said Amber again. "I'll get back to you by the end of the week with a proposal."

Debra thanked her employee and then ended the check-in the same way she always did, "Is there anything else I can help you with?"

Amber opened her mouth, then closed it again. After a short but noticeable delay, she replied. "Thanks, I'm sure I'll have questions after I work on the project plan."

As Amber got up from her seat and walked toward the door, there was a sporadic pause in her step that Debra couldn't help but notice. She'd seen it many times across her career. It was an indicator of a person who wanted to say something but hadn't decided if they would or not. Usually this meant they were on the precipice: deciding whether to start a difficult conversation or not.

If Debra were candid with herself, sometimes she felt too tired to ask what was going on even when such signs were staring her in the face. She often let herself assume that if it were important, the person would raise it again later. She saw Amber's hand move toward the door knob. Again, a slight pause mid-air.

Today, Debra decided she would do the right thing. "Are you biting your tongue?" she asked.

Amber looked surprised. "Well, I guess there was one thing I wasn't sure if I should mention."

Debra gestured Amber back to the chair.

"I know this isn't my place, but I thought I should say something…" Amber trailed off as she alternated between making eye contact with Debra and looking at her hands. "I think maybe there are a few areas where Leland could use some more onboarding support? He seems like a nice guy and all, but I'm a little worried about his impact on the team."

Shit. Debra didn't like to swear, even in her head. But statements worded as questions were never a good thing: that was what staff did when they had something important to say but were worried about being out of bounds. She'd certainly deployed that tactic throughout her own career. And the veiled reference to Leland's needing "onboarding support"—even the most dense CEO knew that was the polite way of noting someone was a disaster at their job.

She tried to keep an even tone. "Can you be more specific?"

Amber seemed to gain confidence now and spoke more directly. "Well, I think he hasn't gotten to know our products or our teams very well, so that might make it hard for him to lead the relaunches effectively. The staff have a lot of great ideas about what's working and not, but he hasn't really asked anyone. If he didn't trust our opinions, he could get into the market himself and talk to customers, but he hasn't really done that either. He just talks a lot about how they did things at his old company and throws around a lot of business jargon. I don't want to overstep, but maybe he needs some coaching."

Coaching—another word that could be innocent in some contexts, but that was clearly a euphemism in this one.

Debra wished that she were alone so that she could take the ice compress out of the mini-fridge in the corner of her office and put it on her forehead. Leland had assured her in his interview and first weeks on the job that his first step would be a deep listening tour with both staff and customers.

Okay, maybe Debra should have followed up with him—asked him what he was learning; pushed him on it. She'd just assumed that someone at that level of seniority—and, frankly, salary—would know what to do. She wasn't paying him to be babysat. Had Leland really not gotten to know the staff, the products, the customers? That certainly explained why he was struggling. Debra knew Amber had baggage on this, but it probably wasn't her baggage speaking. It was as if Leland had read one of those *What to Do Your First Six Months in a New Job* books and decided to do the exact opposite.

"Thanks for letting me know," Debra said.

This was tricky ground. On the one hand, she had to acknowledge the problem Amber was stating or risk losing credibility herself as a CEO who refused to listen.

On the other hand, she couldn't be too negative about Amber's boss.

"That's good advice for me on where to coach him," she continued, "And you're right, things are moving slowly, and I've wondered why. Relationships are so important to leadership. It seems like he just hasn't had a great style and needs to get to know you all better."

Hopefully that message worked. Relationship-building was something concrete and fixable she could help Leland work on, right? He had a strong team below him—if he learned to listen to them, he'd be able to guide and support them effectively.

"I think that's a start," said Amber.

So maybe the message hadn't worked so well after all.

"What else?" Debra asked.

"Well, some folks aren't sure whether to trust his judgment," said Amber.

"Can you elaborate?" Debra wondered if she should take consolation in the fact that Amber wasn't admitting at least that she was part of the "folks" in question.

"There's a lot of frustration around that inter-office memo template he's enforcing," Amber continued. "Not that we couldn't do a better job with internal communications, but it's added a lot of unnecessary work to our plates when there's a lot of product relaunch and new launch work we don't know how we're going to get done."

Debra flinched. "That template was a waste of time," she said without thinking. "I'll let him know we need to dial back the adherence to strict memo templates. But let's look at the bright side—at least he hasn't made decisions or offended anyone on anything consequential."

As soon as Debra said this, she realized it was dumb. Was she really implying that it was a positive that Leland hadn't made decisions on anything important? And the truth was that he had made a lot of bad decisions—his non-action on the product relaunches; whatever he may have done or said that had led to the Maximilian Group's divesting in them.

She felt herself rambling next, thanking Amber again for her feedback before adding, "Leland brings a lot of strengths and experience to this role. I know he's not perfect, but you all need to give him a chance. That's just how business works."

A look of disgust flashed across Amber's face before she managed to hide it behind a thin smile. "Right. Well, thanks for listening," she said. "I'll get back to you with my project plan later this week."

Amber left before Debra could figure out something better to say.

Debra spent the next hour staring at her computer, missing two meetings accidentally in the process. She picked up the phone twice to call Terry to discuss whether they might need to be pathing Leland out. She put it back down both times. They couldn't afford to have the CPO position vacant right now, not with so much work to get done. He'd just have to get better, and fast.

She pulled LinkedIn up on her phone and looked at his resume again. Everything about his profile indicated that he would succeed. Nobody was perfect. He'd had a rough start, but he'd get better.

CHAPTER SEVEN

Amber

Glass doors and walls made for a beautiful office environment, but they were lousy for privacy. Sure, the glass was frosted, which meant people might not know (unless they looked closely) if you were crying at your desk or emailing another employer about a job interview. But it was too easy to see who was likely "debriefing," as Amber's friends called their gossip sessions, with whom and for how long. The frost's ocean-inspired pattern didn't cover the ceiling-to-floor glass entirely and also made it too easy to peer through gaps if you stood in the hallway at the right angle.

Amber had found that office life was full of both: (a) people debriefing, and (b) people spying on people debriefing. For those who occupied the former category, there were a number of ways to throw off the spies.

For one, every office had a six-foot ficus plant in the corner, ensconced in a sleek silver pot resting on the taupe Berber carpet. "The leaves are known for providing natural air purification," an analyst on the human resources team had argued during a competition several summers before to propose ideas for promoting a healthy life at work. Employees had voted on the winner. There were better ideas, but they had been proposed by less popular colleagues, so a few months later, the ficuses received funding and appeared. While a person couldn't completely hide behind the ficus—the leaves weren't that big—you could stand half-shielded behind one so that someone walking by the office would have to peer closely to notice you were there.

Unfortunately, this really only worked for short debrief sessions— nobody wanted to stand behind a plant for more than fifteen minutes.

Every office also contained a large whiteboard against a teal accent wall (the other walls were all white); a black standing desk (with wheels even though there wasn't much room to move it around), the surface just large enough to hold a laptop and one notepad; a black mesh chair (more comfortable than it looked); a three-shelf dark gray folding bookcase; and a small round glass table with two stackable silver metal chairs. The bookcase was occupied with more assorted objects than books: a large seashell from her best friend's wedding in Hawaii, a few stress balls picked up at conferences, a wooden vase from a vacation in Costa Rica. On top of Amber's round table was her handbag, a sensible Longchamp nylon tote in navy blue. Draped on the back of the metal chair was a black, tailored blazer—even though their office was "jeans casual" and it was the middle of the summer.

Out of these items, the whiteboard was most helpful for disguising debriefing activities. At the moment, Amber's whiteboard was divided into three different sections. On the far left, her list of current priorities. In the middle, her team's goals for the quarter and, updated weekly, how they were progressing toward that goal. The last third of the whiteboard was empty except for a cluster of assorted shapes drawn in red marker in the bottom right corner: three triangles, two squares, five circles, and some lines connecting them all. Any visitor would assume these symbolized some complicated process maps, but actually they'd been drawn quickly during a debriefing session last week, so that the three people in her office could pretend they were discussing something urgent in the event that someone important (or at least nosy) came by.

Above her desk hung a medium-sized bulletin board—originally a standard cork board, but she had taken a silver paint marker and colored over the light brown frame, making the $15 bulk-purchased board take on the feel of something much more. At one point, she had even covered the cork with teal-and-white chevron giftwrap from the upscale stationery store next door, but that was now barely visible beneath the dozens of cards from co-workers she'd pinned up. Birthday cards. Thank-you cards. Good luck cards. Goodbye cards (sadly).

Whenever she had a long day, she would unpin her favorite card—featuring a sleeping koala on the front—and read the handwritten messages inside. It had been signed by one of her teams after they'd pushed several late nights to get to a sudden deadline. "We did it! Thank you for your support!" one of them had written, and she had felt proud that they felt such a sense of celebration and gratitude even while she felt guilty for asking them to work so hard.

Amber could have attended the SMC meeting that morning, but after her frustrating conversation with Debra the day before, she had decided to schedule a call with a vendor during that time. SMC stood for the Senior Management Council, which was made up of thirty of the most senior people in the company. Debra convened them about once a month, often relaying company communications that she'd first discussed with the smaller ELT.

In the time Before Leland (BL, as her friend Meg liked to say), Amber had never missed a SMC meeting. Before Leland, she also had worked many evenings or weekends. Natalie had inspired that kind of commitment.

Amber guarded her time more carefully now. One hour in a SMC meeting meant one more hour that she'd have to stay late or work on a weekend. She'd already wasted her time yesterday before her appointment with Debra, in Leland's meeting with their departmental management team, watching him awkwardly read through a stack of index cards without once looking up.

Amber and Meg often discussed the challenge of engaging their teams when everyone's work habits had changed AL (After Leland). You didn't hold a leadership position at a technology start-up unless you were a bit of a workaholic. But when she had to decide at 9:00 pm each night whether to get back on her laptop when the kids went to sleep—well AL, she did that only half of the time. She knew that Meg and the rest of the team were making the same kinds of decisions. They got their work done, such that a hypothetical jury of their peers or anyone writing a performance review could never claim negligence. But they were doing what Amber's friends who worked in HR called limiting one's *discretionary energy*—or, in simpler terms, the willingness to go above and beyond.

"What happened at the SMC meeting?" Amber asked Meg.

Meg shrugged at the question. "There were donuts," she said. "I had a chocolate cruller."

Amber shook her head. "Wow, that bad, huh?"

SMC members had long noticed that whether they were given breakfast—and even what the breakfast was—had a direct correlation with the content of the meeting. If the news was *kinda bad*, they got bagels. If the news was really bad, they got bagels *and* donuts. Meg once joked that if they ever arrived at an omelet station, they would know they were all losing their jobs.

Meg positioned herself behind the ficus. "Well you probably figured this out, but we haven't met our revenue goals for the third quarter in a row, and sales have continued to slip. They're emailing out the deck, so you'll see the exact numbers later, but basically we're down an additional 10% since last half."

Amber wasn't surprised—Debra hadn't told her the exact numbers, but their one-on-one meeting had seemed a clear prognostication of doom. She thought about how Debra had told her she wouldn't get any added staff for accelerating the new launches. Now she understood some of the reasons why. "Did they mention layoffs?" she asked.

"Sounds like finance is still figuring that out," said Meg. "But, yeah, they told us to be prepared for the fact that some of us may be having difficult conversations with staff soon."

"Difficult conversations." Amber sighed at the euphemism.

"Someone should have a difficult conversation with Leland," said Meg. "Hard to believe that much will turn around as long as he's steering the ship." She paused before smiling. "You got a positive shout-out though! Apparently, those new apps your team launched last quarter were the only bright spot in the numbers."

Amber gave her friend a half-smile. "Yeah, I'm proud at how much the team is really stepping up," she said before pausing. "What was the mood of the meeting? I'm guessing not great."

Meg shrugged. "Culture eats strategy for breakfast." It was an old management aphorism that the C-suite liked to throw around. The best strategies fail if the culture isn't strong. Even Jack would frequently cite the kinds of management books that tracked what made companies succeed (and fail). You could have two companies in the same industry with virtually identical strategies. Culture would be the difference between success and failure.[2] "I think Debra and Terry were surprised that the room was pretty lackluster when they announced a new monthly guest speaker series with women leaders from other companies," said Meg. "This was their solution to the gender gap in the engagement survey."

"Ugh," said Amber. "The problem is they're focusing on the wrong parts of culture. Pep rallies or speaker series. You can't 'event' your way to better engagement results."

Meg left her position behind the ficus and walked to the glass wall, peering out as if she were afraid that what she was about to say would be heard if someone was even in eyesight. Satisfied that the hallway was indeed empty, she added, "I've gotten a few calls from recruiters lately. I haven't really jumped on any of them, but I don't know…"

"Yeah, I know what you mean," said Amber. "I started working here when there were only fifty of us. It's been fun building something. But maybe it's time to start looking." She paused, wondering if she should tell Meg that she'd already updated her resume and that the black blazer on the back of her chair had been used for a networking conversation she'd had with another firm the day before. You couldn't wear a suit to work at a tech company without raising flags, but she'd been able to fold the matching skirt neatly into her handbag. Then, in a Starbucks bathroom across from their competitor's office, she'd swapped her jeans for the skirt and donned the blazer.

Meg was Amber's best friend at the company, and usually she would have been honest. But Amber hadn't quite decided whether the situation was redeemable or not. Saying out loud to Meg that she'd already started testing the waters would almost feel like admitting to herself that it wasn't. She took a sip of her coffee. "I wish there was more we could do to help Debra and others understand how to think about culture."

"Have you thought about talking to Debra about Leland?" Meg asked.

Amber gave her friend another half-smile. Normally, she would have debriefed her friend right away about her earlier conversation with Debra. But today she felt too tired as she replayed it in her mind. Had Debra really told her that it was okay that Leland was making bad decisions because at least they hadn't been consequential? Amber thought about an article she'd read about destructive versus absentee leaders.[3] The impact of destructive leaders who treated people poorly was entirely obvious from the beginning of their leadership tenures. While they caused a great deal of harm in the short-term, organizations were able to see the problem more quickly and remove these individuals from their positions. By contrast, the longer-term impact of leaders who were not destructive but merely absent (meaning they didn't make any impact, good or bad), was actually worse. The argument had been that absenteeism wasn't as obvious as blatantly bad behavior and that it therefore wasn't as easy to catch and was rarely addressed. This meant that absentee leaders could take up space and lead to disengagement without adding value for years.

She felt like such a sucker for believing Debra when she'd approached her for a career conversation a few years ago. Amber had asked for a pay raise for all the extra responsibility she'd undertaken—far more than her peers, and many above her in rank. Instead of the raise, Debra and Jack had assured her that she'd be the next CPO.

She had believed them right up until the day she'd been told Leland would be her new boss.

Amber had seen the research on women in the workforce. A man would have been more likely to have been given the raise then *and* the CPO position now. Her eyes drifted to the bulletin board on the wall with the cards and mementos from her team. In the past, she had put new cards up immediately, but three cards from the last five months were now sitting on the top shelf of the bookcase, back in their envelopes. It's not that she didn't appreciate the cards. They just no longer inspired her.

Below the bulletin board on her desk were the stapled pieces of paper that Leland had handed out last month, announcing the new protocol on inter-office memos. Font size, what to bold, how many words. Their revenues were continuing to decline, and this is what the CPO had focused his time on.

Amber had always believed in the company—and in Debra's leadership. They'd been through tough spots before, and every time she'd assumed they could turn it around and had appreciated the faith that Debra and Jack placed in her to be a part of that. But when the only decision your new CPO had made in six months was around an inter-office memo template—well, it was hard to have the same kind of faith. She looked at the black blazer on the back of her chair and hoped that Debra would start to take the concerns she'd raised more seriously.

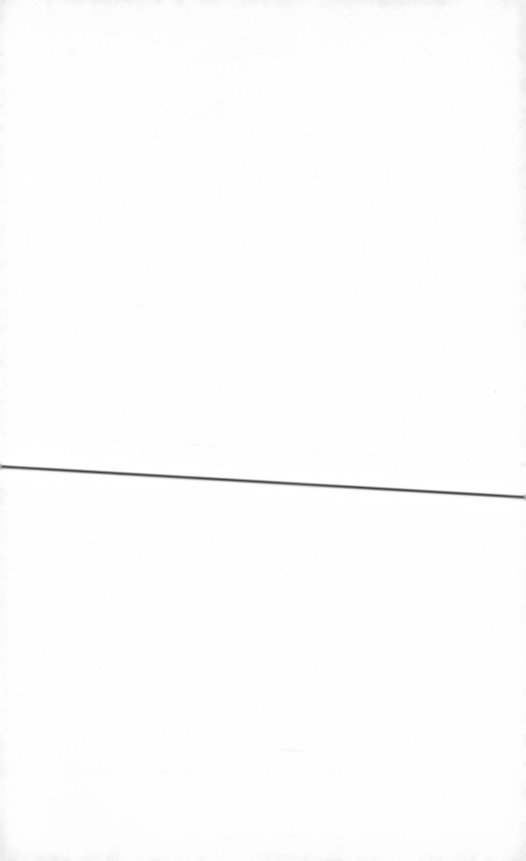

PART THREE

Wake-Up Call

CHAPTER EIGHT

Debra

This was the first year that Debra truly dreaded attending the annual company off-site. Bringing together the entire team outside the office was usually a highlight of the year. Today, she tried to suppress the sigh that was stuck in her chest as she walked the two blocks to the nearby beachside hotel with the rest of the company. Hundreds of people moving en masse across the city streets—like little dots of a pointillist painting, adding up to something only comprehensible with distance. She moved with the masses, smiling at staff who caught her eye, as if sales weren't down. As if she didn't have six—no, now it was five and a half—months to prove she still deserved her job. As if this were like any other year.

In the past, they'd had real off-site retreats, ones you couldn't walk to in less time than it took to unjam the copier. They had gone to Lake Arrowhead or Sonoma for multi-day trips complete with rope courses, trust falls, and marathon planning sessions, with the mental (and sometimes physical) exhaustion being tempered by wine tastings or BBQs in-between.

There was neither the time nor the money for any of that now. She and Jack had weighed whether they could still hold an off-site retreat for at least the leadership team—just one night, somewhere close. In the end, they couldn't make the numbers work. But they had to do something.

They'd just done another engagement survey. Not only had the gender gap widened further; this time they'd correlated engagement results with performance review scores. Their highest-performing employees—both men and women—were also the least engaged. No CEO ever wants to hear that their best employees are the least happy, but it was especially unwelcome news right now.

Debra was skeptical that a company off-site was the solution, but she knew they had to try something.

She arrived at the hotel, where they had rented a floor of conference rooms and the stunning ocean-side outdoor amphitheater behind the property. A venue this nice would have been out of their price range if Jack's sister hadn't worked there.

Each staff member, no matter how senior, was required to put any devices they'd brought into a basket at the entrance to the conference area. Dedicated to this purpose were three brave HR staff members who stood at the entrance trying to look simultaneously friendly and menacing, each holding a long wooden pole with a basket attached to the end.

Two of the staff were being particularly aggressive, using the poles to block anyone from walking by until they'd sacrificed their electronic tethers. The third was more hesitant and ended up having to run after anyone he'd missed in desperation, until he ultimately adopted his colleagues' tactic of not letting anyone pass from the beginning. The baskets looked suspiciously like the collection receptacles Debra remembered from her childhood attending Catholic mass. Where had they found them anyway? No matter. Debra admitted to herself she didn't really want to know the answer. She just silently prayed that some enterprising assistant didn't have a predilection for religious kleptomania.

Like everyone else, she put a post-it with her name on her phone and dropped it into the basket. Then she stood in the bagel line. Several staff tried to insist that she cut to the front of the line, but she shook her head, feeling a mixture of emotions as she looked around at all her employees crowded about: pride (she had built this!), exhaustion (if only she could just blend in!), and worry (their jobs all depended on her!). The last point was particularly troubling. There were at least five staff in her line of sight whose jobs they were likely to eliminate later that month due to the current budget situation.

Out of the corner of her eye, she noticed Leland standing by himself. All the other executives were making small talk with staff, as she expected them to do. That was part of the reason for taking everyone's mobile devices. Instead, he had a pile of those odd notecards in his hand and seemed to be writing furiously.

After her conversation with Amber two weeks earlier, she had asked Terry to talk to a few other managers on Leland's team. Many of them hadn't held back in voicing their frustrations and their worries about his negative impact on the business. Some had even hinted they were now thinking about job-hunting. "He's going to have to turn it around quickly," Terry had said to Debra.

Debra wondered what was he writing on those notecards, noticing that, even though he was standing in the middle of the room, he was giving off the impression of someone crouched in a corner.

After a day of small group workshops and panels, the last session of the day was with the entire company in the outdoor amphitheater. "It's Instagram-worthy," one of the members of Terry's team had explained when they had discussed location selection. Debra didn't quite understand why that mattered so much, but she was enjoying the view as she looked around. The rows of semi-circle benches were made of stacked stones in a perfect mosaic of grays, complementing the freshly trimmed grass beneath. The stage was set a few feet from the ground against the backdrop of the ocean.

Ideally, they would have started the day there too, not just ended it. But even with the discount, they couldn't afford to pay for the amphitheater twice.

Usually, Debra sat in the front at company-wide meetings with the other members of the ELT. Today though, Terry had suggested the executives scatter themselves throughout the audience and near the back if possible. "It'll be a better way to get a pulse check on how the employees are doing," she had said.

Debra picked a seat in the second-to-last row as George climbed the steps to the stage for his Q&A. The Board Chair didn't typically attend their annual off-site, but this year Debra had invited him as the staff had given feedback after the last off-site that they'd be interested in hearing from a Board member. She had asked Terry to moderate the session, and so the CHRO walked a few steps behind George. The hotel events staff had set up two tufted teal library chairs on the stage with a small white round table in between to hold two water bottles and (presumably just for decoration) a silver bowl overflowing with Granny Smith apples.

Debra had approved the questions in advance and had spent fifteen minutes the day before discussing with George what he was going to say, so she didn't feel too guilty tuning most of the session out as she ran through budget numbers in her head. Mostly, the session was uneventful.

But the last question came from a young woman who strolled to the microphone with the earnest confidence that marked many of the company's fresh-out-of-school staff. "How will we remain competitive on the talent front? We're trying to get so much more done as the company grows, and we don't have enough people to do it. How do we ensure workload is reasonable when it's so hard to fill positions?"

Many members of the audience nodded their heads. Debra knew workload was especially high for some of the teams with vacancies. As more tech firms moved into their region, which was increasingly known as "Silicon Beach," they were losing more good candidates, and even worse, existing staff, to outside offers. The most established tech companies often offered stronger brand names and higher salaries. Filling key positions at the required speed was harder than ever now—and the staff were feeling the pain.

However, George looked surprised by the question. Debra expected him to punt the question to Terry or even to her at the back of the room. Few things were as sensitive to staff as concerns related to workload. He must know that.

Or maybe he didn't.

"That's a really good question," he said. "I'm definitely worried about how we'll have the organizational capacity for everything that we need to get done. But I know we can definitely keep growing our talent. I think a lot of the challenges here might be solved by getting more women into leadership. You know, there's a lot of literature on how women lack the confidence they should have and on how much more women can lead if they raise their hands more."

Debra frowned at the way he'd dodged the question, which had nothing to do with women. The staff always got irritated when they felt like their questions weren't being answered.

But then she relaxed a bit as she considered the pros in George's response, even if it had been off-topic. Many of the staff, especially the women, would get his allusion to Sheryl Sandberg's TED Talk, which discussed the question of why organizations have so few women leaders. Debra had been the one to send George the link a decade ago, and it was that which had led him to read *Lean In* when it was published.

It was a great TED Talk. After describing the appalling numbers—how few women were heads of state, had C-level jobs, and Board seats—Sandberg talked about how women consistently underestimate their abilities. The message was a rousing one: Sit at the table more. Raise your hands. Go for what you want.

Debra knew several women who had said that watching the video gave them the inspiration and confidence to ask for a raise or new assignment: to not sit at the back of the room.

Still, she wished George hadn't so obviously avoided a legitimate question, one totally unrelated to gender, by changing the subject.

On the other hand, if he were going to dodge a question, showing his awareness of women's issues probably wasn't a bad idea—especially given the gender gap in their engagement results.

Then she looked around. A number of the women in front of her were whispering to one another, clearly angry about something. At the end of her own row, two women stopped talking as they saw her looking, even though she couldn't hear anything they said.

As they all filed out, Debra turned to a director in the finance division who she'd earlier noted as one of the whisperers. She had forgotten the woman's name, but she helped Jack with Board presentations sometimes, so Debra had at least met her before. "What did you think of George's answer to the questions?" she asked, trying to sound as casual as possible.

"Um, really interesting," the woman said, looking at the ground, her tone filled with fake enthusiasm. Clearly, the woman was pulling punches. Debra frowned. She had missed something, again.

She looked across the amphitheater and spotted Cassandra, a director on the HR team. Cassandra worked with Terry and oversaw the company's professional development programs, but Debra knew that Terry had started using her for a number of other special projects as well. As part of their women's leadership program for high-potential women in management roles, Debra had been assigned to be Cassandra's mentor.

If Debra were honest with herself, their first mentor-mentee lunch a few weeks earlier had unsettled her. As she always did in such situations, she had begun the lunch by asking Cassandra where she could be helpful. She had mentored a lot of women over the years and found most came to the CEO in search of fairly targeted skills development—for instance they'd ask about public speaking skills, or what they could do to better understand the company's finances, or what she looked for when hiring people into roles to which they aspired.

The areas that Cassandra had mentioned she'd want help from a mentor in were so much more vague: "How does my leadership presence and style need to change across a day, quarter, career?" "When do I change as opposed to thinking people should adjust to me?" "How do I avoid gender stereotypes like being seen as too nice or a pushover?"

"It feels like you're overthinking things," Debra had said.

They hadn't been bad questions. But spending too much time on those kinds of existential questions seemed a waste of time. You just did what you needed to do to survive and to have an impact. She had felt that she would need to help Cassandra with that. "You need to be more confident in your leadership style instead of overthinking it."

Cassandra had tilted her head then, as if reflecting on what Debra had said. She had smiled and then changed the subject, asking Debra a softball question about company strategy. Debra had felt judged by the younger woman, as if she had somehow disheartened her.

Terry had looked puzzled when Debra relayed the lunch to her after. "Cassandra definitely doesn't lack confidence," she said. "She's probably one of the most confident people I've worked with in my career—of any level or age."

Now, as everyone was filing out of the area, Cassandra stood to the side, as if watching the rest of the room. What's she thinking? Debra wondered. She wanted to go up to the younger woman and ask her questions, but then looked at her watch. She had a few important emails to write back in her office before attending an event that evening. Besides, their mentoring conversation hadn't exactly gone swimmingly.

CHAPTER NINE

Cassandra

Cassandra sat in the front row of the amphitheater. Not her usual choice. She had always been a solidly back-row person—not because she didn't want to pay attention, but because she liked to watch the reactions of the audience. After receiving her doctorate in anthropology three years ago, she'd left academia to become the company's internal corporate training specialist. But she still couldn't help wanting to observe the world around her.

Today, though, it'd been too hard to pick the ideal back-row seat as she tried to walk through the hotel grounds, balancing her notebook, small handbag, the two-inch stack of papers she'd managed to accumulate across the day, a cup of coffee, and the banana she'd grabbed from the snack station. Instead she had plopped her stuff down at the first seat in her path.

Their Board Chair, George, was on stage for the final session of the day, and it turned out that most of the session was relatively uninteresting, so there wouldn't have been much to observe anyway. But her spidey senses were on full alert as she watched a young associate from the accounts team ask George a question. Cassandra had never been able to explain exactly how it was she knew when something bad was going to happen—usually in a social situation. But she knew as soon as she heard the woman's question:

"As more and more technology firms are moving into the LA area, do you think we are going to have a harder time recruiting and retaining talent? How will we remain competitive on the talent front? We're trying to get so much more done as the company grows, and we don't have enough people to do it. How do we ensure workload is reasonable when it's so hard to fill positions?"

Cassandra didn't know what George would say, but she knew the answer was going to be bad. She knew it from the way George's eyes lit up, as if he'd found the perfect response to the difficult question, and the way his chin lifted up, shoulders back, small smile. He just looked too proud of himself. Cassandra put her coffee down and leaned forward. She felt as if she were watching a play.

Her eyes grew wider as George spoke: "That's a really good question. I'm definitely worried about how we'll have the organizational capacity for all that we need to get done. But I know we can definitely keep growing our talent. I think a lot of the challenges here might be solved by getting more women into leadership. You know there's a lot of literature on how women lack the confidence they should have and how much more women can lead if they raise their hands more," George paused, before concluding with: "There's so much untapped potential among our women at the firm."

Well, that made no sense at all. The question wasn't about women. Why did he talk about women in his response?

Obviously, he wanted to get credit for having seen the Sandberg TED Talk—but it was such a left-field thing to say. Cassandra felt like burying her head in her hands. It seemed he was placing blame on women twice: first, women needed to be more confident. Second, if women were more confident, the company would have fewer talent problems.

She wondered if Terry, who as head of HR was her boss, would say something in response to George's remarks. Would she mitigate the harm he had unwittingly done? Cassandra looked over at Terry, who was sitting next to George on the stage.

"Please chime in," she said under her breath. "Say something."

But Terry just looked nonplussed. She had leaned back in her seat once George started taking questions from the audience and remained in this passive posture now. Cassandra's face felt hot, as if she was experiencing the physical pain of embarrassment on both George and Terry's behalf. Was there such a thing as vicarious embarrassment if you were embarrassed on behalf of people who had absolutely no clue why they should be?

Cassandra knew that she shouldn't have been surprised by Terry's failure to realize what was wrong with George's comment. Whenever the subject of gender came up at their HR department meetings, it was clear that Terry thought there were only two challenges for women in leadership: they weren't confident enough and they struggled to balance work and family. Terry often waxed poetic about how Debra, their CEO, had helped her with both.

In the past, Cassandra had sometimes tried to diplomatically explain that Terry was missing a whole slew of additional challenges. She had come to accept that this was a fruitless endeavor. When it came to Cassandra's job, Terry fully respected her expertise and truly listened. She was a good boss. But whenever Cassandra tried to explain what her generation saw as the neglected issues for women at the company, Terry just smiled and acted as if Cassandra were too young to understand.

Cassandra had gathered that, at the age of thirty, Terry saw her as old enough to respect her opinion in areas where Terry didn't have a lot of knowledge already, but not enough to truly listen if Cassandra wanted to change her mind on something where Terry already held a cherished belief.

Eventually, Cassandra had given up trying.

She looked behind her to see if she could spot any of her friends in the amphitheater. Haley from marketing. Rita from finance.

Shannon from product development. Kyle from product development; the one guy in their group. The five of them had met at orientation when they started working at the company three years earlier. Most of their orientation group had just graduated from college, but they'd all been through graduate school and/or multiple jobs and had bonded as the "older" members of their start class, even though then they'd only been in their late twenties or early thirties. They had remained close since.

It was torture, having to listen to something like this without being able to share a glance with her crew. At the very least, Cassandra wished she had her cell phone with her. They would have been live-texting throughout George's comments if devices had been allowed.

No matter. They had made advance plans to debrief over a quick drink and snack at The Purple Panda, their favorite restaurant and bar near the office, when the off-site ended at 3:30 pm.

When the session ended, Cassandra started moving with the masses as the entire company trickled out together. But hundreds of employees filing out simultaneously felt too claustrophobic. At some point, she stopped and decided to stand off to the side and wait for the crowds to clear before she exited.

As she watched the crowd dwindle, she spotted Debra across the amphitheater. It almost looked as if Debra were looking right at her, but the CEO was likely just examining the masses of people, too.

Cassandra wondered what Debra was thinking. She had been flattered and grateful when Debra had been assigned as her mentor a few weeks earlier through the company's women's leadership program. There was so much she had wanted to ask Debra about how she'd gotten to where she was. It couldn't have been easy for her.

But Debra's blanket advice to Cassandra during the lunch—"assert yourself"—had been a disappointment. Sure, there were probably times when Cassandra could be more assertive. But Terry had actually praised Cassandra in her reviews for her willingness to state her opinions and to volunteer for difficult assignments. Debra didn't know Cassandra at all, yet she had just assumed assertiveness was the problem—just like George had assumed that, if the company's women raised their hands more, their talent problems would be solved.

Across the amphitheater, Cassandra couldn't help but gaze at Debra's dark brown pumps. Two-and-a-half inches, she estimated. She'd heard rumors of Debra's emergency drawer with Neosporin and Band-Aids for women who'd been done in by their shoes, along with a pair of flats that Debra sometimes changed into at the end of the day. It was a foreign concept to Cassandra. Sure, she sometimes wore heels. But she also had no problem starting the day—not waiting to end it—in flats.

Later that afternoon, Cassandra was the first to get to their usual spot. The others must have stopped to get stuff they'd left at their desks first. The Purple Panda's main restaurant area rarely had res-ervations open and was a little pricier than justifiable for a random night after work. Luckily, the bar and lounge area always had open seating and a good happy hour menu.

Cassandra claimed their favorite circular booth in the corner of the lounge, sliding into the velvet eggplant-colored seat and placing her phone on the smooth walnut table. The entire venue was adorned in a dozen shades of purple, but Cassandra's favorite feature was the canvas prints scattered about the walls: close-ups of flower petals and other nature scenes. She found the irises particularly calming.

Slowly, the group arrived. They ordered their usual plate of gourmet nachos (blue corn chips, pulled pork, green chiles, cojita cheese) and calamari rings (honey-sriracha mayonnaise dipping sauce) to share.

"So, can you believe that last question?" Shannon said as soon as they each had a drink in hand, along with a small plate (too small, they all agreed) and flatware for the appetizers.

She didn't need to explain to anyone what she was talking about.

"I mean, mystery solved," Kyle said with his usual sarcasm, "I had no idea that all our vacancy problems were just because you women aren't raising your hands. You all should do better."

They all laughed—a sad collective laugh. At first, the Purple Panda crew (as they referred to themselves) had only discussed the challenges they saw for women in the office when Kyle wasn't present. But Shannon, who worked most closely with him in product development, had convinced Cassandra, Rita, and Haley that they could trust him. She was right. They appreciated that Kyle also saw many of the challenges they faced as women, and, at least most of the time, that he was appropriately angry on their behalf. At any rate, they knew nothing would ever improve if men weren't also part of the discussion. Part of what Cassandra disliked about the firm's various women-in-leadership events was that men were never part of the conversation—it was as if the challenges for women were simply a female problem that needed to be solved by women, not an organizational problem that needed to be solved by everyone.

"I'm sure George meant well," said Rita as she dipped a small corner of a calamari ring in the sauce. Cassandra saw that her friend, known for her level-headedness, was trying to give George the benefit of the doubt. Out of the five of them, she was the one who'd had the most direct interaction with George: in her role on the finance team, she often helped prepare financial statements for the Board and even responded directly to George's questions. She reached for another calamari ring. "He'd be appalled if he realized it sounded like he was blaming women for the company's talent shortage."

"I know he meant well," said Haley, picking at one of the nachos on her plate. "And I'm so grateful that, in my first job after college, my boss told me about all the research showing women are less likely than men with the same qualifications and abilities to apply for jobs or promotions. When I first saw the ad for the job I have now, I almost didn't apply because I didn't match every single line in the description. Then I asked myself, 'what would a man do?' and I applied anyway!"

"Yup, we do need to raise our hands more as women!" said Shannon. "But you know what really kills me? Hearing all the men who have read *Lean In*—or, let's be honest, often just a book review of it—and then think the only real problem is that women are self-sabotaging and holding ourselves back."

Cassandra sighed and then took a sip of her mojito. "Yeah, it's all about 'fixing' women. Maybe there are factors strapping a woman in her seat that make it harder to lean in."

"Not only that," said Shannon, "I can think of a few men who aren't pulling their weight, letting women do their work without the credit. Should we give George a list?" Her words were bitter, but her tone was matter-of-fact—tinged with two parts resignation, one part rancor. They all knew that she was probably thinking about Leland in particular—Shannon hated the fact that her boss, Amber, had been passed over for that job. They all knew that Amber leaned in all the time.

Shannon was on a roll now. "Or, Haley, why don't you tell George about the last time you raised your hand and ended up with twice as much work without the pay that men doing the same amount of work were getting?"

They all looked at Haley. Most days, she was too Zen to complain as vociferously as the rest of them, but this time she couldn't help it. She looked down at her hands. "I'm sure he had no idea how much salt he was rubbing in the wounds of so many women with that comment."

Cassandra knew Haley's wounds were especially deep. While all of them considered themselves strong employees, Haley was in a class of her own. She leaned in so much, but asking for raises in return never got her anywhere (even though they knew many men who had been given salary increases for less reason). Over time, the group had taken to encouraging her that she actually needed to lean out to not be taken advantage of so often.

"There's also a bunch of men—and women too—who perhaps should lean out, like maybe listen to others once in a while," Cassandra added.

"I ran into Debra right as everyone was leaving George's session," said Rita. "She asked me what I thought of George's answers to the questions. She was clearly fishing. Felt like she knew that something was wrong, but didn't know what."

"Well, that's something," said Kyle. "What did you say?"

"Nothing really," said Rita. "I didn't know if it was worth the trouble."

"I mean can you imagine what Terry and Debra had to go through to get to their positions? I sometimes wonder if they're so appreciative of how much better things are, they can't see how much further we have to go or what's different for us today," said Haley.

Cassandra thought again about her conversation with Debra. The CEO clearly wanted to support women across the firm. But the gap—more like a gulf, really—between what Debra might have made of George's comments and what Cassandra and her friends thought of them was probably wide.

What would it take to shift Debra's perspective?

CHAPTER TEN

Debra

After the long day of the off-site, the last thing Debra wanted to do was to attend a charity reception at least an hour's drive away. Both she and Jack were on the panel at a 5:30 pm event on corporate social responsibility, hosted by the president of a local foundation at a hotel downtown. The only thing to look forward to about it was that her thirty-seven-year-old daughter, Olivia, would be attending as her guest.

She didn't see her daughter, a busy cardiologist, that often, and half-expected her to cancel at the last minute. When she saw the text from Olivia saying that she'd arrived right before she went onto the stage for the panel, part of her didn't believe it was real. And when Debra spotted Olivia's face in the crowd during the panel, she kept waiting to see if she would suddenly glance at her phone, give her an apologetic wave, and dash out. But afterward, as Debra and Jack made their way to the reception outside, she spotted Olivia at one of the tall round tables, underneath a cluster of palm trees, a glass of rosé in one hand and her phone in another.

"That was really great, Mom," Olivia said after giving her a hug. "I loved what you said about the role tech companies can play in helping young girls learn to code."

While Olivia was greeting Jack, Debra tried to ignore the fact that her daughter's compliment was paired with a tone of surprise, as if she hadn't expected to enjoy public remarks by her mother.

Just take the win, she told herself. Wins, really. First, that Olivia was there. Second, that her activist-turned-doctor daughter no longer went around completely disappointed that her mother was a "businesswoman" instead of pursuing a more noble calling. Even though Olivia had been raised attending events like this one—her father, Debra's late husband, had been a vice president of sales—she'd always seemed to only partly accept it as her world. Even now, as a fairly well-off physician, Olivia looked out of place in her black cocktail dress, her black shrug only partially covering the lotus flower tattoo she'd gotten to commemorate her Peace Corps service. Her bracelet—thin leather braids with beads spelling out S-H-E P-E-R-S-I-S-T-E-D—looked like they should be paired with a flowered tunic at a beach bonfire. But Olivia wore it with such confidence that it looked as natural with her semi-formal attire as a string of pearls would have.

Olivia was talking to Jack about how she'd seen his daughter recently at the wedding of a mutual friend, when a twenty-something man in a dark gray suit interrupted their conversation.

"I read in your bio that we went to the same business school," he said to Jack, holding the program in his hand. "I'm so impressed by everything your company has done, and I wanted to introduce myself. I'm a Wharton grad as well, and so was my father. I think he graduated around the same time as you."

Debra watched her daughter narrow her eyes at the young man and wondered what Olivia found more offensive: the fact that he'd interrupted her conversation with Jack without even acknowledging her existence, or that he hadn't acknowledged that Debra too was a Wharton grad. Had he had missed the line about their shared alma mater in her bio, or just not even bothered to read Debra's (even though, alphabetically, it came *before* Jack's in the program), despite his apparent interest in *her* company?

"I'm sorry," said Jack, "I don't know that I've met your father, but always great to meet a fellow alum."

The young man looked disappointed but clearly wasn't going to leave the conversation until he made a connection. He started listing several other names—friends of his father's, co-workers, professors— that he had deemed to be in the same generational orbit as Jack.

"Have you met Debra, our CEO? You know Debra is an alum too—she and I were actually there at the same time," said Jack. He stepped back a few inches until his back rammed up against the table; an attempt to widen the circle. "It was she who encouraged me to apply while we were both working at the same consulting firm after undergrad."

"Oh, really?" the man said in a flat tone, as if he wasn't even sure why Jack was sharing such a meaningless tidbit with him. He shifted his eyes to look briefly at her in acknowledgement but didn't bother to turn his body from its posture facing Jack.

She'd become used to this kind of thing over the years, so it didn't faze her. Men always looked astonished when she was able to participate in conversations about things they considered stereotypically male—football, cars, home improvement. It was sad to have business school be on that list of "topics men are surprised women have something to say about," especially when the offender was so young—in his late twenties, early thirties, perhaps. What percentage of his business school class would have been women—40%? Sure, not half (regrettably), but much closer to it than when Debra had been in school.

If she got angry every time men in professional settings treated her as if she didn't exist, even as a CEO, she'd spend her whole time enraged. She went on smiling politely as the young man continued to direct his attention to Jack alone.

She wondered what the man, a young, highly educated professional in a major metropolitan area, would say if asked about his beliefs on women in leadership. Odds were he chimed in to fervent discussions with his friends about the need for gender balance in Congress. The chances were that he did care about women's equality, at least intellectually. And yet he didn't associate someone who looked like Debra with "businessperson of potential use to me" in his head.

When he left, as soon as he was out of earshot, she and Jack laughed. "I wondered how long he would keep name-dropping," said Jack.

"I mean I thought he was going to pull out the phone book next," Debra replied.

Olivia looked at Debra with an appalled expression. "Aren't you livid?" she asked. "It's like you were invisible even though you're the CEO."

"I'm pretty used to it by now." Debra shrugged. "You've got to let these things bounce off you or you'll go crazy."

"But how could you just sit there and let him disrespect you that way?"

"What was I supposed to do? Tell him I'm important? What would that accomplish?"

Olivia seemed flustered. "I don't know, but there must have been something we could have done." Her face was red. "It just makes me so mad. I mean, you worked hard to become CEO. I worked hard to become a cardiologist, and today I've had three people mistake me for a nurse. You know, another thing I've noticed is that when female doctors introduce other doctors—men or women—they use their title. But when male doctors introduce other doctors, they are much more likely to use the 'doctor' title for men than for women.[4] Every woman I know faces these kinds of micro-aggressions all the time."

It's not that Debra thought unintended insults and slights were okay. She was annoyed too and more than that sad that this still went on. But things like this were harmless and insignificant. You had to save your energy for the big aggressions. Debra said what she always said to younger women. "You can't let this kind of thing anger you. If you do, you let them win," she said.

Jack nodded. "Your mom is CEO, and he's just a dumb kid."

Debra added what had been her mantra for decades, "All we can do is concentrate on doing good work."

Olivia narrowed her eyes again. She seemed to be taking a deep breath. "Fine, whatever," she said.

"You can't let that kind of thing bother you," Debra tried again.

"Right," her daughter replied. "Should we check out the carving station?"

Debra recognized that tone: lightness barely masking irritation. Another younger woman who seemed to be biting her tongue. Debra thought back to the women at her company who had whispered about George's comments at the off-site but were unwilling to tell her what was going on. As they walked to the carving station, she remembered Cassandra observing the amphitheater after George's presentation. What Debra needed right now was someone who could help her understand what she was missing—could her mentee provide that perspective?

Debra could hear George's voice in her head: sales are down again, your jobs are on the line, you can't focus on the gender problem.

She thought about his not-even-veiled threat from a few weeks ago: she only had a few months to turn things around. That wasn't a lot of time. Shouldn't every single minute she had be spent on the sales problem?

She thought about Natalie's departure. Debra had tried to convince herself at the time that Natalie had simply tired of business and would pursue non-profit work or even get a degree in counseling; something she'd said she might do someday. But since then, Natalie had started her own company.

Clearly, Debra had missed something.

She heard someone calling her name. Damn it. Another detour from getting to eat. Should she pretend not to hear it?

No, she couldn't do that. "Yes?" she said, turning around to see a woman who reminded her of her daughter. She was wearing what appeared to be a high-end dress, but her hair was in a messy ponytail and she had a Smart Watch, complete with exercise band, on her wrist.

The woman shook her hand. "You probably don't remember me, but we met at my father's Fourth of July party a few years ago. I'm Jennifer Maximilian. I really enjoyed your talk," she said. "Listen, I wanted to say that even though we weren't able to continue our investment, I've long been an admirer of yours. Having talked to Leland, I just didn't think the current strategy was aligned with what we're looking for at the moment, but I hope that you'll stay in touch."

It had taken Debra a while to place the woman's face despite hearing her name, so it took a few beats for her to realize what was going on. Sam Maximilian, Jack's long-time golf buddy, must have handed the reins to his daughter. She felt furious. Why in the world had Jack sent Leland in as their representative?

"I was sorry to hear about your decision," Debra said. "But I'd love to sit down with you, bring in Jack, and Pat"—their investor rep, whose job was to wine and dine folks like Jennifer—"and talk more about some of our plans."

Jennifer tilted her head at Debra in a way that reminded her of Olivia again. "Yes, Jack suggested that you, Pat, and I meet as well when my father told him that I'd be making our investment decisions." Well, thank God for that. "I asked to have coffee with your CPO first," she said. "It seemed like there were some major product changes that needed to be made, and I wanted to get a sense from the ground before we went through all the official investment talk."

Well, at least now Debra knew what happened.

She could hardly blame Jennifer. Would she have invested in a company that had Leland representing it?

How much had they counted on the buddy system of the golf course in the past? Not that Jennifer's dad wouldn't have eventually realized the issues as well; perhaps he would have divested too: but friendship often bought time. At least in theory, Leland could have had a chance to find his legs.

Jennifer said goodbye, and Debra finally made her way over to the carving station. She wanted the beef but realized that she'd had a burger for lunch, so she should maybe get turkey instead or even forego meat altogether.

Suddenly, she felt old.

Before getting back to Olivia and Jack, she stopped at the nearest table to put her plate down for a few seconds. Never mind if Jack and George didn't want her spending any time solving the gender gap. She was the CEO, and it was time to get help understanding what the younger women could see that she couldn't. She pulled her mobile phone and sent her executive assistant an email: *Can you get me time with Cassandra ASAP? 60 minutes ideal. 30 OK. Thanks.*

PART FOUR

Mental
Auto-Completes

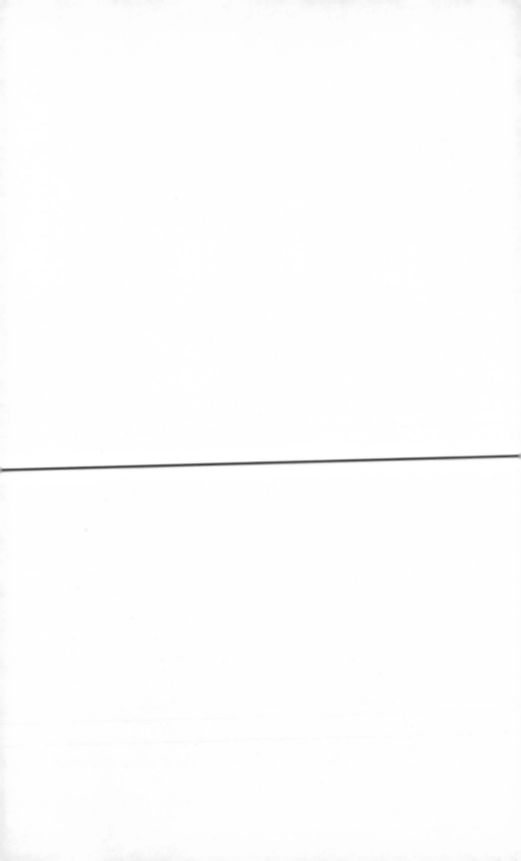

CHAPTER ELEVEN

Cassandra

The day after the off-site, Cassandra was surprised to get an email from Debra's executive assistant first thing in the morning. It said that Debra wanted to get some time with her at 11:00 am that day.

She hoped that Debra hadn't suddenly decided to follow up on their lunch and help Cassandra be more confident.

But she'd find out what Debra wanted to discuss in a few hours. In the meantime, Terry had asked her to examine their internship program and make recommendations as to its improvement. She wasn't sure if her boss realized there wasn't actually an internship *program* to speak of—each department pretty much did what it wanted. But she needed to start somewhere and knew the finance team used more interns than other departments. She'd also heard finance was more organized than most at assigning tasks to interns, allocating responsibilities all at once in their weekly staff meeting rather than the disorganized free-for-all by which managers in other departments tried to claim interns' time.

Cassandra brought her latte (almond milk, sugar-free caramel syrup) into the weekly 9:00 am finance meeting and took a space at the back of the large conference room.

"Thanks to everyone for welcoming our new interns," said the associate vice president of finance, Lucile, who was presiding over the meeting from the head of the table. She looked at the notes on her tablet computer, which was housed in a smart medium brown leather folder. Cassandra didn't know Lucile well, but she did know that she had gone out of her way to mentor Rita and was one of the first senior women to sign up any time Cassandra and her HR colleagues needed someone to help with a women in leadership event or initiative.

"The group is already excited about their first assignments," said Lucile. "Ethan is going to be doing financial analyses for one of our new launches, Paige is helping prepare the slides for a conference presentation a few members of the senior team are doing in San Diego, and Jessica will be helping to plan our leadership retreat."

Cassandra glanced at Paige and Jessica, who happened to be standing a few feet away from her—close enough that she could hear them whispering. Ethan was at the other end of the room.

"That's nice for Ethan," whispered Paige. "But weren't there more substantive tasks for us?"

"Nope, the girls prep slides and plan events," muttered Jessica bitterly. "I've tried asking for more substantive work but was just told to be patient. Every time the tone I hear in response is like a combination of *'isn't that cute'* and *'don't get too big for your britches.'*"

"I didn't even have the guts to ask," Paige admitted, "So good for you. Do you think Ethan has more experience than we do?"

"Maybe," said Jessica, "But somehow I doubt it."

Cassandra had looked at all the interns' resumes earlier, so she knew the answer. There was not much discernable difference in qualifications between Ethan, Paige, and Jessica. If anything, Paige was the standout of the three.

Cassandra and her other friends, who worked in a wide range of industries, often talked about how these kinds of opportunity gaps for women in the workplace started early. Female stockbrokers made less than their male counterparts, mainly because they were assigned worse-performing accounts.[5] In law, women and minorities were subject to what attorneys called the "thin file", where there was less to evaluate on their road to partner because existing partners gave more significant assignments to associates with similar backgrounds and experiences.[6]

These opportunity gaps were often not intentional. Cassandra knew the finance department's leadership team; they weren't people who *consciously* thought men should do the financial analysis work and women should plan the parties and help with slides.

That was the problem though. The unintentional nature of these opportunity gaps made it even harder to root them out.

In this case, it was Lucile, a female AVP, who'd made the assignments. Cassandra thought how often she'd heard Terry say that "everything will be better for women once we're 50% of leadership teams."

Obviously, women should be represented in the highest ranks. But, in this case, having a woman in a leadership position did not wipe the problem out. And not for the stereotypical reasons often discussed— Lucile was no stereotypical "queen bee" who was out to get other women. She was an advocate for women individually and collectively.

No matter how dedicated to the cause, both men and women could both unwittingly reinforce gender gaps.

Sure, this was just one assignment. But it was too easy to play the story forward. The experience that Ethan would gain was likely going to give him a set of impressive resume bullets and interview talking points that could help him land a job after college.

Of course, Ethan would need to demonstrate his own talents too. But from this very first assignment, he was being afforded the opportunity to do so in a way that women were not. Through this opportunity, Ethan would be interacting meaningfully with senior leaders at the firm.

Paige and Jessica's assignments—planning an event, preparing slides—weren't unimportant activities. But they weren't connected to the skills they'd aimed to gain by seeking an internship in this department.

As Cassandra looked at these two younger women, she thought about how the opportunity gap continues to widen over the course of a career. The mentoring and experience that Ethan received through this one assignment would probably help him not only get his next assignment (at the company or elsewhere), but also to thrive at that assignment, since he'd come in with more practice and knowledge. Then, success at that next billet would open up even more doors—and so on. Success, experience, and mentoring would beget even more success, experience, and mentoring—all leading to greater skills, and greater confidence too.

The Debras of the world had fought their way to overcome these kinds of opportunity gaps and worse. But Cassandra knew that she and her friends didn't want to just accept that—and it seemed like these interns, in their late teens and early twenties, were even less likely to do so.

Cassandra was so caught up in her thoughts that she barely noticed when Jack posed a question to the group. "We're starting a new professional development series for the finance department in a few months. Does anyone have any ideas?"

The first person to raise her hand was Paige. How's that for leaning in, Cassandra thought. "It'd be interesting to understand what role finance departments play in determining what companies outsource and what they don't," said Paige.

Jack wrinkled his eyebrows. "Yeah, that's interesting," he said, but with a tone that implied either he didn't agree or he hadn't been paying attention. Still, he went to the flip chart and wrote "OUT-SOURCING" on it.

Paige could clearly tell her idea had fallen flat. She looked sheepish. "I liked your suggestion," Jessica whispered, earning a grateful smile back from her friend.

The discussion continued. They made it to the second flip chart—some of the ideas being met with enthusiasm by Jack, others with the same passive regard that Paige's had received.

A few comments later, Ethan spoke up from the side of the room. "We should have a speaker come to discuss outsourcing," he said.

"Interesting," said Jack, this time with a completely different tone. "What's your thinking there? And it's Ethan, right?"

Ethan sat up straighter in his chair. "Yes, that's right. Ethan. Well, more companies are looking at outsourcing as a potential way to restructure costs, right? But I've heard that sometimes it doesn't actually save money as intended. I'd love to hear an expert perspective on lessons learned."

Jack wrote on the flip chart:

"Outsourcing—Lessons Learned."

"You see, everyone. This is why it's so great to have interns. They come up with ideas all the time we wouldn't have." He gave Ethan a thumbs-up from across the room.

Cassandra looked around. Only Paige and Jessica looked appalled. Had nobody else noticed?

After the meeting ended, Cassandra found herself walking a few feet behind the two interns as they headed down the hallway. "My mom calls that the butterfly effect," she heard Jessica say quietly to Paige. "Women's ideas are like sleeping caterpillars, until men take them on, and then they suddenly take flight. There are a lot of butterflies here." She made big circular waving motions with her arms as if they were butterfly wings and laughed.

How often did women use laughter as a coping mechanism in situations like this one?

The laughter didn't make up for the sting though. Cassandra thought about the unconscious factors at work in the case of these kinds of "stolen" ideas. As she thought back over their statements, she could see that Ethan's had certainly been more assertive than Paige's ("We should" as opposed to "It'd be interesting"). After their initial statements, Ethan was then given the opportunity to say more.

But it was hard to say whether Paige would have done better with a slight alteration in word choice; after all, there was plenty of research saying that women were penalized when their language was too direct. Most women learned to wrap any semi-controversial statement in layers of bubble wrap. Cassandra suspected that even with the perfect word choice, the butterfly effect would still likely be at play. The room was simply ready to hear ideas from Ethan in a way they weren't from Paige.

At 11:00 am, Debra's assistant ushered Cassandra into the CEO's office. Debra appeared to be busy finishing an email and didn't register Cassandra standing awkwardly near the door until she stopped typing. She stood up and gestured to the round mahogany table near the window. Cassandra noted it was the same wood as Debra's desk and just large enough to fit two cream-colored accent chairs. They both took a chair, and Debra handed her a coaster for her water bottle. Cassandra wasn't quite sure where the coaster had even come from—it had almost seemed to manifest out of nowhere, like a quarter from behind the ear of a magician's audience member.

"I need your help," said Debra.

That wasn't what Cassandra had expected. "Sure," she said, before adding uncertainly, "With your social media?"

During Terry's training for both mentors and mentees, they'd been told that a secondary goal of the program was also to find something that the mentees could teach upward. "Reverse mentoring," this was called. Cassandra had found it clichéd that "social media" was the only example given in the training—as if that were all someone more junior could teach someone more senior. Cassandra wasn't even that young—she was thirty! Even she went to the twenty-somethings when she needed to figure out how to Snapchat with her niece or needed someone to explain the point of TikTok.

But sure enough, at their lunch, Debra had mentioned that she liked the reverse mentoring concept and that perhaps they could talk about whether she should be leveraging Twitter or LinkedIn differently.

"Social media?" Debra looked confused. "Oh, right, the reverse mentoring. Well, I do need reverse mentoring, but not with that. I think you know about the gender gap in our engagement survey results?"

Cassandra nodded. It wasn't something the company had broadcast widely, but as a member of the HR team, she knew a lot that wasn't widespread knowledge.

"I'm trying to understand what's causing the gap," said Debra. "I've had the suspicion for a while that women today—your generation, that is—are facing frustrations that I don't understand. But every time I try to ask, I feel like the person I'm talking to is biting her tongue. Yesterday, for example, at the end of our off-site. I noticed a lot of women whispering after George's session. Can I be honest with you? I have no idea why. I know he dodged that question about talent, but it seemed like women were upset about something bigger than that."

Cassandra wondered how honest she should be. As she was pondering what to say next, Debra spoke again, "I need you to not bite your tongue."

"Okay," Cassandra said, "I'm just not sure where to begin. And I worry about pretending that I can speak for all the women in the company."

"I don't expect you to," said Debra. "But Terry told me that you've got a good pulse on the organization—that you're well-networked across departments."

What the hell, Cassandra thought, she might as well go for it. She wondered if she should explain everything she and her friends had discussed over drinks the night before. No, that was probably too much for the fifteen minutes they had left that morning, and she'd want to organize her thoughts more anyway. But she could start somewhere.

"Well, let me tell you what I observed this morning in a finance department meeting," she began.

CHAPTER TWELVE

Debra

After her conversation with Cassandra, Debra felt too distracted to deal with her inbox. She looked at her calendar and noticed that there was a "lunch and learn" panel where two of the marketing directors would be discussing their incorporation of data and analytics into the company's marketing plans—an important topic, especially given their sales challenges.

Debra sat in the back of the room. She listened to a woman from HR introducing the session panelists, two marketing directors called Chad and Haley. The company had grown so big that, even though Debra hated to admit it, she didn't know all the director-level staff by name as she once had. But these two at least were familiar. Chad had been at the company for over a decade and had worked on some of their highest-profile projects. Haley was newer (maybe three or four years at the firm?), but Natalie, their former CPO, had been assigned as a mentor to Haley through the women's leadership program and had often raved about her.

Natalie. Debra only let herself feel sad for a minute or two as she thought, for the second time that week, about how much easier everything would be if her former CPO was still there.

But she couldn't think about that right now.

She tried to listen to Chad and Haley's presentations, each detailing a separate data and analytics pilot project their respective teams had deployed. But it was hard to pay attention with her morning conversation with Cassandra weighing on her. When Debra had been a finance intern herself on Wall Street, years ago, she had been the only woman in the internship program. Just a few weeks ago, when she had looked at her company's recent intern list, she had patted herself on the back to note that they had a fairly even gender ratio among interns, even in male-dominated fields like finance.

But having an equal number of women in a role was only the first step to equality in opportunity—what women and men were assigned mattered too. It was distressing to realize how far they had to go there.

The session was winding down to Q&A.

"Is there one takeaway about the importance of data and analytics that you'd each say we should remember from this session?" someone in the front row asked.

A good question. Debra secretly felt overwhelmed by how much she didn't know about big data and how much it seemed to be eating the world. Time to pay attention.

Haley spoke up first. "That's a great question. It's never about data and analytics for their own sake, you have to know what your goals are—how you're going to measure success. For the set of products where my team piloted new dashboards to help us prioritize our marketing investments, we grew sales by 15% and cut costs by 10%. But this was just our first pilot, so I'd expect the results will be better as we incorporate lessons learned."

Impressive, thought Debra. No wonder Natalie had spoken so highly of her. She made a mental note to learn more about Haley's pilot. Maybe scaling this could help with their sales problem.

Chad was next. "Well, I don't think there's one takeaway," he said. "But there are a bunch of different ways that the data raises a lot of interesting questions where we might want to dig in even deeper to find out more. There's just so much that data can do."

Okay, so clearly Chad either wasn't paying attention or didn't understand the import of what Haley had said: it was never about data and analytics for their own purpose. Everything he said after that was similarly empty, and Debra found herself wondering about the respective levels of engagement of Haley and Chad. Was Haley a retention risk? She seemed so passionate about her work and her team—not Debra's picture of a disengaged employee. But, as much as Debra might hope that Haley was engaged and happy, the survey data hinted she might not be.

Debra looked around the room at all the women, many of whom were in management positions. Such a change from when she entered the workforce. In an audience this size—about thirty people—you'd have been able to count the women on one hand. And most of them would have been assistants. She never failed to feel grateful and proud of how far they'd come.

But she knew she'd only scratched the surface that morning with Cassandra when it came to the intensity of frustrations among the rising generation of women leaders. Haley was in her late twenties or early thirties. Natalie was about ten years older than that. Both from a different generation to Debra. She thought of her own daughters. They wore their HRC-era pantsuits with symbolic pride, but they could barely grasp Debra's stories about how, when she was in high school, something like *The Woman's Dress for Success Book* could have been a best seller. It had confidently asserted that the pantsuit was a "failure outfit" and that liberated women must burn not their bras, but their pantsuits in order to advance in the corporate environment.

The session ended. Wrapped up in her own thoughts, Debra ran right into Tom, vice president of marketing and Chad and Haley's boss, in the hallway. She always enjoyed talking to Tom. He was the kind of person who always stayed behind at the end of a party to help clean up—and, perhaps more importantly, looked surprised when the host thanked him for it.

"Did you just see Chad and Haley's presentations?" he asked.

"They were fantastic," she said. "You've done a great job with them."

"I wish I could take credit," said Tom, looking surprised, "But really all I had to do was get out of their way."

Debra smiled. This was why Tom's teams loved working for him so much. He always truly thought about the good of the group—without any need for credit. She was reminded of a conversation she'd had with Terry about Tom earlier that week. "Terry mentioned that you'd sent her a good article about random acts of gratitude? She said you'd really taken it to heart."

"That was nice of her," said Tom. "The team works so hard, and I've been looking for new ways to express my appreciation to them. Last week, I left handwritten thank-you cards on their desks so they'd find them Monday morning. It was so nice to see their faces light up as they opened their notes."

Debra circled through the company organizational chart in her head. "That's over thirty people, right? How long did it take you?"

"A while," he confessed. "Though I did more customizing with the staff I work most closely with."

"That's great," said Debra, wishing she could remember the last time she'd written handwritten thank-you notes to her team.

Tom looked proud. "I wrote Chad's about how excellent he is with data—always coming up with another analysis of new marketing metrics for our team."

Debra nodded, thinking about how Chad's love of data had been so evident in the earlier presentations. While he wasn't as strong as Haley, all he needed was a little coaching and they'd be able to put that passion to better use.

"And Haley," added Tom. "She's just the glue of the office, and she has such an infectious smile."

Wait. Did she hear that right? Is that how Tom described his two top lieutenants?

Both Chad and Haley had essentially the same job: each of them oversaw marketing for a portfolio of the company's apps. Yet Chad was praised for his fluency with data, a specialized skill important for prioritizing investments and tracking the success of their marketing campaigns. Meanwhile, Haley was described by an aspect of her physical appearance—her infectious smile—and the soft abstraction of being the office "glue," which certainly seemed like a good trait but a generic one that wasn't central to success in her *specific* job.

Debra considered the session she'd just attended. Hands down, Haley had been much better than Chad. Could those presentations have been an anomaly?

Before the next session started, she found Terry in the hallway. Her head of HR had an amazingly good memory and a good sense of the performance of everyone at the director level and above.

"I just saw an interesting presentation by Chad and Haley," said Debra casually. "I'm curious—how has Tom rated their performance on their official reviews?"

"Hmmm, let me think," said Terry. "Both are strong overall, but Haley is rated higher on pretty much every category on the performance grid—not just by Tom, but also in the feedback from others who work closely with her."

"What about in data?"

"Haley's definitely a lot stronger there," said Terry, without needing to think about it. "I actually just looked at how various directors scored on data competency last week. We're trying to figure out who can teach one of our internal professional development classes. Tom has dinged Chad for spending too long performing analyses that had no business ramification. His feedback on Haley is the opposite—she generates the exact right hypotheses quickly and comes to a conclusion."

So the presentations weren't an anomaly. Haley was stronger at working with data.

Tom was a caring manager. Uniquely so. After all, how many managers—especially at the VP level—took care to write notes of gratitude to their staff? She'd never considered Tom as someone who was overtly biased against women. Quite the opposite, as he'd also been one of the main senior advocates for establishing their women's leadership program several years ago. He obviously saw Haley's strengths, beyond her infectious smile—that was evident in her performance reviews, which he had written himself.

Debra recalled a male manager early in her own career who had truly seemed to believe Debra's sole purpose was to get him coffee—even though she was a financial analyst—and didn't recognize any of her other strengths. She'd taken comfort over the years that, as the CEO, she'd taken a zero-tolerance attitude to that kind of behavior. She would have considered Tom a model for advocating for both his male and female staff and seeing their many talents equally.

But here Tom was talking about his two employees in ways that made it sound like Haley's main value was her smile and social support—or whatever he meant by glue—whereas Chad was the data star. If that's how he described them to Debra, was that also how he described them to others? Was the reputation he was building for each of his employees consistent with their skills and contributions to the company? Did Haley know that Tom described her this way, and how did it impact her perceptions—of herself relative to others, and of her place at the firm? How did she feel about getting that note, and did she suspect or even know what Chad's note had said in contrast?

Eager to take a mental break, Debra turned to her to-do list. She had a few questions she needed answered on the product relaunches. She headed down the elevator to Leland's office. But as she was a few steps away, she turned her heel and went the opposite direction. She knew it was wrong to bother Amber. But the truth was that Amber was much more likely to have an authoritative answer quickly, and she didn't feel like dealing with one of Leland's nature metaphors.

Debra poked her head in Amber's door. "Do you have a few minutes?" she asked. "I wanted to get your thoughts on some of the product relaunches."

"Of course," said Amber. She did all the things you'd expect an employee to do when the CEO entered your office: put her mouse down, swiveled her chair away from her screen and toward Debra. But Debra could see the frustration: they both knew that Debra was about to ask her a question she should theoretically be asking Leland. They both knew how poorly their meeting had gone a few weeks ago when Amber had raised the issues with Leland.

Before Debra could ask her question, the phone rang. She glanced down at the Caller ID: FRONT DESK. Well, that could be anyone, but Debra was old-fashioned. When the phone rang, you answered it. She told Amber to go ahead and take the call.

Amber hit speakerphone, and a frantic voice came through. "Hi Amber. I'm the front desk manager. I'm really sorry to bother you, but one of my receptionists got a call from one of our corporate partners who is really angry and honestly not making a lot of sense. I tried to talk to him, but he's demanding to talk to someone senior in product management for one of your apps. I'm not sure what to do. I know you're really busy. Do you want to take it, or is there someone on your team I should try?"

Debra nodded at Amber. "I can wait a few minutes. If it takes too long, you can come to my office later."

"I'll take it," Amber told the front desk manager. After she was connected, she introduced herself to the person on the phone. "I lead our product team for the app you called about," she said.

There was a moment of silence at the other end of the line before a man's voice came through the speaker phone, speaking quickly, shaking with anger. "I said I wanted to talk to a manager. You're the third secretary I've been transferred to. This is completely unacceptable."

Did he really say that? Debra and Amber looked at one another.

Amber took a deep breath, then calmly said, "My name is Amber, sir. I am the person who runs the product development team. I'd be happy to help you."

There was another pause. "Oh," he said gruffly, not as embarrassed as one would like before he continued on.

"I'm sorry you had to experience that," said Debra after Amber hung up the phone.

Amber shrugged. "What did you want to discuss on the product relaunches?" But the back-to-business question didn't hide the sadness in her eyes.

That evening, Debra and her son dined together at his favorite Italian restaurant in Venice Beach. At the end of the meal, Debra wasn't surprised when the waiter, without ceremony, put the check in front of her son. She enjoyed breakfast or lunch with male employees a few times a month, and this always happened then too—even when it was clearly a business meal, and even though she was always the one who had asked for the check. This had even happened once when the man had been an intern who didn't look a day over twenty. Even if they didn't always put the check in front of her, there should have been enough uncertainty about who might be paying to place it in the middle.

"Wait," she called out to the waiter, as he was turning from their table. "Here you go." She reached across the table to take the check, slipped her card into the jacket, and handed it back to him.

As soon as he left, she whispered to her son, "Watch this. He'll bring the check back to you. I'd put the odds at six to one."

"Do you really think so? I mean you were the one who gave it to him, and I don't think I look like a Debra."

"Doesn't matter," she said.

She was right, of course. A few minutes later, the waiter once again placed the little black folder in front of her son, this time with Debra's card sticking out. "Thank you very much, sir," the waiter said.

"That's so appalling," her son said, shaking his head.

Debra shrugged. She was used to it and didn't (or couldn't) let it bother her. She was reminded of how, when her mobile phone company rolled out its auto-complete emojis, typing in "CEO" or "doctor" made a male emoji immediately appear. Her daughter Olivia had been appalled, but Debra had admitted she didn't really care. Not just because she didn't have an emoji habit—there were simply bigger things to get worked up about. Even as a female CEO, she herself had to admit that most CEOs were male—so, in terms of probability, the auto-complete wasn't even wrong.

The mobile phone company had rectified the faux pas, eventually. Of course, it was a lot easier to reprogram a phone than to reprogram a human to make the same assumption. Debra herself had to stop herself sometimes from using the pronoun "he" without thinking when talking about certain professions. Even in the face of all the evidence, the waiter's unconscious wiring seemed to have overpowered the facts. Quite simply: the auto-complete in his brain had told him that it must be a "sir" who paid the bill.

Unconscious biases were like auto-completes, Debra realized.[7] But they reared their head a lot more often than when you were writing a message on your mobile phone. They could happen while talking about your colleagues to others (as in the case of Tom discussing Chad and Haley), when introduced to someone for the first time (as in the case of the Wharton alum at the reception or the angry voice at the other end of Amber's phone), or when considering assignments (as in Cassandra's story about the intern meeting).

These types of events were so normal that she realized she probably didn't even notice them much of the time—perhaps due to her own mental auto-completes. The situation with Amber's phone call had been dramatic enough that it would have caught her attention. But Tom's description of Haley that morning—Debra didn't want to admit it, but she might not have blinked if she weren't currently trying to figure out the source of the company's female engagement problem.

She felt sick on her drive home as she remembered a memo she'd sent out the week before, announcing promotions to the rest of the firm. Debra had just cut and pasted paragraphs that managers had sent her without giving much thought to them beyond fixing a few typos or ensuring they were all the same length.

As soon as she got home, she pulled the memo up in the email sent box on her phone and found the sentences she'd remembered:

Congratulations to Mara for her promotion to senior manager of analytics. We're appreciative of Mara's incredible work ethic and also grateful for her exceptional baking skills—we've probably all gained a few pounds from her brownies.

She looked at the description below Mara's:

Congratulations to Michael for his promotion to senior manager of analytics. He recently led analytical work that was exactly what was needed to bring a critical project across the finish line, leading to $5M in revenue.

The implications hit her. They had hundreds of employees at the company. Most people reading the memo wouldn't know every promoted employee. She could imagine Mara's manager defending the paragraph, saying that Mara liked bringing baked goods in; that it was important when it came to building a positive team environment.

All of that might be true. But people reading the memo would perhaps remember only one thing about each person. With Michael, they would remember the results. With Mara, they would remember the brownies.

Debra's chest felt heavy as she noticed other disturbing patterns. The paragraphs about men were always focused on concrete accomplishments. The paragraphs about women—whether sent to Debra by male or female managers; whether they were new managers or more tenured—were more likely to include words that connoted effort rather than ability ("hardworking"). The female paragraphs were more likely to include basic job descriptions ("she will be doing XYZ activities in her new role") rather than ringing endorsements ("she is one of the best at XYZ activities"). The paragraphs for men were more likely to have phrases like "leader" and "trailblazer" applied to them as opposed to good phrases like "very productive," "very good skill set."[8]

She could edit out the mental auto-completes the next time she wrote a promotion memo. But that happened once a year. The more pervasive problem was the seemingly off-hand comments and mental auto-completes that happened every day. What was worrying here wasn't just how many people might take Tom at face value if he'd implied Haley's main virtue was being the glue of the office, but that they'd then repeat it to others. After all, Tom was Haley's boss, so he must be a reliable source. If someone in another department had a high-profile project they needed to assign to someone in Tom's department, it seemed only logical that they would expect Chad to be the superstar and ask for his time. Cassandra had explained to Debra the opportunity gap facing the interns, but it affected people further up the ladder too. The female interns weren't given as many opportunities to prove themselves. And then, once women reached Haley's level, they still had to prove themselves over and over again.

CHAPTER THIRTEEN

Cassandra

T he day after observing the finance meeting, Cassandra decided
she wanted to hear the interns' perspective directly. She sent an
email to Paige and Jessica and decided to be honest: *"I'm trying to better understand perspectives of women at the firm on the different challenges
we face. Can I come by this afternoon?"*

Paige and Jessica greeted Cassandra as she entered their work
area. They were accompanied by a third female intern. The company
had run out of desk space, and so the interns were camped out in a
conference room with a few makeshift, slightly-nicer-than-usual card
tables and multi-colored folding chairs around them. One telephone
was perched on a small filing cabinet in the front of the room. Ethan,
the male intern that Cassandra remembered from the meeting the day
before, sat, by himself, at a table at the front of the room by the phone.
He seemed to be absorbed in his work and didn't even look up when
Cassandra walked in. The three women had been scattered across the
back half of the room, but moved to concentrate around one table
when Cassandra walked in.

Cassandra had barely sat down when the phone rang.

Paige, Jessica, and the third woman looked at one another. The third woman started to get out of her seat, as if to walk toward the phone, but Jessica shook her head, as if to say no, don't get it.

That was odd, Cassandra thought. Were they avoiding someone? Ethan didn't seem to be in on what they were doing, but he wasn't answering the phone either—despite being closest to it.

The phone rang again. The women looked at one another. Cassandra examined their faces. Frustration on Jessica's face. Sad amusement on Paige's. She couldn't see the third woman's face as she'd started mock-banging her head on the table. Ethan continued to stare intently at his laptop.

At the fifth ring, Ethan suddenly snapped his neck up. He turned around and said tersely to the room, "I'm in the middle of something. Can someone get that?"

Paige sighed quietly, walked up to answer the phone. "It's for you," she said as she handed it to Ethan. After exchanging a few words with the person on the other end, he picked up a stack of manila folders and left the room.

Cassandra looked around quizzically. Obviously, she was missing something.

The women nodded at one another as if to say, "we can let her in."

Jessica pulled an old-school black-and-white composition notebook from her handbag and flipped to a page to show Cassandra. "We started counting the number of times the phone rings and how often one of us three compared to the one of the three male interns picks it up."

The page was filled with rows of pink tally marks and only a handful of blue tally marks.

"Right now, after a month, it's sixty to seven," said Paige.

The three of them then spoke all at once and in quick succession, as if they'd been waiting for someone more senior at the company to listen:

"They don't even realize it," said Jessica.

"And Ethan even said he was expecting a call fifteen minutes ago," added Paige.

The third intern sighed. "We're not their assistants, but that's how they treat us."

"We have no idea why they don't answer the phone," said the third intern. "Do these guys not answer the phone in their daily lives either? Do they have mothers or sisters or girlfriends that do it?"

"What happens when we're not here? Are they inconsiderate of each other, or just of women?" added Jessica, with a sigh, "Maybe we should put in a nanny cam to see."

As Cassandra listened to the younger women, she wondered about the connection between Ethan being treated as more valuable by his bosses and him acting as if his time were more valuable than that of his female colleagues. Even if he started the internship seeing the women as equals, would he continue to believe that when he saw them receiving less important assignments or when he noticed their ideas were less likely to be listened to than his?

She and Debra had met for coffee before the workday started that morning, and the CEO had mentioned her thinking about the "mental auto-complete." It was a smart phrase for what others referred to as unconscious, hidden, or implicit bias. Even if you knew that biases were held by good people, and that they were often unintentional, it was hard not to shut down or bristle when you heard the word. Most people had a bias against the word bias, Cassandra mused. Debra's term emphasized that, like electronic auto-completes, mental ones were due not to malicious intent, but to faulty programming.

What programming did Ethan arrive at his internship with, and what was being further reinforced each day?

The conversation pivoted to the assignment Ethan had received the day before, compared to the women's tasks.

"It makes me so angry," said Jessica.

Paige looked uncertain. "I know I should be angry too. But I guess it makes me question myself. I wonder whether I'm less qualified than Ethan. And then I think that's silly, and I'm letting them win."

"Ethan mansplained pricing strategy to Paige the other day," Jessica said to Cassandra with a disgusted sigh. "This would be bad enough, except that it was Paige who taught Ethan pricing strategy on our first day. We were all there!"

Cassandra had been in grad school when the word "mansplaining" first started entering the popular lexicon. Some of her male colleagues started to use the word as a joke anytime they went into long monologues. But the women noted mansplaining was often something that felt more insidious: men who didn't think that the audience member, usually a woman, *should* know whatever it was they were about to discuss, or that it didn't matter what she knew (or didn't know) because his need to be the expert superseded her reality. There was a deep unconscious bias implicit in the things men felt they needed to explain to women.

"I don't know?" Paige said sarcastically. "Maybe he understands it better than I do?" But then her tone shifted to sadness. "He seems to be the one whose ideas get the attention in the meetings."

Jessica's lips were pressed. "I couldn't believe that meeting yesterday," she said. She turned to Cassandra. "That happens every meeting."

"I know that I shouldn't question myself," said Paige. "But I wouldn't have even applied for this internship if Jessica hadn't convinced me. I'd already been unsure as to whether I was qualified enough, and seeing how Ethan gets treated differently than we do makes me doubt myself. I'm sorry; I know I sound insecure."

"We really need to get you a 'sorry jar'!" Jessica shook her head. "If you had to put a quarter in every time you said sorry without needing to, we'd be able to go out to a really nice lunch!" Then her tone turned more serious. "Paige, you started your own business when you were in high school and won all kinds of young entrepreneur competitions! I think you're more qualified than me, Ethan, and all of the other interns combined."

Cassandra wondered how the job advertisement had been worded. Did that at least partly account for why someone as accomplished as Paige had been put off? They'd started discussing in HR department meetings how specific words in job listings could lead more men versus women to apply.[9]

Moreover, would Paige now be less likely to share her ideas, seeing it as pointless? Cassandra hoped that wouldn't be the case, but knew that it might be. She'd have to explain to Debra how this exemplified why so many women were frustrated by the overfocus on being told to "lean in." Women often felt stuck with only one of two undesirable outcomes: you lean in, you don't get credit and often a man does. You don't, and the idea doesn't go anywhere either.[10]

Cassandra wondered how the movie would play forward. Would Paige become less confident with time? Would her confidence, which had been lower than Jessica's to begin with, continue to be impacted by Ethan and the way their managers treated them? Would that have an impact on her performance? Cassandra's psychologist friends talked a lot about "internalized bias" as explaining how people can come to believe and accept negative biases about their own groups (and themselves) without even realizing it.[11] She winced at the thought: how much mental auto-completes might shape not only Paige's experience at work, but also her perception of herself.

Cassandra was thinking about the situation with Chad and Haley that Debra had described to her over coffee that morning. At the time, Cassandra hadn't been sure how much of her friend's feelings she should reveal to the CEO, but now she realized Debra needed to understand the type of bias that women could internalize based on how they were treated. "Privately, Tom has told me I'm the strongest person on the team in terms of data," Haley had recently told the Purple Panda crew over drinks. "And yet publicly, he rarely talks about my data skills in the same way he talks about Chad's. I know that I haven't gotten assigned to some of the highest-profile projects because people in other departments assume Chad is better. But probably worse is that sometimes I doubt myself— are my skills as strong as I think, or even as strong as Tom tells me?"

Even worse, despite her excellent reviews, Haley had mentioned she had had trouble getting specific feedback from Tom on how she could improve. Once, Haley had shown Cassandra a performance review she'd received from Tom—mostly stellar but with a phrase about how she needed to "improve at having gravitas in internal meetings." What did that even mean?

Cassandra thought about the research she'd read that, even when women and men enjoyed similar work opportunities, supervisors are more likely to provide men with the type of detailed feedback that is needed to support the individual's continued growth.[12]

As Cassandra was about to leave the conference room for her next meeting of the day, a second male intern walked in.

"I'm going to be busy concentrating. Can you can take my calls?" he asked the women.

He set down his laptop at a seat in a corner of the room and put his headphones on without waiting for a response.

"I mean, I suppose that's better than Ethan," said Jessica, breaking the silence. "At least he asked. Sort of."

They all laughed tensely.

"I need a coffee break," said Jessica, walking out the door with Cassandra.

"Are you glad you took this internship?" Cassandra asked as they made their way to the elevator. "Would you want to work here after graduation?"

"My mom and my aunt work in business, and they're pretty honest with me. So I know it's hard for women at all organizations," she said. "And I think the work itself is exciting. But I don't know. I try to be a really confident person, especially when I'm around the other women interns here. I want us all to rally together."

"But?"

"I don't get as many of the really meaty assignments as the men do, though I've gotten a few. But whenever I do, I feel like I have to work twice as hard to prove not only that I can do it, but that women can!"

"How have you done?"

"I've done well," Jessica smiled, "One of the managers told me my last assignment was better than anything he's seen, not just from an intern, but from the full-time analysts as well. So I know I shouldn't complain."

"That's great," said Cassandra. She felt sad about the "working twice as hard" phenomenon that Jessica was experiencing. She knew from personal experience how that only seemed to get worse as women advanced the ladder. Many of her friends mentioned they hadn't even noticed it as much until they reached management level. She wanted to be able to tell the younger woman that things would get better, but didn't feel she could honestly make that promise.

"Can I tell you something else that's bothering me?" said Jessica. "Sometimes we get grouped with other interns here to get specific assignments done. When I'm paired with only other women, I'll always volunteer to be in charge, no matter who it is."

"That's not surprising," Cassandra laughed, even though she'd barely met Jessica.

Jessica smiled briefly before letting out a sigh. "But there was one time I was grouped with a few male interns, and not ones like Ethan who is pretty take-charge himself too. But male interns who probably never volunteer to be in charge. And I basically told one of the guys to be in charge. I didn't realize it until later, and I honestly don't know why I did that."

Cassandra felt sad, but not surprised. She'd noticed the same thing herself. When genders were mixed, men seemed to become the leader the majority of the time—even when there was a woman who was the more dominant personality.[13] It was interesting how both Jessica and Paige, in different ways, had been impacted by internalized bias. Jessica didn't question herself in a fundamental way like Paige did, but she still unconsciously took a backseat when it came to her male colleagues.

"I guess I also worry about being seen as an angry Black woman," said Jessica. "You know, Jessica is actually my middle name. I never go by it, outside of here. But when I put Tamira on my resume, I didn't get as many calls for interviews."

"I'm using my middle name too," said Cassandra. "I have my whole life." The name Chun Hua was on her birth certificate, but since kindergarten she'd gone by Cassandra, after the experience of an older sister who was tired of being taunted at school for her hard-to-pronounce given name. She thought about the events that the company scheduled on diversity, equity, and inclusion. They often had events that were meant to support women. And occasionally they had events that were meant to support people of color (of whom there was a smaller number). But they never really talked about intersectionality, or the fact that many individuals had to confront biases and challenges related to multiple identities. As a Black woman, Jessica faced different barriers compared to Black men and white women. Cassandra wondered if Debra realized that part of why Haley did work so hard on making sure she had an "infectious" smile was that, as a Latina woman, she felt like she had to overcompensate for stereotypes that the world might have about her. As an Asian-American herself, Cassandra wondered if Debra realized her own assumption that Cassandra was quiet and lacking confidence had been a stereotype too.

Early the next morning, Debra dropped by Cassandra's office. They were both early risers and had decided they'd try to connect before the workday started to trade notes whenever they could. But the "woke" Debra who had very much absorbed the magnitude of the mental auto-complete challenge the day before, and who had seemed distraught as a result, had been tempered by optimism. "I was just thinking about how many men participated in the Women's March, especially men your age. I admit my generation isn't the most enlightened," said Debra, "But it seems like things will get better with your generation. That's got to make you feel more hopeful."

"I guess so," Cassandra said tentatively. She didn't share Debra's optimism, but she also didn't want to come across as too ungrateful. She knew how much worse it must have been for Debra when she was Cassandra's age. Obviously, things were better now than thirty years ago, and Cassandra hoped they'd be better still three decades later. Jessica had mentioned there was one male intern who actually called the other guys out on what they were doing from time to time. And it was true that Cassandra had many male friends and colleagues, like Kyle, who were at least more cognizant of gender dynamics and issues than their older counterparts. At the same time, spending time with the college-aged interns had made Cassandra reflect on the common misperception that biases in the workplace would be eliminated once younger generations rose into power. Even young men that considered themselves woke were still subject to mental auto-completes. Just the week before she'd seen an article in her Twitter feed that had made her want to throw her phone against the wall: a university study that revealed bias in how male college students evaluated their male versus female classmates.[14] Cassandra wasn't the throwing type, so instead she retweeted the article and then ate a bar of chocolate.

She knew that generational shifts alone wouldn't bring about change.

CHAPTER FOURTEEN

Kyle

When Leland had arrived at the company earlier that year, Kyle and his friends had spent more time dissecting their new CPO's short, one-paragraph introductory email to their division than eager college English majors explicating a passage of Shakespeare. They'd all expected that Amber would succeed Natalie for the CPO position; she'd started doing a lot of the job anyway while Natalie was busy with other projects.

Instead, Leland appeared, and it had been pretty bad from the beginning—his very first introduction to the group.

I'm excited to meet all of you. For a little background on myself, I studied engineering at MIT, received my MBA from Harvard Business School, and have worked in product management for over three decades. I've always aspired to be a CPO and am grateful for the opportunity and look forward to working with you all. On a personal level, I enjoy sailing and play racquetball and golf often (Jack and George can testify to seeing me at the Brentwood Racquet Club a few times a week, though despite how much time I spend there, I never seem to get better).

Kyle and his friends were neither executives nor communications specialists, but it didn't take an expert to point out the problems with Leland's introduction.

#1. It sounded like Debra had passed Amber over for someone the CFO and Board Chair had found on the racquetball court.

#2. MIT, Harvard, sailing, racquetball, golf—he obviously didn't realize that flaunting these types of privileged experiences was not the way to bond with the staff in an introduction. Maybe that would work in some companies, but not theirs.

#3. The introduction was all about him.

"I mean, I'd expect a new entry-level staff person to do more research than this before introducing themselves at a new company," Kyle had told Shannon as they dissected the email. Kyle and Shannon were both directors of product development. She reported to Amber, while he reported to Meg, but he'd worked with Amber on a number of projects over the past few years. "He could have looked on our website, talked about something he was excited to be a part of. How did we hire a CPO with less basic EQ than we'd expect of someone more junior?"

The replies-to-all to Leland's initial message on the all-company listserv didn't make things any better.

From Jack: *Welcome to the team, Leland. You'll have to improve your speed on the racquetball court though—we don't work as slow as your previous company.*

From Roger, their Chief Revenue Officer: *Leland, I think I saw you playing golf last week. Was that you trying to chip out of the sand trap on 8?*

Jack again: *Roger, don't pick on Leland. At least he didn't double bogey on the 11th. Talk about amateur hour.*

Kyle had observed that this was the way the male executives seemed to interact with one another—constant riffing and publicly challenging one another. It was like a corporate version of the fraternity house, he supposed. In truth, he found it all strange. But he had learned that he could bond with the executive men by participating in the game—laughing about Jack's khakis (so 1990s!), and letting Jack make fun of seeing him running on the street in the mornings (work on your form!). He straddled both worlds, joining in the male executive banter (though he'd never do it over email in front of the entire company—how embarrassing), but also laughing about it with his friends (who were mainly women).

After Leland's introductory email—and the replies to it—Kyle, Shannon, and a few of their other friends (Haley in marketing, Cassandra in HR, and Rita in finance) exchanged a series of group text messages: their most frequent form of communication about the absurdity of everyday work life:

> Kyle: *What if this just went on forever? Every male executive personally challenging each other while copying the entire company every day for six months?*
> Shannon: *I've figured out how to become an executive as a woman. I'll need to hire a man to ghostwrite my executive banter for me.*
> Haley: *But seriously, why do they copy the entire company on these?*
> Rita: *I think they think it's engaging. Like we'll want to be like them.*

Other than group text messages, the group's preferred method for day-to-day debriefing was coffee breaks in the vegetable and herb garden on the roof. The rows of wooden planters were a selling point to prospective employees—"we have roof-garden-to-table veggies in the cafeteria!" Truthfully there was only enough produce for occasional garnishes. Additionally, the roof was fairly inconvenient to get to—two sets of stairs separated by a long hallway—so it was often emptier than one would expect. Kyle and his friends could easily meet at the gourmet coffee bar, secure their beverage of choice, and trek to their private debriefing zone.

Since Leland had arrived to run their department, Kyle estimated he and Shannon had tripled the amount of "coffee breaks" they took. That morning, after they'd sat through yet another meeting where Leland literally read from a stack of index cards, they didn't even have to exchange words to know that they'd want to discuss it on the roof. They didn't even bother to get their coffee as they wordlessly made it to the patio chairs haphazardly placed in between the mint and basil plants.

"It doesn't seem like anything has changed since we talked to Terry," said Shannon.

They were both quiet. The month before, Terry had interviewed a number of managers on the product team—about half a dozen of them altogether—to ask how Leland's "onboarding" was going so far. They all compared notes afterward: no one had pulled punches, not even Kyle, who had more of a "keep your head down" philosophy compared to his female counterparts. Terry had assured them she'd talk to Debra about Leland and they'd see real change. But nothing had happened.

"I feel like our teams are trying to get work done on the product relaunches, but he has us spinning around working on random other stuff. I can't help but think this is a sinking ship, and we should start looking," said Shannon.

"What does Amber think about Leland?"

"She's too professional to tell me the truth. But we all know that Amber would be better at that job. And maybe Leland wasn't intentionally hired over Amber because they were looking for a man…but you do still wonder. Would a woman get away with being so ineffective?"

"Probably not." Kyle hated to admit it.

"He's like the literal manifestation of our glass ceiling," said Shannon. "I mean if he were a strong performer, it would be one thing.

We'd still be frustrated on Amber's behalf. But now it feels so symbolic—an incompetent man permitted to hold a C-suite position despite not getting anything done."

Leland's mere existence was demoralizing to Shannon and Kyle's other female colleagues in a way Kyle could try to understand, but never fully identify with—Leland wasn't the literal manifestation of *his* glass ceiling, after all. At the same time, Kyle's own engagement and productivity at work depended on having strong leaders above and around him. He certainly didn't enjoy working so hard for a department head he found completely incompetent. Even worse, if Shannon and others quit, there'd be a lot more work for Kyle—and the workplace would be less enjoyable too. Perhaps it was better to be first domino than the last one standing?

He made a mental note to turn on the feature on LinkedIn that alerted recruiters to the fact that you were open to other opportunities.

Cassandra joined them a few minutes later.

"Would you ever discuss Leland with Debra?" Shannon asked Cassandra, knowing their friend was helping the CEO understand the gender issues that their generation faced.

"I've been thinking about how to discuss with Debra that there are multiple kinds of bias," Cassandra said. "There's out-group bias, which means what it sounds like—bias against someone unlike you. But there's also in-group favoritism, which is also what it sounds like. It's where men receive a 'leg up' for being men, because other men see a younger version of themselves or informally develop more rapport."

Kyle appreciated the frameworks that Cassandra brought from her graduate degree, but didn't like feeling guilty as she spoke. He'd been invited to golf or racquetball with the male executives on several occasions. He went, of course. It wasn't like he could say no. And he wasn't someone who believed people in the workplace shouldn't socialize. You spent most of your life in the office, and those interpersonal relationships made the time more engaging and could help get the work done. But Shannon played golf too—actually, her handicap was better than his—and was never invited. And, even if Shannon hadn't played golf, the male executives could have easily invited her to breakfast or lunch to try to get to know her more informally.

Even in the cases where women were invited to the same social events, they were treated differently. Just the day before, he and Shannon had both attended an event in the company's private suite at Dodger Stadium for some of the managers and executives of a cross-divisional team that had been working on the new systems roll-out. There had been two women and eight men.

As soon as they'd all arrived, a waiter had come and asked one of the vice presidents what they wanted. The room had already been full of beer, wine, and a stocked table of food, so it had been hard to imagine what else would be necessary. But the VP had spoken up anyway, "I think we should start the evening with some tequila shots," he'd said. "Bring us eight!"

The women, and a few of the men including Kyle, had looked at each other uncomfortably. Had he really ordered shots just for the men?

Later, when Shannon had grumbled about it, Kyle had asked her why she hadn't said anything. Instead, she and the other woman in the group had hung back awkwardly while all the men drank their tequila.

Her eyes had flashed at him. "You can count too, why didn't you?"

Right. It was easy to be an ally when commiserating with his female friends. He could feel good about himself for understanding their plight. He enjoyed getting credit when he got home and could empathize with his girlfriend Nicole about her struggles with colleagues based on what he'd seen at the office. "You're such a good ally," she'd say.

But Shannon's question had hung in his consciousness for days. Kyle believed he'd earned every promotion or raise or critical assignment he'd received, but he also knew that there were accomplished women, like Shannon, who were also deserving but who didn't have the same kind of access or rapport as he had. Kyle managed both men and women, and he considered himself better at bonding with the women than men of a previous generation. He knew which ones liked sports (whereas Jack was constantly surprised whenever a woman could join in a sports-related conversation), and which ones shared his taste in television shows or books or restaurants. He had an easy rapport with Meg, who was his boss, and Amber, who was a mentor to him.

But, in the end, for his closest friend at work, he hadn't been willing to sacrifice his own likeability on something as silly as a shot of tequila. He had been enjoying the opportunity to bond with a VP who had previously barely known his name—and he hadn't wanted to put that at risk by pointing out the man hadn't ordered shots for the women. Kyle had always thought of himself as woke. But maybe there was a difference between being woke in bed and staring at the ceiling and actually getting up and doing something.

"Why don't you invite him to lunch yourself?" Kyle had said to Shannon about the VP as they carpooled home from the game. As soon as the words had come out of his mouth, he had realized it was a dumb question. He probably didn't even realize all the reasons that it was dumb, but he had suspected Shannon would tell him.

"It's not as easy for a woman to befriend a senior man," she said. "If they are your manager, or you're working together on a specific project, and social conversations become part of work conversations, maybe even over meals, that's easier. But if you're just looking to network? Even if it's totally innocent, or you're doing the exact same thing a male colleague would do, you're always worried about optics—like someone will think you're using your feminine wiles or something." She laughed. "And, frankly, I think even men who make fun of the Mike Pence rule often worry about seeming like a creepy older guy, so they don't know how to behave. Plus, don't even get me started on men who say they don't want to meet with female colleagues alone because they're afraid they'll start crying and they won't know what to do."

It was unfortunate. With all of the challenges they faced at work, having a mentor was even more important for women. But it seemed that much harder for women to find mentors at all.

He felt even worse later that week when another female colleague, Beth, asked how the game in the coffee room had gone.

"It was great, you should have been there!" Kyle said.

"Why didn't you come?" asked Vince, another of their colleagues.

"I need at least a few weeks' notice to book our babysitter," she replied. "I wish we had more social events during the day or earlier in the evening when I could make it. I understand if some of them are at night, but almost all of our events are after hours. And often not scheduled far enough in advance to make arrangements."

"Amen," said another woman who was rinsing out her coffee mug. "I know men have responsibilities outside of work too, but it's generally easier for men to attend evening events."

"I babysit my daughter plenty of times when my wife has to work late," protested Vince.

"The fact that you call it babysitting is telling," said Beth. "I'm sure when your wife was watching your daughter while you were at the game, she didn't call it babysitting. It's called being a mom."

Vince clearly didn't know what to say to that. Kyle thought about what Cassandra had said about "in-group favoritism" and realized that there were two forms of it going on here. First, there was the insider network by which Kyle was more likely to go out to lunch or golf, drink shots together at a group event, or even exchange informal banter in the hallway with the more senior men. But there was also the fact that business environments had long been built around the schedules of men who felt more free of familial responsibilities in the evening—it was a type of structural bias that disproportionately and negatively impacted working mothers. He thought for a moment about texting his friends in the Purple Panda crew to say this. Then he caught himself, realizing how silly it would seem to them if he wrote the text as if he'd "discovered" this bias: after all, several of them were working mothers themselves.

CHAPTER FIFTEEN

Debra

"We have a meeting with the Board finance committee next month, in mid-October," said Debra. She had arranged to meet with Jack, Leland, and Amber over lunch at Thai Pantry. "Let's discuss what we'll present to them as a path to an added $5M in revenues this year." She and Jack had worked the numbers out. If they could come up with a plan, they could avoid layoffs for now. Plus, they'd be in a better spot in January—when the Board meeting was probably going to determine whether she kept her job.

It was an awkward group, sitting around one of the square tables in a corner. While they made small talk before the waiter arrived to take their order, Jack tore up the paper placement into a stack of almost perfect 1x1 inch squares and stacked them on the table. It was an odd habit of his that tended to resurface when he was especially stressed. The last time she'd seen him do it was during the Great Recession.

Across the table, Leland also seemed uncertain of what to do with his hands. He alternated between placing them on his lap, on the table, and picking up his phone, seemingly to check his email, but never looking at the screen long enough to do so.

Amber's hands were beneath the table, but she was studying the menu as if it were the most riveting laminated sheet in the world. Her eyes were currently fixed on the meats page, even though she was a vegetarian.

Sometimes Debra wished it didn't always fall on her to break the ice in uncomfortable situations. But, alas, that was ultimately the job of the CEO. "Leland, which of the relaunches do you think we could move up?" she asked. "We need to go faster."

Jack nodded his head.

Leland continued to fidget with his phone. "Well, we'd have to figure out what decision criteria we'd use to determine timeline," he said.

Was he stalling with that response, or did he truly have no clue?

"I'm just worried that the teams aren't ready. I guess I'd have to think about it more…" Leland trailed off.

Before Leland had a chance to say any more, Jack jumped in. "Amber, I saw the project plan you'd put together last week for the new product launches—thank you for doing that so quickly and mapping out the path to two million. You have a great plan already, but what if we wanted an extra million?"

"I think both of the new products could potentially play well in a secondary market," she said. "I'd have to sit down and run the numbers, but it's possible that could get at least an extra million that way."

"Excellent," said Jack.

"That's great," Leland added.

"So that means you'd have to get the other two million out of the relaunches, Leland," Debra said.

Leland looked uncertain but nodded his head. "Yes, of course."

Debra felt the guilt in her shoulders and didn't want to look Amber in the eye. She knew that it wouldn't be easy for Amber and her teams to squeeze even more money out of the new launches—and that she wouldn't have had to if Leland had done his job properly and gotten the relaunches off the ground already.

Debra looked across the table. Jack didn't seem to be suffering any guilt. He started asking Amber follow-up questions as he took the pen out of his breast pocket and started jotting down numbers on his napkin.

"Do you think Leland can get everything done?" asked Debra. After lunch, she and Jack had returned to her office with Terry joining them.

Jack closed his eyes for a second. "I don't know what we're paying him for if not," he muttered. Then he seemed to remember how hard he'd advocated for Leland's hire. "He's had a slow start, but I'm sure he will get better. I am worried about Amber though. We are asking her to do a lot, and I wouldn't want her to feel overwhelmed."

"I think we need to give Amber a few more staff to help her," said Debra, ignoring the issue of Leland for the time being. "I have a few ideas for who we could move over."

"More people? She's already got a big team," said Jack. "If she can't get this done without more help, then she probably is too overwhelmed. Should we remove some of the existing products under Amber's purview? The apps reporting to Shannon are doing pretty well, and she's so independent. We could have Shannon report to Leland instead of to Amber. That would free up Amber's time."

"I don't know," said Debra. "Leland seems to be the one who is overwhelmed. Why would we give him more responsibility through another direct report?"

"True. Perhaps he just needs more leverage. Wonder if there's a senior person elsewhere in the company that we could move to help Leland out. Maybe we should give more work to Kyle. I'd love to see him groomed to take on more."

A few weeks earlier, Debra would have seen the conversation as the type of natural back-and-forth that leaders should always have, debating the pros and cons of all staffing decisions and organizational structures. But after her week of discussing mental auto-completes and unconscious bias with Cassandra, she had a nagging feeling that something wasn't quite right. Jack's reaction to Amber's stepping up was to worry she would be overwhelmed. As a result, he proposed decreasing her span of control. His reaction to Leland, the one who was actually overwhelmed (not performing in his job), was to increase his span of control (moving Shannon to report to him). When Debra pushed back on that, Jack's next response was to give Leland more leverage—another senior staff member on his team. If anyone would need that added leverage, wouldn't it be Amber, who had just agreed to take on more?

The phrase "benevolent sexism" had appeared in some of the articles that Cassandra had emailed Debra earlier that week.[15] Was that what was going on here? Despite Amber being, without question, more competent, Jack still saw her as someone who needed to be protected from too much work, whereas Leland needed to be supported so he could take on more. She knew that Jack appreciated Amber's strengths, but did he (unconsciously) see Amber as simply less strong compared to a man and less able to handle the challenges of more difficult work?

As far as Debra could remember, Jack hadn't been so paternalistic with Natalie, but she was ten years older than Amber. Did age come into play here? Jack's suggestion of assigning Kyle more work was also telling. Kyle and Amber were about the same age. With a young woman (Amber), his worry was about overloading her. With a young man (Kyle), the question was how to put more on his plate to get him "groomed" for more responsibility faster.

If she were honest with herself, it wasn't just Jack to blame here. In this case, it was Jack who didn't want to overload Amber. But wasn't that partly the argument that Debra had used to make herself feel okay hiring Leland in the first place?

She was grateful to Amber for volunteering to take more on, but she wondered whether she'd unintentionally let Amber fall into the trap women often did. Earlier in her own career, Debra remembered often feeling like she'd become a "responsibility magnet," taking on more when needed by the team without being given any credit or authority.[16] Whenever she had asked for more resources to get the work done, it had been seen as weakness. Whenever she had asked for more compensation for taking on these responsibilities, it had been seen as being difficult, entitled, or ungrateful for the opportunity. By contrast, she'd watched over and again as her male colleagues seemed to experience a totally different game. They didn't volunteer to take things on. And that meant that when new responsibilities were given to them, their bosses felt that they needed to give them additional staff and compensation.

Perhaps this was why the women had been so frustrated when George talked about how women just needed to raise their hands. Women were raising their hands all the time, with more work for less money, less help, and less recognition. Were women at work trapped in a Catch-22? If they didn't raise their hands, they wouldn't get some of the most important assignments, because of bias. But if they did raise their hands and they tried to ask for any of the requisite help to get the work done, they were assumed to be incompetent, confirming the bias that was already there.

"I'd like to leave Shannon where she is," Debra said. "I think Amber can handle it. And, given all that we're asking her to take on, I think we should move a few people to join her team."

At least there was a small victory here: Jack didn't seem to feel like arguing—perhaps realizing that any argument that depended on Leland's competence wasn't likely to go anywhere. Their conversation turned to some of the other strategies they were considering—in particular the international expansion that Natalie had been starting to look into before she left.

"Is there someone on the sales team that can start establishing relationships abroad?" Terry asked.

"What about Anna?" Debra asked. "She studied international business and is fluent in multiple languages."

"Would she be able to move abroad if we needed that?" Jack asked. "I know her husband's got a really great job at one of the big accounting firms downtown. How about Kristine? She would also be excellent."

"Just had her second child," said Terry. "I'm not sure yet if she'd be able to make that kind of commitment. I think she was even considering an 80% schedule. How about Rob?"

"I think that makes sense," Jack said. "The commitments required for a second child are a lot more than a first; I'm sure the kids will need Kristine. Rob's not as strong but I think could figure the job out."

Debra nodded and wrote Rob's name down on her steno pad. But then she stopped her pen mid-stroke. Why were they considering Anna and Kristine's relationship and family statuses, but not Rob's?

There was that benevolent sexism again: assuming that Kristine would be overwhelmed. But there were other issues too. First, an implicit assumption that a husband's career would always come before the wife's. They assumed Anna's husband was unlikely to relocate but didn't even question whether Rob's wife would, even though she was an entertainment lawyer in Hollywood—arguably even less portable than Anna's accountant husband, who worked for a multinational firm with locations abroad. A female partner was expected to be moveable in a way that a male partner wasn't. Maybe Anna's husband could relocate and maybe he couldn't; maybe they'd be fine living apart for a while, maybe not; wasn't that their decision?

Then there was Kristine, who hadn't said for sure she wanted to work an 80% schedule. But Terry and Jack seemed to have decided that was what was best for her (and her children). Even if Kristine did want to shift to 80%, maybe she'd reconsider if she was given the greater opportunity.

And, even if Kristine did want to work a reduced schedule, would that necessarily mean she was less committed or right for the job? Why were women always seen as mothers first and men as workers first?

"Hypothetically, what would help us advance the business more— four days a week from Kristine or five days from Rob?" she asked Jack.

"Kristine's one of the most efficient and productive people I've ever seen," he admitted. The same thing she would have said.

Then, he added, "Four days from her would certainly yield us more than five days from Rob. But that's not the question. This is an important priority. We need someone who is wholly committed."

She wanted to ask him to reconsider his math. If 80% of Person A > 100% of Person B, then wasn't Person A the obvious answer? Would it be different if the genders were reversed?

Now, maybe 100% of someone with Kristine's skills was the ideal in the end, and what they needed to do was seek that person. But this wasn't an abstract question of the "ideal" employee for the job. This was about moving someone internally rather than hiring from outside, as soon as possible. And Anna, Kristine, and Rob were the only logical candidates in-house.

Debra had always been proud of the fact that they allowed many of their employees part-time schedules—mostly working moms—but there was one man who took care of an ailing grandparent and a woman who helped with her parents' small business. But it hadn't occurred to her how many biases underlay the opportunities these employees were afforded: that they were consequently seen as less committed and less able to take on certain roles.

Because women more often asked for part-time arrangements than men, this automatically meant more women were disadvantaged—and that their skills weren't often being leveraged as they could have been. When the business was facing as many challenges as it was now, every single hour of every single employee's time counted. As one of her professors in business school, who had studied manufacturing plants, had said, "You have to maximize what you get out of every single unit of productivity." That meant having the best person on the job for every individual activity.

She'd always thought this was a no-brainer: *of course* they were mindful about who did what. But how often did all of their mental auto-completes get in the way of the right decision?

PART FIVE

The Goldilocks Dilemma

CHAPTER SIXTEEN

Amber

The one common delight all office workers share is the feeling when a meeting ends fifteen minutes early. Five minutes late is more common. Amber had almost jumped out of her seat with glee when Debra had had to run to a commitment off-site, and the team's weekly new product pull-up had ended with a glorious quarter of an hour to spare.

She walked down the hallway to her office with her phone in the back pocket of her jeans. It felt odd not to have the device in her hand. Typically, she checked her email on her phone whenever she could—under the table during meetings, while in the elevator, and even walking down the hallway (while trying not to run into anyone). She felt bad about this, knowing she should be more present. Breathe, and all that. But when your calendar was perennially scheduled back-to-back, there was no other option if you wanted to make sure to reclaim at least some personal time in the evenings.

These extra fifteen minutes were everything, though. She'd be able to answer a few emails once she got back to her desk (imagine that!), and maybe even take a few minutes to use the meditation app on her phone.

However, a few feet from her office door, she heard a voice behind her: "Amber, do you have a few minutes?"

Damn. She turned around. It took her a few beats to place the twenty-something woman in front of her: Erica, an analyst managed by Calvin, a fellow senior director on the product team, who also reported directly to Leland. Amber and Erica had spoken a few times in line at the coffee shop. Small talk about the weather and television. Pleasant enough. Today, Erica had a slightly panicked look in her eye. Her body was leaning forward at a slight angle, as if she wanted to dive in front of Amber to keep her from leaving her line of sight.

"Of course," said Amber. There goes that two minutes of meditation. More emails to respond to at home after dinner. She knew she could have said no or asked her to come back later. But there wasn't a later—these were literally the only fifteen minutes she had free in her calendar for the next two weeks.

As she gestured Erica into her office, Amber flashed back to a time in her twenties when Brent, a male peer with whom she shared a cubicle, had told her that she gave away her time too freely. He told her she should value it more highly. She hadn't understood what he meant at first. But then she had started paying attention to how she and Brent approached their work during an average day. When anyone came up to Brent asking for help, he wouldn't let it distract him from what he was doing. His eyes remained focused on his work, barely lifting as he said he was too busy.

By contrast, when anyone came up to Amber, she would swivel around in her chair and ask how she could help.

"That's why you go home at 8:00 pm and I go home at 6:00 pm," Brent had said.

That conversation had been ten years ago, but it had stuck with her.

Since then, she had learned that there were benefits Brent hadn't appreciated about her more accessible approach: she had become a better manager and a better collaborator across departments, partly because of those experiences helping others even when it wasn't her job. She had been forced to grow her ability to multitask, spreading her attention and time across disparate issues. She liked to think that having developed these skills was the reason she was a senior director now and he was still lower down at a different company. But she wasn't always so sure. Perhaps she'd be even further along in her career if the time that she had spent on "unofficial service" had gone only to the quality of her work. Or perhaps she'd be in the same place but have more time for friends, family, and hobbies.

Either way, she knew she did need to say no more often. She couldn't help everyone in the world. Sometimes you needed to lean out.

And yet enforcing boundaries was easier said than done when there was someone in front of you looking panicked and asking for help.

They sat down at the small circular table in the office.

"Calvin asked me to own a new business plan related to AI technology," Erica said, "I'm not sure how to do this, and I heard you have a lot of expertise in business plans."

Amber refrained from rolling her eyes. A fairly new analyst—just out of college—should certainly not be taking primary ownership for a business plan, at least not without some support. And on a topic as gigantic as artificial intelligence—well, that was even more ridiculous.

This woman was being set up to fail.

Sadly, Amber wasn't surprised. Calvin was widely known as a terrible manager. He was constantly sloughing work to his staff without any support or explanation.

If the projects went poorly—often the case given they hadn't positioned for success—he used the staff member as his convenient fall guy (or, more often, fall gal).

If they went well, he took all the credit, barely acknowledging their role at all.

"Could you be a little more specific?" asked Amber. "Is there a particular business problem you're trying to solve or goal we need to accomplish? AI could be used in a lot of different ways."

She knew Erica wasn't there for a lecture, and it wasn't her place, so she refrained from explaining the different uses of AI that Amber's team had been using for the past few years. They had already incorporated AI to improve the user experience on a number of different apps. Did Calvin know this? Perhaps the more important question: did Leland?

"There's no specific business problem or goal," Erica said. "AI is going to be transformative. It's everything."

Amber wondered how Erica had ended up in front of her. There were a few other junior analysts Amber had given advice to over the years. Knowing business planning was a strength of Amber's, and wanting their staff to have more exposure to a broad range of senior leaders, many managers across the company regularly asked Amber if she'd help their staff think through holes in their plans or explore ideas they hadn't considered.

Occasionally, a proactive junior person approached Amber directly, without an introduction from a manager. But they usually came prepared with very specific questions. Even though the company had a fairly non-hierarchical culture, most junior staff wouldn't approach a senior director who they barely knew, as Erica was doing, without enough planning to put themselves in the best light and get the most out of her time.

Amber looked at the clock. Ten minutes till her next meeting. Ten minutes that she so badly needed to chip away at her to-do list or take a breath. Instead, here she was having to help Erica because Calvin and Leland had, once again, neglected their managerial responsibilities.

She remembered the famous saying about there being a special place in hell for women who don't help one another. On the one hand, Amber believed this—it was the only way for women to thrive in business, where the cards were constantly stacked against them. On the other hand, it always seemed that this sentiment allowed men off the hook.

But that wasn't Erica's fault. Amber could afford to give those ten minutes to someone in need.

"Tell me more about what specific ideas you're considering, and I'm happy to brainstorm further," she said. "For example, are you thinking about AI as a way to engage with customers? Or, more on the back-end, to help our vendors gather and use information behind-the-scenes more efficiently?"

"I want to think bigger than that," said Erica. "Calvin and I have been discussing how *transformative*"—there was that vague word again—"AI is going to be. I don't think we should limit ourselves to one business problem."

The conversation continued in this vein for another five minutes. Amber kept trying to ask Erica the same probing questions she or any senior manager would ask any junior staff member. Erica seemed largely uninterested in listening and kept throwing around vague words.

"So I'm thinking this should be about fifty pages, right?" Erica asked Amber.

Geez, did Calvin not teach Erica anything? "You can look at some samples, but most successful business plans have been much shorter," said Amber. "Actually, Debra always asks for something that can be articulated in three to five pages."

"Well, I just don't agree," said Erica, sounding frustrated. "I think you're totally wrong. I mean, like I said, AI is going to be so transformational. It's going to impact everything. I could imagine this business plan being fifty pages."

Then, even though she had just invalidated everything Amber had said, she added, "Can you help me with that? I'm not sure where to start."

Typically, Amber loved coaching the junior staff, who often had interesting new ideas and perspectives. But this was getting out of control. Erica was not only not making sense, but she also seemed impervious to feedback. And given the extent to which the business was in trouble, the fact that an employee was running around randomly in circles was especially infuriating. Still, she tried to be polite.

"Even if you have fifty pages worth of information to share, you'd still want to be able to summarize what's most important in three to five pages," she said.

"But AI is going to be so transformational," said Erica. She was like a broken record.

This poor person needs some serious coaching, Amber thought. And that wasn't her job. Still, she remembered how much, across her career, she had benefited from senior mentors—both men and women—who took a few minutes every now and again to help her, even if she wasn't in their reporting line. Amber couldn't promise a lot—she certainly wasn't going to do the job of Calvin or Leland here. But she could offer to provide guidance again—provided Erica actually brought more clear thoughts the next time.

"I have to run to my next meeting," said Amber, getting out of her seat. "But I'm happy to talk again over coffee sometime if you want to come to me with more of your thoughts outlined, especially as to specific business problems we'd be able to solve."

On her way to her next meeting, she took her phone out in the elevator and wrote a quick email to Calvin, summarizing the conversation, where she thought Erica needed most help, and offering quick advice. She doubted Calvin would read it or care—and he was certainly unlikely to thank her, as most fellow managers would—but she still maintained the basic courtesy of keeping him updated on a conversation she'd had with someone on his team.

A few hours later, she noticed that Erica had also stopped Dan, their vice president of partnerships, in the café and was asking for his thoughts on her business plan. Amber wasn't surprised to overhear Dan giving Erica the exact same feedback that Amber had provided, though much more bluntly. "Your ideas aren't making any sense," he said.

By the next morning, Amber had attended five more meetings on twelve different topics and written about thirty more emails. She had mostly forgotten about the interaction with Erica.

As a result, Leland's first comment in their weekly check-in surprised her.

"We need to talk about an interaction you had with Erica. You really demoralized her. She told Calvin that she'd gone to you for support, and you were just critical of her ideas."

Of course. Calvin wasn't doing his job as a manager, and Amber was the one getting blamed. But Leland was her boss, and so she had to explain herself. She tried to do so succinctly: "Erica stopped me in the hallway yesterday and asked me for help. She mentioned that Calvin had asked her to write a business plan on AI. I tried to ask her some questions to help her focus. But she kept saying that AI would be 'transformational' and didn't seem interested in getting more specific. She planned to write a fifty-page business plan, and I suggested three to five pages was more appropriate, but she disagreed. Despite her not listening to any of my advice, I still offered at the end to speak again—if she came back to me with specific business problems in mind." She paused. "Would you have done something different?"

"Well, no," said Leland. "And I've had conversations with Erica where she's been pretty vague too, so I know what you mean. But the point is that she feels really bad. Calvin was very worried about that."

If Calvin was so worried about Erica, why hadn't he structured the assignment more clearly and provided the coaching that it was his job to do? And Leland was Calvin's direct manager so it was actually his responsibility to ensure both Erica and Calvin were approaching the task correctly. But instead of ensuring Calvin did his job, here was Leland faulting Amber for going out of her way to provide support.

"I don't think I was wrong about my guidance, but I was very direct with feedback she needed to hear," said Amber. "Did she also complain about similar feedback she'd gotten from Dan? I overheard them having a conversation in the café—he said the exact same things as I did, but, honestly, a bit rudely."

"No, Calvin didn't mention any complaints about Dan," said Leland. "But you know how Dan is. He can be a bit too direct, but he's always very giving with his time."

Amber was willing to bet that Leland thanked Dan for helping Erica the next time he saw him.

She counted to three, took a deep breath and tried a different tack: "I'm also a little confused as to why you're criticizing me of not being supportive of Erica, when I was trying to be helpful, when Calvin, her manager, seems to be at fault. Do you think someone at her level should have been given that kind of assignment with so little direction?"

"Well, no," said Leland again. "And you're right about Calvin needing to improve at how he directs his staff. I'm definitely working with him on that. In the end, this is a she-said/she-said between you and Erica, so I probably shouldn't wade into it. But I think it's important that, as a senior leader, you understand the impact of your interactions on junior staff."

Great. Amber was not only being criticized for taking scarce time out of her day to help Erica, but Leland was acting as if her opinion was equal to someone much more junior. Not that there weren't times when senior staff were completely wrong. But, in this case, Amber had been trying to help Erica do her job better, and Leland didn't seem to be interested.

Maybe she shouldn't have helped Erica in the first place. No, that wouldn't have worked either. When men said no to a request from a colleague, it was seen as a sign of their status and good time management. But when women said no? People whispered behind their backs that they thought too highly of themselves, or were cold, or too overwhelmed. And when a woman didn't help a woman? She must be catty.

It felt like he was doing just that: treating her as the catty Queen Bee (his "she said" comment spoke volumes) because she hadn't adequately played the role of nurturing Mother Hen, as was expected of all senior women.[17] Leland hadn't even thanked her for the fact that she'd taken her own time to give advice that he admitted was correct.

Amber and her senior female colleagues had faced these challenges countless times. And contrary to the conventional wisdom that "women are catty with one another" (which she hated Leland for perpetuating), these challenges weren't just from women. The resistance of some junior men who couldn't accept a female leader sometimes hit you in the face; it was always most obvious when the senior group got together to do performance reviews of junior staff, and multiple female leaders with very different styles and personalities had all had trouble with the very same junior male employee, only to hear the male leaders gush about his talents and attitudes (and often imply that the women were incompetent or bad leaders for not feeling the same way).

But what was worse was the more subtle sense that your leadership was being judged by different standards. She thought about an activity she'd completed in a business course during college, where half the class had read a case study about a leader named "Jim," and the other half a leader named "Jill."

Jim and Jill had been described identically in both cases except for their genders. The studies had used the exact same paragraphs, with only their first names and pronouns changed.

But, when the class had subsequently described Jim and Jill's leadership styles, the ratings and descriptions had been telling. Jim had been considered a strong, accomplished leader. Jill had been considered selfish and demanding.[18]

Amber often thought about that case study. The characteristics that women needed to exhibit to be effective leaders—giving difficult feedback, for example—were simply not accepted in the same way they were with men. She was expected, as a woman, to be supportive of Erica, a fellow woman, in a way that Erica's own boss Calvin clearly wasn't. At the same time, any guidance that didn't seem suitably nurturing and supportive led to her being seen as the catty Queen Bee. Damned if you do, damned if you don't.

Amber remembered that Cassandra had put some time on her calendar to get her thoughts on the gender engagement gap. She knew that Cassandra had been helping Debra understand the issues. Amber hadn't planned to be wholly honest; what was the point, especially when Debra's inability to deal with the Leland issue was so apparent? There were many things Amber admired about their CEO, but did she really understand the types of everyday slights women like her still faced all the time? Should she try to raise the issues again, or was it just another thing that would take up her time and crowd her mind? Would it just end up being another thing that she had to deal with that men like Calvin didn't?

CHAPTER SEVENTEEN

Cassandra

There was a reason why Cassandra worked in learning and development, not finance. She had to doodle in her notebook to stay awake as she listened to a budget analyst drone on about a new requirement the firm was piloting for submitting expenses. The blue curlicues she had drawn in the margins looked lonely, and she wished she had one of those four-color pens she'd been obsessed with in high school so she could insert some green squiggles in between.

At first, Cassandra had been excited to attend a project management meeting, bringing together leaders from finance, marketing, sales, accounts, and product. It wasn't the type of meeting she'd typically attend in her role in HR, but, as part of the women's leadership program, one of her assigned tasks that month was to attend five representative, cross-departmental meetings across the firm. Her friend, Shannon, one of the regular attendees of this particular meeting, had laughed at her eagerness. "It's pretty boring," she had said. "I think most of us spend the meeting thinking about what we're going to eat for lunch."

Although Cassandra had no interest in anything the budget analyst was saying, she was enjoying observing the individuals around

the room. The meeting livened up as the door suddenly opened and
Jack walked in. The budget analyst started in his seat, and paused
until Jack gestured for him to keep talking. The other participants
exchanged glances as he sat down. Shannon, who was sitting next to
Cassandra, seemed to be writing a text message in her lap. Cassandra
didn't realize she was the recipient until her own phone vibrated. She
glanced at the screen.

*Wow. Jack never attends this meeting. Is the company in such financial
trouble that the CFO needs to dig into the weeds?*

Glances were exchanged once again when, in the middle of the
budget analyst's monologue, Dan, vice president of partnerships,
entered the room. Even though there were plenty of seats at the
table, Dan went to sit in the corner of the room on a small table that
was typically used to hold snacks. Almost immediately, he took out
his laptop and started typing so loudly that it sounded like he was
using an old-fashioned typewriter. Even though he'd just arrived at
the meeting (ten minutes late), he periodically looked at his watch
and sighed.

"So those are the ten new protocols for finance reporting we want
to test out with those working on this particular project," the budget
analyst said, "Our goal is to see if they make sense to roll out in the
firm more broadly—"

Suddenly, the rhythm of Dan's typing came to an abrupt halt. It
was replaced by the slamming shut of the laptop. He stood up. "Are
you serious?" he asked the analyst. "You want to spend extra time on
new reporting protocols? I don't have time for this shit."

He strode to the door and slammed it behind him.

A few glances were exchanged, but the group treated Dan's departure as if it were an ordinary occurrence. The budget analyst looked a
bit teary, and his voice shook through the next few sentences, before
passing out a few pieces of paper outlining the new process.

"Do you have any questions?" he asked.

Again, Cassandra noticed the other participants in the room

exchanging silent glances, as if they were deciding who was going to say something.

It was Shannon who spoke up.

"I'm sorry," she said, even though she didn't sound particularly sorry. "But I don't think this process is very clear. Items #3 and #4 especially need some fine-tuning. Can you come back to us when it is revised? Maybe circulate to the group by email for feedback?"

Cassandra cringed a little at her friend's tone, knowing that it had come across as more direct than expected. How many times when their group had been out to dinner had Shannon unintentionally offended one of them by her bluntness and had to apologize later? But she wasn't wrong; the process outlined on the papers seemed a bit of a mess. And at least, unlike Dan, she was trying to be constructive— pointing out specific areas that needed improvement and offering to give feedback over email.

Jack wrinkled his brow. "I know this is a new process, and there will likely be some kinks," he said, looking directly at Shannon. Then he moved his glance around the room, and raised his volume to emphasize it was the end of the discussion: "But we need to do our best to try it out. Now what's the next agenda item?"

After the meeting ended, Shannon, Cassandra, and Rita stayed behind.

"Well there goes my next performance review," said Shannon. "I know I shouldn't have put it that way. You know they even assigned me a coach to work on controlling my responses. But the men just get away with it. I doubt Dan has ever gotten a coach."

Cassandra couldn't reveal confidential HR information, but since she oversaw the coaching and training budget, she knew that Shannon was right: Dan hadn't ever been assigned a coach to work on the same behaviors that had consistently led to Shannon being penalized on her performance reviews. If this meeting was representative at all, then Dan needed feedback and coaching as much as, if not more than, Shannon. Dan had been rude throughout and then sworn at the analyst without explaining why the process was "shit". Shannon had been blunt, but she'd also delivered specific suggestions as to what to fix, as well as concrete next steps where she'd offered to help.

Rita sighed. "Dan storms out of rooms all the time," she said, "Sometimes even more dramatically than he did today."

"It's interesting that it's women who are seen as the emotional ones," Cassandra mused.

Rita rolled her eyes. "What? I thought only people with periods have emotions."

Shannon laughed sadly. "Hopefully there aren't any recording devices in this room. Someone might not realize you were joking."

That afternoon, Cassandra received a call from Debra's assistant. One of Debra's meetings had gotten unexpectedly canceled and she had some free time if Cassandra was available to meet. They'd had to skip their pre-workday coffee meetups the last few days, and Cassandra was happy to put aside the report she was working on for another day. On her way to Debra's office, she found herself in the elevator with Jack.

He turned to her. "I noticed you at the project management meeting this morning. What did you think?"

Should she take the opportunity to see what he thought of Shannon's and Dan's reactions to the budget analyst's presentation?

She contemplated how to broach the issue, but before she could say anything, Jack spoke again. "You oversee the coaching program, right?" he said. "So you know we've asked Shannon to work on those issues. She's good at her job, but her tone is such a problem, it'll really limit her in her career. We'll have to decide whether more coaching would even make a difference to helping her reach more senior positions. Perhaps that's just how she's wired."

Cassandra wasn't sure what to say. Then she remembered Debra asking her not to bite her tongue so often. "What about Dan?"

"Dan?" Jack looked puzzled. "Oh, he lets his emotions get away with him, doesn't he?" he said with a laugh. "But he's so good at his job—nice guy, really smart."

Didn't it matter that Shannon was also nice and smart?

She knew the answer was no. Dan was seen as a nice guy who lost his temper every now and again—almost like a personality quirk. Like someone you'd want to get a drink with, both for fun *and* because he'd step up for you in a bar brawl if needed. Meanwhile, Shannon's similar behaviors weren't viewed as a bad moment, but as a fundamental character flaw.

The two both needed to work on how they interacted and engaged with others. But the penalty was so much higher for Shannon. Jack had said Shannon was good at her job, *but* her tone was such a problem. By contrast, he described Dan as letting his emotions get away from him, *but* he was so good at his job. In Dan's case, the "but" was a positive, grounds for excusing bad behavior. Cassandra remembered a book she'd read which described typical archetypes like "the office screamer" or "the bull in the china shop"— who were forgiven by colleagues as long as something redeemed them.[19] She wondered what would have happened if Shannon had behaved the same way Dan had: the swearing, the slamming the door? What would the reaction have been? Perhaps a request for coaching, but more likely something worse.

As Cassandra walked from the elevator to Debra's office, she realized the conversation with Jack provided the perfect springboard for her conversation with Debra.

"I need to get out of the office," said Debra as her assistant let Cassandra in. "Do you mind if we walk and talk at the same time?"

Cassandra tapped her Fitbit. "I could use the steps," she said.

They talked about what they each had planned for the upcoming weekend as they exited the building and walked across the street to the pathway by the beach.

As soon as she could be sure that nobody would overhear them, Cassandra relayed the events of that morning's meeting, as well as her elevator conversation with Jack, to Debra. She also described the conversation she'd had with Amber about how Leland had rebuked her for providing constructive criticism to Erica.

Debra didn't seem surprised, though she flinched a little at the mention of Leland.

"You're talking about the Goldilocks dilemma," she said. "As a woman, you have to walk the tightrope—can't be too stereotypically feminine or too stereotypically masculine. If we're too feminine, we're seen as less competent, less able to make decisions. If we're too masculine, it's seen as unnatural—not soft enough. When women aren't the whole package, they get penalized."[20]

Cassandra was somewhat taken aback by the older woman's matter-of-factness. "Doesn't that frustrate you?"

"Of course," said Debra. She looked surprised at the question. "But you can only spend so much time being frustrated. What I've focused on throughout my career is helping other women find the right balance. Honestly, sometimes it's little things. I've known women like your friend Shannon, who have been able to improve how they were perceived by talking more slowly and less assertively—same words, but different tone. Relaxing their body posture. Wearing their hair differently—not in a tight ponytail, but framing their faces more."

"What about women who are seen as too feminine? Do you tell them to wear their hair in a ponytail?" Cassandra immediately felt bad for asking this in a sardonic tone.

"I know a lot of women find this irritating to have to accept," said Debra. "But we have to be realistic about how we can best help women advance. For women who are too feminine, yes, it's also the little things. They usually need to adopt some power-posing. Don't hold your chin down or cock your head to the side when you speak. Hold your head upright. Speak louder and more rapidly. Maintain eye contact. Lean your body back, and lower your brows. Don't cross your legs or fold your hands. Wear fewer pastels and maybe try some power blazers."

Cassandra looked down at her own lavender blouse. "So you're saying I shouldn't have worn this today?"

"Your outfit is fine for day-to-day, but yes, if you had an important meeting today, I'd have suggested either wear a darker blouse or pair that one with a blazer. I know it sounds silly, but I've helped dozens of women advance over the years and helping them strike the right balance has been a large part of it."

"This all sounds so superficial," said Cassandra. "I mean we're talking about body language, tone, clothing."

"Yes, some of it is," admitted Debra. "But it goes beyond that. I think of it as different leadership styles. On one end of the spectrum, there's a more direct, assertive style, focused on task and outcomes. On the other end of the spectrum, there's a more communal style, focused on group dynamics and involving everyone in discussion. The strongest leaders—whether they are men or women—know how to balance the two, and maybe when to be each, what the hybrid approaches are, what to do in what context and so on. Most people fall somewhere in the middle of the spectrum. The challenge for women is that the allowable spectrum is so much wider for men—they can be either more assertive, or more communal without penalty."[21]

"I can understand why men can be more assertive without penalty," said Cassandra. "Female leaders are just expected to be friendly and team-oriented, right? But why are men allowed to be more communal? Wouldn't they be penalized for adopting leadership behaviors that are seen as stereotypically feminine?"

"Even a communal man is seen as assertive by virtue of being a man," said Debra. "A woman asking a group's opinion is perceived as weak, but a man doing so is perceived as thoughtful, savvy, or confident."

"Shouldn't we be trying to change this instead of just accepting it?" Cassandra asked, trying not to sound too accusatory. She knew that Debra's advice to women was probably correct if the goal was career advancement, but it still sounded like selling out to her.

Debra held firm. "The way we change things is by ensuring there are more women at the top."

Would that work? After all, Debra was at the top at their company, and they still had these issues. "But aren't women enforcing these norms as much as men?" Cassandra finally asked. She was glad they were walking side by side as they talked. She didn't want to be able to see Debra's facial expression, knowing that if the CEO looked offended, Cassandra would probably shut down. After all, she was probably more on the communal side herself. But, just a few weeks ago, they had discussed the unconscious biases that women can exhibit as well—whether it was the woman in the finance department who had assigned uneven tasks to the male and female interns, or Debra not initially noticing the differences in how men and women were described in promotion memos. Couldn't Debra see that in telling women to walk on tightropes, she was reinforcing unconscious biases too—those mental auto-completes and shortcuts that expected women to be a certain way?

"Women don't support one another as much as they should," said Debra. "When I was coming up the ladder, we were often pitted against each other. When men saw two or more women in a conversation, they'd make snide comments about us congregating. Things are very different for your generation. You have senior women who can help you. And you all seem to support each other much more." Her next words sounded both sad and frustrated: "Don't take that all for granted."

It was true. Cassandra was grateful for Shannon, Rita, and Haley. She knew she was fortunate to have the support of senior women like Terry and Debra. What would it feel like to look around and above you and not see any women at all? She probably did take that all for granted at times. But she wanted to feel like senior women like Debra weren't just helping women better fit into the "acceptable spectrum" for their gender, but also finding ways to change the fact that men and women were allowed such different spectrums in the first place.

It wasn't just in the realm of gender where people had mental catalogs. She knew that people's brains went through life developing shortcuts and auto-completes; it was a necessary way of processing the quantity of information they came across on any given day. As a parent, she had a catalog in her head of all the teachers she'd ever known and respected—her own, her kids' teachers, teachers that happen to be in her social or professional network. One day, she'd met her daughter's teacher and they had come across as really quirky. She hadn't been sure about that person, but then she had remembered a friend from college who was similarly quirky and (she'd always suspected) a great teacher. This connection had allayed her worries and made her feel that this teacher would be good just like her friend.

In this case, her mental shortcut hadn't been wrong. The quirky teacher had turned out to be excellent, with a lot of different novel ways of making learning fun. So, sometimes these shortcuts were helpful—in this case, she hadn't worried about the teacher because the person fit a mold in her head. But sometimes they weren't—for instance, if this teacher had turned out to be ineffective, would Cassandra have realized the problem quickly enough given the assumption she had made?

What did the mental catalog look like in terms of gender? Despite the growing awareness that gender isn't binary, male and female were still the primary categories by which people registered one another. When asked to describe someone for the first time, the first thing most people will mention is gender.

Debra had told her in confidence that part of why Jack had convinced her to hire Leland was that he had reminded him of someone named Mac they'd known once. So, even though Leland had said things in his interview that should have been red flags for a start-up environment, they had written those off as they had remembered an analog individual who was known to be quiet and mild-mannered but also entrepreneurial and a real go-getter. The catalog of men in Debra and Jack's heads was likely much larger than the catalog of women because, numerically, there were just more men at the top who they'd both worked with longer. In the end, everyone obviously needed to be assessed on their own merits and accomplishments. But someone who matched another person already in your mental catalog was likely to get more of a chance.

The spectrum on which women were allowed to sit was much more limited for two reasons. First, because they had to walk the tightrope of "feminine" versus "masculine" attributes. And, second, due to the lower number of women in leadership positions, everyone had fewer archetypes in their head of what a model female leader should look and act like. The mental auto-complete at work again.

What frustrated Cassandra was that Debra seemed at least partly aware of this problem, but didn't seem to be using her power to fix it. Instead of changing the way the system operated, she continued to give Leland a chance (even while all the evidence was clear that he was failing at his job) and she was telling Cassandra to do a better job fitting into some imaginary mold (even though she saw the mold as flawed).

PART SIX

The Value of "Stereotypically Feminine" Traits

CHAPTER EIGHTEEN

Debra

As Debra looked around her friend Fay's office, she felt like she had fallen into a Restoration Hardware catalog. It was like something you'd expect of period French royalty. No sterile office desk here, just a beautiful marble table with a hand-carved, grey oak base. Fay's laptop looked out of place leaning against a round velvet pillow on the Victorian chaise. The other sign of the 21st century in the room was a gigantic flat screen—about five feet wide—on one wall. In front of the flatscreen, a thin console—the same length as the flat screen, but only five inches deep—held a small tablet.

Fay had been one of Debra's college roommates. Now she was CEO of a major restaurant conglomerate. Even though they worked in different industries, they had been each other's closest consiglieres for the past several decades. Since they had both entered the C-suite, they had been too busy to talk as often as they once had. The month before had been the first time they'd connected in a while, when Debra had invited Fay to be a speaker in their women in leadership series. Over drinks afterward, Fay had confessed to Debra she was facing a number of challenges at work at the moment. "I could use an outside perspective on our current difficulties—do you think you'd be up for spending the day with us sometime soon?"

That simple question had felt so difficult to answer. How could Debra say yes when her own company seemed to be in free fall? On the other hand, how could she say no—not only to one of her oldest and dearest friends, but to another CEO in need? Besides, Debra was eager to get back into the pattern where she and Fay would text and call each other regularly to exchange ideas.

She felt especially curious as to how Fay would react to hearing about Debra's conversation with Cassandra. The younger woman had helped Debra think through a lot of complex issues. But she also felt that Cassandra was young and still too idealistic. In the real world, women were penalized for being too feminine or too masculine, and you had to walk that tightrope. Maybe that wasn't fair for women. But that was simply the world they lived in. Debra wondered how to get this through to her mentee. Over the years, Debra and Fay had often discussed the importance of mentoring younger women. Surely Fay would have some ideas as to how she should support the Cassandras in her own orbit.

But Debra was here to help Fay with her challenges, not the other way around. Fay's assistant came in and gave Debra a cup of coffee. As soon as he left, Debra turned to her friend, "So what can I help you with today?"

"We're going through a big re-org," said Fay. "The usual stuff: shifting roles, changing reporting lines, and the like. We're in the middle of planning everything right now. I've done a lot of re-orgs as a leader, but something isn't working about this one, and I can't figure out what. I felt like I needed an outside perspective. My staff know you're here to observe our meetings, and give us advice on what we could be doing differently through the process."

There were few things as complex in leadership as reorganizing staff roles and reporting. Debra almost felt guilty for how immediately intrigued she felt—her subject of curiosity was the thing keeping

Fay awake at night and giving her daily pain. She tried to look solemn as Fay handed her a schedule for the day.

For their first meeting, they were able to stay in Fay's office, and Debra learned why the gigantic flat screen had such a prominent place as the group of regional VPs dialed in from across the country. Debra's company only had a few remote employees, so they hadn't invested in the technology used here—the flatscreen on Fay's wall lit up with each person in a different box, like the Brady Bunch opening credits, and participants could easily share screens and even take turns writing on a virtual whiteboard.

But for all the collaborative technology, the meeting was a mess. Fay had provided Debra with some advance context: the regional VPs had been assigned in pairs to work on parts of the communication plan for rolling out the impending re-org to their staff.

"Okay, Ryan and Mark, why don't you start with your recommendation of how we communicate with the general managers of each restaurant?" said Fay after opening the meeting.

Both of them started talking at the same time, and neither seemed willing to yield. All Debra could hear in the minute of chaos was random phrases overlaid on one another. It felt like the oral equivalent of a word cloud. Cascading. Staff. Worries. Timeline.

Fay picked up her tablet. She slid some controls on the screen, which seemed to dim the voices of the two talkers, and allow her own voice to carry over theirs. "One at a time, gentlemen. Ryan?" Her fingers went back to the tablet and raised everyone's volume back again to the default level.

"We're convening all the GMs at our annual conference in two months," said Ryan. "I recommend that we wait until then to do the communications—this kind of message is best discussed in person, and with everyone hearing the exact same thing at the same time."

Mark interrupted, "That's too late. Ryan, we talked about this. We can't wait that long."

They started talking over one another again.

"You're both right," a female voice said, loud enough to carry over them. Her title and location appeared in text over her neck on the screen: Patricia from the Midwest. "We need to figure out a communication strategy that's as quick as possible and consistent in messaging. And we need to figure out how to best use the conference, where we have the rare opportunity of everyone there in person."

"Why don't we provide a broad overview at the regional meetings over videoconference next month?" someone else said. "Then we can go into more detail in person at the big conference next month."

"I guess that would work," said Mark.

"Yeah, I can live with that," said Ryan.

Debra had experienced this kind of thing before. Fay had clearly assigned the task to Mark and Ryan, two VPs who obviously didn't get along, because she wanted the benefit of their two different perspectives. But instead of 1+1 = 3, as the management cliché went, it was more like 1+1 = negative 2.

For the next meeting, Debra and Fay moved into a large conference room, convening the SVPs that were located at headquarters. They were discussing a few of the big goals on their strategic roadmap, including increasing healthy offerings and unique diner experiences (whether through decorations, mealtime entertainment, or tablet ordering) across all the brands.

"My staff are really struggling to innovate the diner experience," one SVP said. "They're so used to the way they've always done things. I think they're scared to death but don't realize it."

"It seems like we need to help them acknowledge their fears," said the Chief Talent Officer, "There's interesting work on building emotional intelligence among executive teams that I could bring to our next—"

Another SVP interrupted with a laugh, "It's not our job to be therapists."

"I'm having my team go into restaurants and actually sit down and eat meals with real customers," said another SVP.

Did they always change the subject so abruptly?

"That's *nice*," said another voice, dismissively. "But is it necessary? We have so much data about customers. Reams of it."

"Graphs and numbers are not the same as really getting into a customer's head and understanding them," countered the SVP who had raised the idea.

The data-oriented SVP opened his mouth, as if he were about to argue, but then closed it again, clearly thinking. Interesting, thought Debra. Perhaps they could have a good discussion about the value of quantitative versus qualitative customer research. Where each had different strengths. How they complemented one another.

At that point though, Fay looked at her watch, "We're already behind on our agenda. Let's get to the next item."

Four hours later, Debra had returned to Fay's office. Her friend had left to get snacks for them from the breakroom, but had been gone for a while now—most likely waylaid by staff on her way. Debra took the quiet moment to reflect on what she'd seen and to look through her notes. The themes seemed pretty clear, and it came down to relationship and empathy skills that were missing in their leadership team interactions.

Mark and Ryan hadn't taken the time to understand how their differing perspectives could get them to a better joint solution than either would have come up with on their own.

The staff were experiencing natural emotional reactions to change, and the leadership team was choosing to ignore this rather than confront it directly.

The leadership team wasn't having the discussion it probably needed to on how to understand their customers beyond just looking at data.

And Fay, who Debra had always considered to have high EQ, was so focused on getting to the next item on the agenda that she'd shut down an important debate.

When Fay returned with some microwaved popcorn, Debra told her friend what she'd noticed.

Fay looked out the window for a few seconds before speaking. "I feel silly for having such a blind spot," she said. "You know, I've been reading a lot of books on how the workplace is changing and the different skills needed. Technology, globalization, the pace of change; everything I've read lately is about how these types of trends mean that empathy, collaboration—all those communal or stereotypically feminine traits we were told to suppress when we were coming up in our careers—are more important than ever. I know that intellectually, but I hadn't thought about what that meant at my own company."[22]

Debra felt her stomach churn. It had been a lot easier to see what was going on at Fay's company. What if she turned the magnifying glass on herself?

"My blind spot is worse," Debra said slowly. "You're at least reading about how the world is changing. I know the best CEOs are never complacent, that we need to continuously learn as our strategies, cultures, and organizations evolve." She paused to take a handful of popcorn. "And yet I told a young woman yesterday that the only way women can advance in business is by taking on more stereotypically masculine traits. Maybe that was wrong."

"Maybe the only way that businesses can advance in today's climate is if we all take on more stereotypically feminine traits," mused Fay.

Was this yet another problem with the advice for women to "lean in"? Telling women that they just needed to raise their hands or "man up" was about "fixing" the women. There was so much discussion everywhere about how many women needed to be more stereotypically masculine (i.e., more assertive) and so little about how organizations would benefit if everyone, men and women, acted in more stereotypically feminine ways (like being more empathic and relational).[23]

Perhaps many women did need to "lean in." But how many women and men would also benefit from leaning out, or sideways—in other words, listening and collaborating with one another?

On her way home, Debra reflected on her first job in management consulting, fresh out of college, and how much it'd shaped her perspective of what women needed to do to get ahead at work. Her first assignment had been an engagement for a leading beverage company, on a small team that included Jack, who had started at the firm a few years prior. She remembered how much she had loved that first week, especially the opportunities they had had to observe the clients in strategy meetings.

At the end of the week, the partner in charge, Aaron, had convened the team to ask what everyone's perceptions were after the week.

"Okay, let's go around the room and everyone say one thing you think is going to most get in the way of this company's success," he said. While other partners at the firm had treated these idea meetings as a *Lord of the Flies* event where everyone argued over the conch, Debra had appreciated that Aaron was more enlightened, ensuring that each of them had a chance to participate.

Malcolm, one of the senior managers on the team, had spoken first: "They're underestimating their competition."

"I looked at their five-year projections and don't think they've realistically accounted for rising labor costs, especially related to health benefits," Jack had said.

Debra had noticed so many things that it was hard to pinpoint just one. But she had started with what she thought was the most important challenge for the company to overcome. "The executive team doesn't respect one another," she had said. "Pete stared at the table whenever Andrew said anything. Jon and Marissa rolled their eyes at everything Dave said. I don't see how they'll get on the same page."

Aaron had looked annoyed. "We can't speculate on interpersonal dynamics. We're not HR people. That's not relevant to their business objectives."

"True. But they won't accomplish their business objectives when they're in fundamental disagreement about what they are and how to get there, and they need to baseline respect each other for that to happen."

She had consulted her notes and started to explain a few specific incidents where she thought interpersonal conflict was getting in the way of business decisions, but it had been clear that Aaron had stopped paying attention.

Jack had jumped in before Aaron could call on the next person. "Debra, you were saying something over breakfast about their product portfolio that I thought was interesting."

She had felt annoyed by the interruption, until she realized that Aaron was looking up from the notebook where he'd been doodling. The phrase "product portfolio" had woken up the boss.

She had flashed Jack a thank-you glance. "They don't have a wide enough range of products compared to competitors," she had said. "They're basically only focused on an older target demographic, whereas other companies have expanded more to younger audiences—not just in their advertising, but in their products."

"Exactly what I was thinking," Aaron had said. "They've got a very narrow strategy; we'll be able to help them think about new audiences for their existing beverages and identify some new products."

It had been her first lesson in what her (mostly male) bosses wanted to hear. Aaron's question had at first seemed to Debra to have a broad scope. In reality, he was only looking for answers related to strategy and finances: anything else was irrelevant. Debra could come up with a market assessment, business plan, or balance sheet as well as (if not better than) any of her male colleagues, but to her it was silly to discuss these things without also addressing the human element. No product strategy would succeed if the leadership team couldn't stand one another. But this had been an early lesson in what type of information mattered to her bosses, and what type not only didn't matter, but would lead her to be considered less competent in their eyes.

Across the next week, as the team had put together a presentation for the client, Debra had noticed that her co-worker Sam seemed distracted. Sometimes, he seemed to not even be listening when others were talking. For a self-proclaimed numbers guy, he'd been making simple arithmetic mistakes.

"I think something's going on with him," she had said to Jack. "He seems pretty unhappy on this project."

"Really?" Jack had reflected for a few seconds. "Yeah, maybe you're right. But there's nothing we really can do about that, and it's not our business, as long as he's getting his work done."

They had both returned to the manila folders in front of them. Something had clearly been on Jack's mind though. He had been tapping his foot on the ground and folding a piece of paper in one hand over and over again as he read.

After a few minutes, he had looked up. "I hope you don't mind some unsolicited advice," he had said. "You're clearly smarter than the rest of us, but you seem less focused if you mention all this personal stuff so often. Last year, there was a girl who started with me who was like that, worried about how our team was getting along, noticed personality challenges with the client. She didn't last long."

When she was younger, Debra had always thought that noticing things—the obvious, as well as the non-obvious clues in tone of voice and body language and interpersonal dynamics—was her true superpower. It had been what made her different from the people who also had high SAT scores and got good grades, but didn't notice things. She hadn't thought that noticing what was going on with the dysfunctional client team, or their distracted co-worker, kept her from seeing the same strategic and financial matters that the others like Jack saw. But there had seemed to be an assumption that she couldn't do both.

Later that week, Sam's unhappiness had got in his way—he made a mistake in a calculation that led to the rest of the team needing to stay up all night to find the problem. Luckily, Jack had caught it in time to still meet the client's deadline, but what if he hadn't? Whatever was going on with Sam that had led him to be unhappy had eventually impacted his work, and there had been a consequence—one that could have been far worse.

Debra often wondered what had happened to the dysfunctional client team at the beverage company—would they have been able to carry out the strategy the firm had developed for them? But she'd gotten the message loud and clear from Jack, Aaron, and the small number of older women in the workplace who'd seemed to have figured out the system. Social skills were important: you had to get along with others, be the kind of person clients and co-workers wouldn't mind getting stuck in an airport with if your flight was delayed. Being liked especially mattered for women. But anything deeper than that—really understanding what was going on with people beneath the surface and adjusting actions accordingly—was considered fuzzy and a distraction from the real business issues. Boys are socialized to compete (organized sports), and girls are socialized to relate (playing house or school), and it was a boy's club after all.

She wondered if Cassandra got under her skin sometimes because she saw so much of herself in the younger woman. Cassandra's ability to read people and situations—that had been Debra once upon a time. Back before Debra had come to realize how important following Jack's advice would be if she wanted to advance in her career. Nobody wanted to hear her interpersonal or personal observations, either related to the staff or to the clients. Not that Debra had ever turned what she had called her "social sense" (and what would later be popularized as "EQ") off entirely. But it got muted. With time, she had learned to focus on the things that mattered in a male-dominated environment and to shut the things that didn't out of her mind.[24]

As she pulled into her driveway, it occurred to her that, given her connections in the restaurant industry, Fay might know what had happened to the beverage company from that first consulting engagement. All Debra knew was that they didn't seem to be in existence anymore, but she'd lost track of when and didn't know how that might have happened. After stopping the car, but before unbuckling her seatbelt, she texted her friend the question. Then she unbuckled her seatbelt, but waited in the car instead of opening the door, looking at the dot-dot-dot that indicated Fay was typing a reply.

When I was in business school, I met someone who worked there. She said they had a good strategy, but a pretty dysfunctional executive team that couldn't carry it forward. Lots of infighting and turf wars. Eventually acquired by a competitor for a fraction of what they could have been worth.

Debra stared at her friend's text for a few minutes. Had she come full circle in her career? Once again, she was seeing the signs that culture would destroy a company. Only this time it was hers.

Maybe it was time for her to lean in herself—to the task of replacing her CPO.

CHAPTER NINETEEN

Kyle

A week earlier, Kyle's girlfriend Nicole had introduced him to the website called arementalkingtoomuch.com. Like most evenings, they both ended up on their laptops after dinner with a Netflix show streaming on the TV, one that they half paid attention to as they both alternated between work emails and social media. Kyle had gotten up to refill his decaf when Nicole started laughing.

Usually, if one of them LOL'd during their evening internet time, there would be an explanation. So Kyle was puzzled when Nicole didn't even look up. Out of the corner of his eye, he saw her pull up the iMessage screen on her laptop—clearly to share whatever had amused her with someone else.

Okay, maybe Kyle's nosiness wasn't a virtue. But he was curious now and didn't want to deal with the email at the top of his inbox—a project plan from one of his direct reports that needed some major editing. He went over and looked over Nicole's shoulder. He saw a simple web page with the word "check who is dominating the conversation" at the top. Underneath that, it said "who's talking" with a gray button for "a dude" and "not a dude."

"Christa and I are discussing using this in seminar this week," she said, referring to her best friend in grad school. "The idea is that you use the website to track who is talking at any given moment, and then at the end of the meeting, it'll give you a percentage male versus female." Nicole was a PhD student in organizational psychology, where everyone was theoretically supposed to be aware of such things. She often laughed—or sighed, depending on her mood—at how much her colleagues were unaware of the very dysfunctions they studied when it came to themselves.

Kyle had socialized enough with Nicole's doctoral colleagues to know what the results of this experiment would be and wondered why she would even bother with the experiment. Even though a majority were women—maybe 80%—even at casual BBQs or happy hours, it seemed like the few men in the program would often dominate conversation. Frequently, they'd argue over minute theoretical details while the women rolled their eyes. It wouldn't be shocking if the website revealed that men talked 70–80% of the time, despite being in a minority.

Time and again, Nicole (and the therapist they'd seen together a few times) had told him that he was supposed to listen, not try to solve every problem. But he couldn't help himself. He'd never been in a doctoral program, but he knew there was a lot of competition for funding and faculty attention. She should do everything in her power to be noticed.

"Do you think you're talking enough?" he tried to ask a few times, gently (he thought). "Maybe you need to insert yourself in the conversation more. Do a little more grandstanding."

She looked tired. "I speak when I have something to say. But I have no desire for the kind of intellectual dick-waving that a lot of my colleagues get into during seminar."

He felt a little offended but decided it was better not to say any more.

Cassandra and Shannon laughed when he told them about Nicole's dick-waving metaphor the next day at lunch. "Tell her that's a good way to put it," said Shannon.

"I just don't understand the point of a website that tells you what you already know is going on." As soon as he said it and watched his friends exchange a glance, he regretted it. He already suspected Shannon was still mad at him from the tequila incident the other day.

"I think when women notice a situation where we're disadvantaged, we second-guess ourselves, wonder if we're just imagining it." Cassandra spoke more slowly than usual, as if she was weighing her words. "Women are told so often that we're being oversensitive. So when something happens, you wonder, did someone really just insult me, or am I overreacting? Were women really marginalized in a meeting, or is it my imagination? Am I being treated differently compared to my male colleagues, or did I do something wrong? With these types of questions constantly in our heads, it can be comforting when our suspicions are confirmed. Usually it comes from another woman who independently noticed the same thing. But a website like this, it's a way of almost objectively confirming what you're feeling and noticing."

That hit home for Kyle. He had definitely told Nicole (sometimes out loud, sometimes in his head) that she was being too sensitive. And while he knew better than to say anything, he'd often wondered why Nicole and his female colleagues traded so many articles about the challenges women face at work. Like the arementalkingtoomuch.com website, it seemed a bit like a solipsistic activity, just fueling their anger rather than doing anything about it.

He'd never considered why that validation would be needed. After all, this was the 21st century. Sure, not everyone was woke. But everyone in his circles seemed to be. They all knew there were problems.

"Shannon and I and a bunch of the women in the group have been talking about how to change the dynamic on the cost savings task force," Cassandra said.

Along with Kyle, they were part of a fifteen-person group that had been charged to look for cost savings across the company. Jack chaired it. He, Kyle, and two others were the only men. It was odd that the ratio was so uneven, given that the company as a whole was about 50/50.

Kyle tried to recall the last few meetings. Sure, he had talked a lot. But Jack often directly called on him. Sure, perhaps more often than he called on others in the group. Kyle wasn't going to apologize for having good things to say or a solid rapport with the CFO. The other two men were Dan and Leland, both of whom spent a lot of time pontificating: mostly bad ideas.

In fact, Kyle was the one who usually pushed back most stridently if Dan or Leland, who were both senior to him, raised anything foolhardy. If anything, the rest of them should be thanking Kyle for speaking truth to power, he thought.

Any meeting with both Leland *and* Dan in it was especially bad. Both Leland and Dan were known for talking about things they didn't know much about. And when they were both in attendance? The problem seemed to magnify tenfold. Dan and Leland would not only express nonsense themselves, but take up even more time by responding to what the other one said, and so on.

Surely, Kyle shouldn't be placed in the same category as those two? While Cassandra, Shannon, and the other women sat there silent and annoyed—leading Jack to likely wonder why they weren't leaning in—Kyle actually tried to stop the nonsense.

Now probably wasn't the right time for defensiveness or indignation though. He did have some sense of self-preservation. "Yeah, you're right, I guess the men do talk a lot more in that meeting," he said.

"Have you noticed where you all sit every meeting?" Cassandra asked.

Kyle took a bite of his sandwich and tried to recall. He knew Jack always sat at the head of the table at every meeting: facing the door. Kyle usually took the other head in any meeting he was in; it was the closest seat the door, and he liked to be able to get out of meetings quickly so he wouldn't be late to his next one or get trapped in small talk at the end.

Where did Dan and Leland sit?

"Dan usually sits right near Jack at one head of the table," said Shannon. "And Leland usually sits right near you."

"So men are always claiming the power seats?" Kyle asked, remembering Nicole telling him that was a thing in graduate seminar too.

"Yes, and if you're all facing one another, it's like you can ignore the rest of us in your peripheral vision. Sometimes it feels like a back-and-forth sports match," said Cassandra. "Like you're all bouncing the ball back and forth so fast there's no time for someone else to grab it, to acknowledge that there's actually a circle of people instead of just four men talking at another from the two heads of the table."

Kyle couldn't help but try to problem-solve again. "So change where you sit," he said.

"Yeah, we've got a plan for that," Shannon said vaguely.

As soon as Kyle arrived at the next task force meeting, he realized the plan was indeed in place. All the women must have arrived early to grab their seats. They had overwhelmed both heads of the table, leaving the only four open seats all next to one another on one of the long sides of the table. If the tendency to volley back and forth across the table, ignoring the women in their peripheral vision, was indeed a factor that contributed to male domination of the conversation, the women had effectively eliminated that possibility by forcing the men to sit next to one another in a row in the only remaining chairs.

Kyle took one of the remaining seats and watched the other men walk in soon after him.

Jack looked at the head of the table facing the door. Kyle saw his double take turn to annoyance as he saw Meg and Amber there.

"Crowded room today," Jack said. Did he think the reason his seat had been taken was that there were simply more people attending that day? Well, maybe better that than he realize that all the women— including senior ones, Kyle realized, as he saw Meg try to hide a smile—had conspired to force the men into their desired seating chart.

"Am I late?" Leland asked as he took the seat to the left of Kyle, even though the clock clearly showed it was exactly on the hour.

Dan walked in right after Leland and didn't even seem to notice. He slid into the only remaining seat, dropped his stack of papers and laptop on the table in front of them, letting them spread out far beyond the amount of appropriate space, and then leaned back in his chair as far as it would go without falling over. Even with the four men all scrunched into their allocated space, it was typical of Dan to find a way to expand his own personal area.

Jack passed out the agenda. "First item up is sustainability. You all know we just replaced paper towels in the bathrooms with air dryers, but that's pretty much all we've done so far."

"Sydney had a great idea the other day," said Meg. "She was mentioning various low-cost ways she'd heard that other companies encourage carpooling among their employees who live near one another."

"It's all about drawing on principles of gamification," Sydney said. "You know, you get points for carpooling or walking to work or taking the bus or whatever. At a certain number of points, there's some kind of reward. But it doesn't have to be expensive—a small amount of money or tokens toward prizes or even the ability to attend a special event."

"Does that really work?" Jack sounded skeptical. Kyle wasn't surprised. Jack was pretty old-fashioned and always believed in the stick more than the carrot when it came to incentives.

Kyle waited to see how Sydney would argue her point, but instead it was Cassandra who chimed in, "There's been a lot of research in behavioral economics about social proof—basically what you might think of as peer pressure or keeping up with the Jones's. Bet if we had a leaderboard tracking how many different points people were earning and who were the winners, some folks would just want to win."

Jack had begun to reply, but Amber also started talking at the same time. She raised her voice a little with each word so that Jack eventually stopped. "Wonder if it'd be more effective as people signing up in groups rather than an individual competition?"

"Oh, interesting," said Shannon. "Because then you have the added dimension of peer accountability—not wanting to disappoint your team. But could that have negative consequences? Creating conflict if people are frustrated with their teams?"

"Hmm, I love the idea of peer accountability, but yeah, it could cause problems," said Meg. "Cassandra, what would the research say?"

After Cassandra replied, Meg turned to Kyle. "I know your team really got into the fitness competition we did as a company last year. Any lessons from that?" she asked.

Kyle didn't use the gender tracker. But by the end of the meeting, he would have guessed that women had talked about 70% of the time—proportionate to their percent of the meeting attendees. And, for the first time, all of the women had talked at least a few times. Did they simply feel more confident because they'd taken the power positions in the room and rallied together for this experiment? Did the men feel unsettled even if they didn't quite know why, and were they less likely to talk as a result? Was the usual ability for the men to look across one another from the two opposite heads of the table really that powerful?

Kyle thought about various female direct reports he'd worried were getting lost in meetings over the years, and how he'd thought he was woke when he tried to help them raise their voice ("Just get in there, don't let people talk over you, keep talking.")

He'd assumed that supporting women was about helping them understand how to assert themselves around men like Jack, who talked a good game on gender but in truth only listened to women (and frankly men) who exhibited a certain kind of more stereotypically masculine swagger. Sure enough, there had been a few moments in the meeting where Kyle had noticed that if one of the women hadn't raised her voice or interrupted, Jack would have dominated the conversation and not let anyone else get a word in.

But that wasn't the *only* way they had made sure they were heard. What was most striking about the task force meeting wasn't the amount that the women were talking, but how the whole tenor of the meeting felt different. Nobody was stridently trying to make or debate arguments. They were calling on one another if they thought someone else had something to say.

"Did you all plan in advance what you were going to say?" Kyle asked Shannon after.

She tilted her head. "No, did it seem like we did?"

"You called on each other a lot," he said. Then he paused, "Though I guess people also called on me and the other men a few times, and I suppose we weren't 'in' on the plan."

She laughed. "Yup, that's just the difference of a meeting where people are each focused on their individual contribution alone as opposed to one where they're thinking about how to lift the whole group collectively."

Kyle looked at the notepad he'd been using for meetings the last few months. From this meeting, he had a page full of thoughts and ideas that stemmed from the discussion. At previous meetings, he had been so busy talking (or thinking about what he'd say next) that he hadn't been listening—and hadn't written anything much down as a result. He remembered something his mom had told him when he was a kid: if you spend all your time talking, you're not listening, and you're not learning.

When they'd first talked about meetings being like a back-and-forth sports match, Kyle had thought about tennis, with literal volleying back and forth between players. But maybe basketball was the more appropriate metaphor. It was like the value of the point as opposed to the value of the assist. The assist—helping someone else advance or clarify their ideas—should be as important as each individual scoring more points. After all, advancing collective business aims required everyone have as many points as possible, and that necessitated assists. The problem was that promotions, raises, choice assignments, public recognition: those all came from getting points. That was the game that Kyle had been playing and for which he had been personally rewarded. You couldn't be a total jerk, but the system was rigged against those who spent too much time on assists (and not points). He had enjoyed the group discussion today: it had been full of assists, but he doubted those who controlled the scoreboard—in that room, it was Jack, Leland, and Dan—would remember anything but the points.

PART SEVEN

Equal Pay— and Equal Penalty

CHAPTER TWENTY

Jack

As Jack walked through his front door at 10:30 pm on a Friday, he couldn't decide if he hoped his wife, Cynthia, was awake or not. Most days, even after twenty-five years of marriage, he found her a welcome sight at the end of the day. But he'd just spent all evening poring through the company's budget, looking for places to cut. They only had four more months to show the Board that the company would rebound, and that would likely require reallocating dollars into investments that would help with new growth. Part of him hoped that he'd just find a note scrawled on the kitchen table with instructions as to whether he needed to take the dog out in the morning or if she would. The last thing he needed was her accusatory glare.

No such luck. He made his way to the kitchen and there she was, sitting at the table in a light gray bathrobe, their cocker spaniel curled at her feet, with a big stack of files in front of her. At the other end of the table, he noticed a coloring book and a box of sixty-four crayons. Shit. He must have forgotten their eight-year-old granddaughter Juliet was staying with them that night. Had it been his job to pick her up from after-school care?

"When your assistant called me to tell me you'd be late, I had to rearrange a client meeting to pick up Juliet," she said. "I have a job now too. This isn't fair."

Cynthia had quit her own high-powered public relations job when the kids were born. He'd been proud of her when the last one went to college and she returned to the workforce. He enjoyed feeling less guilty for working late or for bringing work home, knowing that she was doing the same as she hustled to make up for the few decades she'd been out of office life. But things had got complicated when their daughter, Jana, an attorney, was promoted into a position that required her to travel from time to time. Jana's husband was an E.R physician with an unpredictable evening schedule, so her ability to accept the promotion was contingent on finding help. Jack had been the first one to say they would be there, and he had assured his wife that he would do his fair share.

"I'm really sorry, Cynthia," Jack said. "My team has been going through the numbers, trying to figure out how to reduce costs in some of our administrative areas without eliminating any staff positions."

Her look softened out of habit, but only for a second. "I know you're dealing with a lot," she said. But then she added firmly, "But so am I. The meeting I had today would be the biggest client I've landed so far."

"I'm sorry. You're right. I should have remembered about Juliet. I should have called you myself. I should have figured something else out."

She nodded, apparently too tired or frustrated or busy to carry the conversation further. After making himself a pot of tea—more to keep his hands busy while gauging her reaction than because he wanted to drink it—he determined it safe to pull out his laptop. Cynthia was occupied with her file folders after all.

He pulled up the document that he and Debra had created that morning, which listed priorities for the next few months. They had spent over two hours discussing what they would do if they laid off

Leland. Assigning Leland's responsibilities to Amber and making her the CPO would have seemed the logical choice. But they needed Amber concentrating on those new product launches even more than before, given everything that Leland had failed to do with the relaunches. Another CPO search would take time. In the interim, they'd have to distribute Leland's responsibilities across a few members of the executive team. Practically, that would mean the majority of the burden would fall on Jack and Debra, on top of everything else both of them were already doing.

If it had been a few years ago, the decision would have been easier. Leland was bad at the job, period. The work would get done better without him, and Jack would have worked extra weekends and evenings—and asked others to do so too—while they came up with a more sustainable solution; hired the right person. Sometimes it had taken six months, even twelve, but Jack always found it worth the effort to have only the right talent in critical roles.

This time, he wasn't sure what to do. Those engagement survey results were so bad—the staff were clearly overworked already. Could he and Debra really ask them to do even more?

And the more personal question was whether Jack himself could take on more without breaking his promises to his wife, his daughter, and his granddaughter. It was ironic, this world of trade-offs. He'd heard that the women at the firm saw Leland's incompetence—and their choice to hire Leland as CPO instead of promoting Amber—as representative of a larger problem for women in leadership. But in the microcosm of Jack's life, in order to help his wife and daughter with their career opportunities, didn't he have to keep Leland in place?

Jack hadn't planned to betray Debra the following Monday morning. At least that's what he told himself. He didn't examine whether there was an ulterior motive to his decision to postpone his 9:00 am meeting to work out instead. He needed to let off steam after dealing with the budget stress. And no better place to do that than the Brentwood Racquet Club.

The name of the club was a bit of misnomer. Only one third of the club's 100,000 square feet was devoted to tennis and squash. Another third was a state-of-the-art fitness center, including indoor and outdoor saltwater pools. The last third was made up of various lounges and dining rooms where neither electronic devices nor any business paperwork were allowed.

Earlier in his membership, when he had been in his twenties and could barely afford the dues, Jack had been caught trying to hand a contract to an acquaintance over the key lime pie. Not having been raised in rooms like this, Jack hadn't quite grasped the rule then: you could talk about business as much as you wanted in these rooms, but the actual transaction itself was forbidden. Discussing a contract in vague terms was okay; looking at one in writing and signing it was not. A valet in a navy suit had appeared at his side, seemingly out of nowhere, and whispered to him that he'd have to borrow one of the private offices on the second floor if he desired to look at any business papers. Jack had felt the eyes of the room on him. How uncouth! How bourgeois! To try to sign a contract over key lime pie.

Nowadays, Jack was usually too busy to linger in the dining areas after getting in a workout. That morning, he found himself wandering to the club's most popular dining room, which overlooked a small terrace with a large fountain at its center. Floor-length, burgundy velvet drapes hung in the windows overlooking the terrace. On one gray wall was a modest fireplace and a dozen small framed portraits. These were the men who had been designated members of the year, each looking solemnly into the camera. Along the other walls were floor-to-ceiling bookcases, mostly holding books and globe paperweights of varying alloys and sizes. At the center of one shelf was a real crocodile skull, two feet long, perched on a wooden display stand next to a book titled *Animal Cruelty at Marine Parks.*

There were three wooden dining tables in the large room. The six-person table closest to the crocodile skull was where George sat every morning with his newspaper, coffee, and crumb cake.

George had donated the skull a decade ago, a trophy from a Florida hunting trip. Cynthia, thinking the display absurd, had placed the *Animal Cruelty* book (found on the shelf below) next to the skull during one of her rare visits to the club. Jack had been worried George would work it out, but he'd apparently never noticed.

As Jack walked to the table, trying not to make eye contact with the skull, George stood up. He always shook Jack's hand, even if they'd seen each other fairly recently. Jack hoped his grip was neither too hard nor too soft.

"Thanks for sending me the new budget assumptions," said George as soon as they both sat down, "I'm still worried, but I think you have done a good job finding places to cut. I do have a question though." He paused to order a second crumb cake for Jack despite his protests that he wasn't hungry. "Debra mentioned that she's almost certainly going to fire Leland. Do you agree? I gather it's been a rough start, but he seemed so promising."

Jack knew he couldn't avoid addressing the inevitable.

In their years working together, Jack had never once undermined Debra's authority to George, no matter how often the Board Chair fished for it. He hated the way George would discuss reading *Lean In* with his daughters in one breath, then invite Jack and even men several levels below him on the ladder—but never Debra or any of the women—to play tennis in the next. Jack didn't ever let himself wonder for too long about George's constant questions about Debra's performance, many of which felt out-of-bounds for a Board Chair to ask a CFO outside of formal reviews. Would George have asked these questions if Debra weren't a woman?

It didn't matter. Jack had never taken the bait.

He had called Debra over the weekend and expressed his change of heart—they shouldn't fire Leland after all, he said. She remained firm that he wasn't right for the job. She didn't think he'd improve fast enough. She was on a business trip for the early part of the week, but would be discussing it with HR as soon as she returned.

By the end of the conversation, he'd admitted she was right.

The crumb cake arrived, and Jack poked at it, then spoke slowly. "Well, Leland definitely is struggling and his work so far has been a disappointment," he said. "On the other hand, his resume is so impressive, and his references were so good. It's hard for me to believe he won't be able to figure it out."

None of that was untrue, Jack thought. It was just the most convenient version of the truth. His stomach turned as he thought about the implications of having disagreed with Debra without so much as a courtesy first. Then he glanced at *Animal Cruelty at Marine Parks* on the shelf and thought of Cynthia. This is what his family needed him to do.

Sure, Jack wanted to punch Leland every time he spoke. He had once found him pleasant, when they had been casual acquaintances at the Racquet Club. Now, when he looked at Leland, he just thought about how much they were paying him and wondered why. But that didn't mean Leland couldn't get better.

He'd have to get better.

George spoke again, "I just don't think the Board will feel confident that the executive team has a path forward if there's a critical senior vacancy. We'd have to look at whether added leadership changes would be needed."

Was that an ultimatum? For a second, Jack felt angry. How could Debra do her job if she weren't empowered to make a leadership change if needed—especially during such a critical time? But if Debra was potentially in trouble anyway, he needed to hedge his bets and show his willingness to work with the Board. If you looked at it a certain way, in supporting George's obvious desire to keep Leland, he was *helping* Debra, giving her and their whole leadership team more time to figure things out before they were all on the chopping block.

"You're right," said Jack. "There's so much we need to get done right now, I don't think we can afford to have the CPO position vacant."

"That's what I thought," said George. "I suspect Debra just needs to have a firmer hand with him. Hold him to higher standards." George began to ramble now. "Her expectations are also unrealistic for a new person. Sometimes I worry she's too demanding. You know, I should probably start checking in with Leland myself over the next few months. I'll tell Debra to get out of his way a bit."

It didn't escape Jack's notice that George had said Debra was both too demanding and not demanding enough, literally a few sentences apart. Jack nodded vaguely before leaving the room. He wondered if there was anything he could possibly do to make it up to Debra.

CHAPTER TWENTY-ONE

Debra

What did he want this time? George had called Debra to his home office downtown once again. The timing was inconvenient, as she'd planned to meet with Terry that morning to start discussing how to let Leland go. For legal reasons, she knew Terry would suggest that they first give him a PDP, or professional development plan—basically a list of activities that he'd have to complete to standard in a set period to either prove that he still deserved his job, or be out. A PDP could range from four weeks to twelve, and Debra knew she needed to plan for a shorter timeframe. Even four felt generous when Leland seemed to be obstructing so many major efforts.

This time, George didn't even do her the courtesy of letting her come upstairs. The concierge in the lobby told Debra that he was on his way out. When he arrived, George said she and Debra could talk as he walked to his car.

Dick power move. If he had so little time, they could have just talked on the phone.

Was he going to fire her on the spot? Was that the reason for expecting her in person? No, not with a Board meeting in a few months. He'd make her work like crazy until then, and then fire her. She'd already explained to him on the phone last week what she would be personally doing across the next few months, including key personnel moves, like firing Leland.

George had reached the reception, but instead of greeting her immediately, he pulled his phone out of his pocket and started either texting or sending an email. As if to purposely show his power and make her wait.

Maybe he really would fire her right away. If something very bad had happened, the rest of the Board wouldn't blink. Could another investor have dropped?

He finished typing and put his phone back in his pocket.

"Thanks for meeting me here, and sorry I have a last-minute meeting on the Westside I need to drive to."

The Westside—meaning where she worked and lived.

Even mentioning that was another dick power move.

"I thought about our last conversation, where you mentioned wanting to fire Leland," he said as he started walking briskly to the parking lot, making her scramble in her heels.

"Right, I was going to talk to Terry about it this morning," she said.

He stopped walking. "Don't. You can't afford to lose a key person right now."

"As I mentioned, it'll be difficult," she said, even though she could tell from his tone of voice that this conversation wasn't going to go anyplace except the direction George had already determined. "I believe that Leland is doing more harm than good right now though, and we're better off without him."

"I find that hard to believe given his experience," said George. Did he mean given his XY chromosome? she wondered. He continued, "You just need to have a firmer hand with him. Make sure he feels the pressure, so he is forced to step up more. I discussed this with Jack. Let's create a product revitalization task force; put Leland in charge of that: either he sinks or he swims, but I'd bet on him swimming."

Leland was CPO. Product revitalization was his job, and he'd been failing at that, how would creating a "task force" help with that?

But more important was what he'd said before that.

"You discussed this with Jack?"

Jack had agreed with her this was necessary. Had George convinced Jack, or had Jack changed his mind and not let her know? Either way, after knowing each other for almost forty years, how could he not have had the courtesy to tell her? Perhaps she should have known better. Every man was out for himself when jobs were on the line.

George shrugged. "I happened to see him at the Racquet Club."

The club that until the 21st century had been called the Brentwood *Men's* Racquet Club?

Debra contemplated whether she had any recourse. George was not only wrong, but he was also out of bounds. As CEO, she should have the right to decide a senior person wasn't right for the team without the Board Chair's approval. She could always try to go to some of the other Board members with whom she had a strong relationship. That was risky though. George had a lot of sway over the other members. She'd let the company's numbers sink the past year. Sure, any CEO would have struggled with the sudden shift in the competitive landscape and the economic climate. But it didn't matter—she was the one at the helm. And Leland was a dude with an impressive resume (and, apparently, the backing of Jack, the CFO).

For all she knew, they'd end up giving Leland her job if she seemed too difficult.

"I'm going to start meeting with Leland one-on-one," George said, "Help make sure he's on the right track."

She couldn't do anything but nod.

When Debra returned to her office, she noticed a one-on-one meeting coming up on her calendar with Frank, a senior director on the IT team. He wasn't someone she regularly checked in with individually, so she looked through her emails to see if there was a message explaining the meeting's purpose. Sure enough, there it was, a short email from Frank unread in her inbox.

Debra,

I know the executive team is having its Annual Senior Talent Review meeting later this week to discuss the performance and career paths of all senior staff. In advance, I wanted to set up some time to discuss my pay and why I think an adjustment would be warranted.

Sincerely,
Frank

It was a pretty ballsy email to send to the CEO, she thought. Her second thought was that perhaps the word "ballsy" to indicate courage was a problem, even though she used it to describe women as well. As enlightened as she'd always thought she was, she had never thought much about this kind of day-to-day vocabulary that implied superior traits held by men. It took balls to have courage. Another problematic mental auto-complete at work.

While she waited for Frank to arrive, Debra wondered what argument he could possibly have for a pay raise. They'd almost fired him a few months ago due to poor performance. He'd been on an official PDP. Over the course of those eight weeks, Frank's manager and HR had thought the likelihood he wouldn't pass was high as he was struggling to get his assignments done, and several were of poor quality. In the end, he just barely squeaked by with the bare minimum not to be fired. He should be grateful to just have a job—and wasn't entirely safe in it. If any adjustment of his salary made sense, it would be in the downward direction.

When Frank entered her office, he immediately settled himself into a power pose on the chair: legs spread on the floor, doubling the amount of horizontal space he'd take up if he sat up straight. He leaned back and draped one of his arms on the seat next to him.

"I won't beat around the bush," he said. "I should be paid another $15,000." Before she could respond, he added, "I'm working on an important project."

Sure. So was everyone else.

"I appreciate the work that you're doing," she said. "But you should know we typically raise salaries only when someone has a strong record of sustained achievement beyond what's expected of their level and is about to take on more responsibility."

Did she have to point out the obvious?

"I simply can't stay in this job in this salary," he said. "My peers from Yale School of Management are making twice this already."

She wanted to ask how many of them had almost been fired recently. Instead, she nodded to show she was listening.

Probably a mistake. He seemed to see that as agreement. He kept going. "I'd like to take my family to Napa this summer with my business school colleagues and their families, and I wouldn't be able to do it without an increase. I already had to cancel our annual trip to Hilton Head earlier this year due to how many hours I was working. They went without me, and now both my wife and children are holding it against me."

She couldn't let that go. "You mean the hours you needed to make sure you completed the PDP?"

"Well, yes," he said. "It was a lot of work. I will need to start job searching if I don't get the raise. I need to be able to provide for my family."

His salary was nothing to blush at, even if it were less than his Ivy League business school peers. But there was something desperate in his tone, Debra mused. As if his entire worth were at stake in that $15K.

She wished that he'd felt that same kind of desperation when it came to proving his worth through his job performance.

"I just can't work here under these conditions," he repeated.

It didn't seem like a big loss, Debra thought. But she gave the party line, "We'll discuss all senior compensation at the Senior Talent Review meeting this week."

The Senior Talent Review was done by a small group: Debra, Jack, Terry, Leland, Roger (Chief Revenue Officer), Brandon (Chief Information Officer), and Saul (Chief Operating Officer). Since Natalie left, the C-level team was all men other than Debra, and Terry in the stereotypically feminine position of HR. Cassandra had told Debra that this was a point of much dismay among women throughout the ranks. "I know it's not ideal," Debra had said. "But think about how many rising senior women we have in the layer immediately below."

"That doesn't actually make people feel better," said Cassandra. "It seems even more like a glass ceiling. It feels symbolic of how powerful men get their work done through female #2s."[25]

Debra winced at this statement, having felt that way herself earlier in her career. Cassandra's words were in her mind as she looked around the Senior Talent Review table. She wondered what it would take to change its composition, but she knew it was time to focus on the matter at hand. Each of the C-suite officers had been tasked with bringing a list of their director-and-above-level staff, as well as demarcating any potential raises, promotions, or problems (such as those leading to PDPs).

She scanned the list quickly as they sat down. There was nothing surprising until one line jumped out at her.

"We're considering giving Frank a $10K raise?" Debra asked.

Brandon, who was Frank's boss's boss, spoke first, "He asked for fifteen. $10K seemed reasonable."

Debra was about to say that logic didn't fly: an outlandish request being met with a slightly less outlandish action wasn't exactly reasonable. But Saul inserted himself into the conversation before she could say anything. "Frank's having a difficult time at home—his kids are entering college age soon where every dollar counts, and it also sounds like his wife is all but ready to divorce him. I know how that goes. It was hard enough being a breadwinner when I was Frank's age: I can't imagine what it's like now. And I know my wife has been frustrated with me for less." He laughed.

Debra had known Saul's wife for a long time and hated the way Saul sometimes spoke about her as if she were that superficial, the cause of him needing to burn the midnight oil (to fund her shopping habit), or the reason why he couldn't (she didn't want him gone so much). It felt disrespectful of women, and Debra thought about how upset she would have been if her own late husband had talked about her in such a way. Never mind the fact that family situations shouldn't come into play when discussing salaries.

She looked at Terry. Was she going to say something?

Terry nodded at her. "Sorry to be the compliance cop, folks," she said. "But we really can't be discussing family status as part of this decision. Let's focus on other issues. The new proposed salary would be in the high range for senior directors. Are you comfortable paying him that, given he was so close to being laid off so recently?"

"I know Frank's not the strongest performer," said Brandon. "But given how much we have going on right now, we can't afford to have him quit. The risk is too high."

Debra always trusted her division heads to make these decisions. She couldn't personally assess the cost and benefit of every single salary decision. The division head had to figure out how to make it work within their budget, and Terry had to agree that the salary was within the general acceptable range for that person's position and experience.

However, the language here was making her uncomfortable. The more that she thought about it, the more she could recall men who, like Frank, weren't the strongest performers but had made strident arguments for being paid more, often accompanied by pleas for what they needed to fund at home—larger-than-advisable mortgages, new babies, or children's education.

Of course, this didn't happen with all men, or even most. But Debra couldn't think of a single woman who'd ever tried to get a raise this way. Was it because they knew that argument wouldn't work—sympathy for the male breadwinner was something to which they didn't have access? Come to think of it, she realized the leadership group often discussed children and families when talking about men who needed to be promoted quickly, but she couldn't remember having that discussion about women (except in the opposite way—wondering if a woman was putting on the brakes on her own aspirations).

Debra had seen a number of articles about gender and pay appear on her LinkedIn feed over the years. She had seen some arguing that women, socialized to be nice girls and team players, were less likely to negotiate for themselves (the argument for "leaning in"). She recalled other research about how women in many scenarios asked for raises as often as men but were seen negatively when they did—as being too assertive.[26]

"I don't think it's right to give someone a raise because he needs to pay for his kids' college or to help save his marriage," said Debra.

She didn't say her next thought—what kind of marriage hinged on a raise anyway?

"Well, that's not the reason," said Roger, despite the fact that Brandon and Saul had both implied that was the reason a few minutes earlier. "He's on an important project, has been working hard, and we can't afford to lose him. Period."

"I'll think more about it," she said. She rarely disagreed with so many of her staff at once, but this seemed absurd.

She looked around and realized that Jack had been looking down at his notepad the entire time, not saying anything. As the CFO, Jack was typically the one who allied with Debra in questioning whether raises were a good idea. Especially during a tight budget time, $10K was not a small deal.

Normally, Debra would ask him what he thought. But she no longer trusted him.

Terry didn't know that. "Jack, you've been quiet," she said.

He looked up and then made direct eye contact with Debra, as if to make clear his defiance. "We can't afford to lose Frank."

"If that were true, we wouldn't have been ready to fire him a few weeks ago," said Debra.

Jack's reply was telling. "Look, not everyone is perfect right away. Sometimes people make mistakes, but we have to bet with them. We just need to give people a chance."

Debra suspected she was the only one who noticed Jack glance at her, then at Leland, only for a split second.

Oh, was this about that situation too? Debra felt dizzy thinking about all the different things that were going on in this one discussion. Consciously or not, there definitely seemed to be in-group favoritism by the fathers and husbands in the group: she suspected they wouldn't be helping a woman in the same position with a sob story about taking her children to Napa. When Debra's children had been younger and she had taken time off for vacations, she had felt simultaneously judged for not spending *more* time with them ("Good that you're getting in quality time with your kids; they must miss you when you're at work all the time") and perceived as less committed for prioritizing any time with her family ("Since you'll be busy with your kids this summer, we thought Mike would be a better candidate for this assignment.")

But there was more going on here. It felt like recognizing a second poor performer (Frank) somehow validated Jack's decision with the first (Leland). One of her mentors earlier in her career often talked about the slippery slope when companies reduced their standards related to talent. If you hired a B player instead of an A player, the B person would hire or promote Cs. Soon, Bs and Cs would became the norm. Eventually the A players would get frustrated and leave. Leland and Frank weren't even B players; they were probably Cs on a good day. However, although strong performance was more important than ever right now, the company's desperation was being used as a way to justify poor-performing staff. That seemed dangerous, but Debra felt, for the first time as a CEO, powerless to stop it.

The last portion of the Senior Talent Review meeting should have boosted Debra's mood. They always spent the last twenty minutes speaking about the director-level staff who showed the most promise and would likely rise into senior leadership positions.

Roger started with a quick review of his staff at that level. As Chief Revenue Officer, that included a pretty large group, including Tom and the marketing staff, and Debra felt especially alert as he talked about Haley and Chad.

"A lot of you know that Chad didn't meet the deadline for a big marketing campaign for one of his apps. He's terrible at time management, but he's got so much potential. I could definitely see him advancing."

"The data dashboards that Haley has created have been so effective that we've asked the whole department to use them. She's also an excellent manager. She has a lot of strengths, but she'll be limited by her challenges with time management."

There was that "but" again. Debra had to ask. "Who is better at time management, Chad or Haley?"

Roger didn't even need to think about the answer. "Haley," he said.

Everyone had development areas, and it sounded like time management was a key one for both Chad and Haley. Yet interestingly, for Chad, it seemed to be an aside before getting to the more important headline: his potential. For Haley, on the other hand, it was being treated as a limiting factor.

"If Tom were to leave, would anyone on his team be ready to take his place?" Terry asked. She took her role at ensuring they were doing succession-planning seriously.

"Chad shows so much promise, and I have no reason to believe he wouldn't be good at Tom's job. I'd bet with him," said Roger.

"What about Haley?" Debra couldn't help but ask.

"Oh, she's definitely doing a great job. Maybe in two or three years, after she's accomplished even more. We'll want to see more over time."

Debra was not nearly as well-read as Cassandra when it came to the literature around gender at work, but even she knew the research showed that women were promoted less frequently and typically after more time in their current roles—what was sometimes called the "prove it again" versus "bet with" phenomenon.[27]

She tugged at her scarf around her neck. "I've seen a lot more evidence of Haley's strengths than Chad's," she said. "For our next succession-planning discussions, I'd like us to look at their performance files."

After the meeting, Debra stopped in the women's restroom and went into the stall at the far end. A few seconds later, she heard two other women enter the restroom.

"Can you believe that email Leland sent today?" one of them said, the second the door to the hallway shut. Debra wished she could hit her forehead against the bathroom stall door. So Leland still hadn't improved.

"I mean what do you expect?" the second woman replied. "Our numbers have just continued to crash since he arrived, but it doesn't matter. Men never get penalized."

Debra didn't recognize either voice. Part of her hoped that the women would notice someone was in the stall, and stop talking. She didn't actually want to know. Before, she'd been in denial. Now, she felt helpless. George had tied her hands.

The company had recently renovated the bathrooms, and the doors reached all the way down the floor. A small green or red indicator near the door knob told you whether or not someone had locked the door inside, but this was less noticeable than the older model of bathroom stall doors where you could see someone's shoes peeking through. They either hadn't noticed the red indicator on her door, or they were simply too incensed to care about anyone else's presence.

"Totally," said the first woman. "I mean if equal pay weren't problem enough, nobody ever talks about equal penalty. When women achieve success, it's luck or hard work. With men, it's high ability."

"The reverse too," said the second woman. By now they'd both left their respective stalls and were washing their hands. "When women mess up, it's seen as weakness or that they couldn't handle the challenges. When men mess up, it's bad luck or laziness that can be overcome."

Debra hadn't thought about equal penalty as the flip side of the equal pay issue. She thought about the Senior Talent Review discussion. Haley had been penalized for development areas when Chad was not, despite Chad having those same development areas to greater extent.

As the air dryers stopped, Debra wondered if these two women would leave the bathroom. But she was glad they didn't—the rest of the conversation was illuminating.

"You know men totally benefit from the Peter Principle," one woman said.

"What's that?"

"We learned about it in business school. Basically, it's the idea that people get promoted to their level of incompetence. Someone is good at their job, so they get promoted to the next job. Eventually, they get to the point where the next job requires different skills, and the person isn't ready. But they end up staying in that job, even if they're performing poorly at most of their new job activities, because they have some strengths—the ones that got them there—that are still useful."[28]

Debra thought about Leland. His references were good, and perhaps he'd been strong at his previous role. And yet it definitely seemed that he had Peter Principle'd. She'd heard the phrase before, but never really thought about it from a gender perspective. By the time a woman had achieved a senior position, she'd faced a lot of crap and become like Teflon. It stood to reason then, that those women who had gone through more hoops to advance would be less likely to Peter Principle than those men who were advanced based on promise rather than evidence they could do the next-level job.

There were two different promotion philosophies Debra had seen over the years: you could wait until someone had essentially been doing the job, or you could make an early bet with those that exhibited high potential. She'd long thought that companies, including her own, needed to be more consistent with the philosophy they applied. Some years they promoted people based on potential, saying the need was too great not to do so, while other times they decided that it was important to wait until people were ready so they didn't burn out or create too much risk for the business. It hadn't occurred to her until this moment that this inconsistency might be consistently gendered. But as she ran through the last few years of promotion decisions in her head, she couldn't deny the uneven ratio in her head.

Debra waited for the sound of the bathroom door to swing shut before she left the stall. She thought about what HR folks often referred to as the "bulletin board test"— if you posted every employee's name and salary on a bulletin board, of course some people would think they should personally get paid more, but ideally they'd mostly say "this list is fair." The thinking was that, even if people were relatively happy with their own incentives, if they thought the bulletin board is wrong—that someone was being paid too much and contributing too little—it could be disastrous for morale. Debra was grateful their salaries weren't public, like they were in many government jobs. But she also knew that people figured it out: they talked or guessed, and were often right.[29]

Thinking about this, she pondered the fact that they needed to ensure not only that women were equally recognized when they did lean in, but also that men and women were equally penalized when they didn't. Her own situation hit her hard: in two months, they'd have to present to the Board what they'd done to turn around the business. If she ended up losing her job, she perhaps deserved it—the buck did stop with her, after all. But she'd probably be the only scapegoat, despite those men around her who were tying her hands.

CHAPTER TWENTY-TWO

Leland

At his first job, Leland had been the person who always cleaned the microwave in the break room. He'd noticed the cleaning crew only did so every other week, and that wasn't enough to deal with the endless splatter on the microwave's interior walls, which looked like a small child had flailed their hands inside after finger painting. It had become Leland's morning routine. He would arrive at 8:15 am, find the cleaner under the sink and retrieve a handful of paper towels before getting to work. This had been before ideas of mindfulness had hit the popular lexicon, so he hadn't had the proper vocabulary yet, but cleaning the microwave had almost been a kind of meditation. The running interior monologue in his head had shut down for those five minutes.

That was three decades ago, but he still remembered the types of things he had started noticing after taking that job upon himself. For those five minutes, the microwave had brought peace. Not so much the rest of the day when it had raised a range of emotions. Gratitude for Elaine and Flo, who had covered their food with a sheet of paper towels, creating literally no mess. Annoyance with Timothy, who was always microwaving Indian or Italian or some other highly saucy food that exploded everywhere. Sheer anger at Randy, not only a frequent culprit but someone who also got in early, watched Leland's cleaning routine, and not once thanked him or offered to help. Leland had known he couldn't really complain: nobody had asked Leland to do this. The dirty microwave had seemed to bother him more than it bothered others. And so, by default, he had become the one that cleaned.

When he had complained to female friends, they had laughed. "Yeah, it's called office housekeeping, and we do it all the time." They had explained to him that they sometimes used the term to describe actual housekeeping: literally keeping the office clean and in order, as Leland did with the microwave.

But it had also involved taking the notes in the meeting—after they had pointed it out to him, he had realized that their bosses usually asked a woman to take notes, whether or not she was in an administrative role, and often even if she was senior to the men. Then there were all the little things that made the team environment better: remembering birthdays, checking how someone was doing if they were having a particularly hard time at work or home. One of his female peers had showed him her calendar once, and he had been astounded by how much more mentoring (informal and formal) she was asked to do and how many task forces she was on (as the "token woman" who did all the work, she said).

Despite the fact that his female peers had done a lot more "white space" (work with no clear owner) and "office housekeeping" than he did, Leland had realized he got praised a lot more for it. It was just expected that the women do these things; as a man he was going above and beyond. "In addition to unequal pay for the same responsibilities as men, we have all this extra labor that is totally unrecognized," his friend had said.

He felt guilty after his conversation with Amber about Erica. She was right. Calvin was a shitty manager. Dan had been a jerk. Amber had taken on additional emotional labor—when God knows, she was busy enough. But what was he supposed to do? He couldn't exactly have told Erica that she was exhibiting some kind of gender bias in criticizing Amber but not Dan. And, well, Calvin was his only ally. The only one who he didn't suspect, like Meg and Amber, of looking at him with total disgust. Not that they ever said anything. But he could tell.

Leland had gotten multitasking down to a science over the years. Listening to audio books while cooking dinner. Doing conference calls while on the treadmill. Technology made it a lot easier. While waiting in line at the company coffee shop, he added groceries to his cart on the mobile shopping app that he used weekly.

He was adding cake mix for the dinner they were hosting for his mother's birthday on the app, when he heard Dan's voice behind him.

"What is that? A grocery app?" Dan asked.

"Yeah, it's great," said Leland. "You can set grocery deliveries same-day or up to a week in advance, for five different stores nearby."

He wasn't sure why he felt the need to say that much. Small talk had always made him feel a little uncomfortable, but it was even worse since he still hadn't found his footing at the company.

"Huh," said Dan. "It's interesting how much people can do on their phones now."

Leland knew it was a mistake, but he kept talking, "Yeah, have you used the TaskCat app? It allows you to book either virtual or local personal assistants. I've been using it to find folks locally to run errands, and even more complex tasks like planning vacations."

Probably more than Dan needed to know, but hey, they were in the app business. Dan should at least show some interest in new trends in the mobile landscape.

"Wouldn't it be cheaper to have your wife do those things?" Dan laughed.

"Instead of her job that pays more than mine?" Leland asked, realizing after that he'd probably committed a gender faux pas in admitting his salary was less than hers. Nothing shut down a conversation with other men faster than saying he wasn't the breadwinner.

In fact, Leland was a rarity among straight men in his fifties: the lead parent.

He hadn't heard the phrase until a few years ago, but it immediately resonated. In most two-career families, even with two actively involved parents who are close to their children, one person assumes the lead parent role. Even when two parents split the to-do list fairly equally on a regular basis, one parent (usually the mom) owns the to-do list. That person keeps greater tabs on schedules: both daily (which parent would pick the kids up from what event) and long-term (what would they do during spring break). That person is listed first on emergency forms and is the one who drops everything in a crisis. In business parlance, the lead parent often not only does at least half of the actual day-to-day work, but also most of the planning and delegating. The vast majority of the time, in a heterosexual couple, the woman is the lead parent.[30]

For Leland and Grace though, it had never been a question that Leland would be the lead parent from the beginning. Even though he had a successful and demanding career, hers as a political campaign strategist was even more so. Elections could literally hinge on whether she could get on a plane in time or deal with a late-night media emergency. They were both passionate about the causes for which she fought, and it was the career of her dreams. He'd stumbled into his first job in tech and steadily advanced, but he didn't feel inspired the same way she did. He loved spending time with their twin sons.

He'd heard that there was an increasing number of younger men who were playing the lead parent role. But in his circles, it seemed rare. Even a high-powered executive woman like Debra didn't seem to get it. His first week, they had gone out to lunch at a diner down the street. She had smiled at a man in his twenties holding a baby.

"That's what makes me feel better about these younger generations," she had said. "In my day, you'd rarely see a father carrying a baby in public like that."

He had kept his mouth shut. It drove him crazy, the pedestal that fellow men would be placed on for doing something as simple as carrying a baby. So many men got showered with praise for doing basic tasks, when it was women (or a few rare male lead parents like himself) who often carried the bulk of the child care. It was like, back at his first job, when a male colleague once got praised for helping throw trash out after a party, when Leland and the women picked up after everyone in the office every day.

But he also knew he shouldn't complain. While women faced a "motherhood penalty"—being the victims of bias as they were seen as less committed; carrying unequal loads both at work and at home—overall, men received a "fatherhood bonus" compared to childless men.[31] Studies showed men were more likely to get called back for an interview if they mentioned the parent-teacher association on their resume (showing stability) and also got paid more (as they were seen as needing the money). Leland knew that Frank had benefited from the fatherhood bonus when he had been given that raise at the Senior Talent Review—it really didn't make sense. Even the fatherhood bonus only went so far though. He'd joined a Facebook group for fellow male lead parents, and they all discussed the penalties they felt for being perceived as "less masculine" at work in the minds of the Dans of the world.

PART EIGHT

Millennial Hopes and Disillusionment

CHAPTER TWENTY-THREE

Amber

Amber had never thought she'd even entertain going to an interview with the company's top competitor. She'd always thought of their competitors as a "them," of whom she could never be a part. She loved her job. She knew that the grass wouldn't necessarily be greener.

But at least it would be different grass, right?

After Leland had chided her about Erica, she had reached out to their rival's CEO, who she had met through mutual friends years ago. She had mentioned that she was considering other opportunities and wanted to meet.

He'd written back within two minutes, suggesting they meet at a restaurant in Marina Del Rey for lunch. They sat outside, overlooking the rows of expensive boats docked in the marina. He pointed his out, though she couldn't tell exactly what he was pointing to—they all looked the same to her.

"How did you come up with her name?" she asked, figuring that would give her a clue as to which boat. Not that it mattered, but it was good to pretend to be interested. She assumed the boat was a "her."

"My childhood dog's name," he replied. "I was thirteen when we put her to sleep. Heartbreaking. I decided I'd name all my boats after her after that."

Amber took a bite of the warm pretzel they'd put on the table instead of bread, pretending to be occupied while she looked at the potential boat candidates. Honestly, it could have been any number of the boats in their line of sight: Shelley. Princess. Athena.

Probably Princess. She'd take a chance. "That's some beautiful wood paneling," she said.

Good guess. He beamed. And then talked about the wood paneling for the next ten minutes. After their food came, she talked a bit about what she was working on in between bites of her vegetatian Cobb salad. He devoured a tuna melt fairly quickly and revealed more about their growth strategy than she would have expected of a competitor over a casual lunch.

At the end, he shook her hand, "I know you said you were still deciding what you want to do. But I'd love to have you come in and meet the team. I feel confident we could find a good role for you."

Instead of driving back to the office or home, Amber headed one hundred miles up the coast to the Santa Barbara Tea Room and Gardens. She had only been there once before—fifteen years ago, as a high school senior. Her grandmother had taken her there for a special treat. It was a place that would feel grown-up to celebrate her acceptance to college. She'd enjoyed her first full-fledged afternoon tea there, sitting in a room decorated in what would later be called millennial pink, but then had just been pink.

This time she bypassed the formal menu and went to the new express window that had since been added, getting a latte and taking it to the gardens behind the tea room. Amber took off her blazer and placed it, along with her handbag and latte, on a wooden bench which was made of a newly polished teak that seemed a stark contrast to the older bricks and stones surrounding it. It was a little too cold for a sleeveless shell, but she wanted to feel the sun and breeze on her arms. For what felt like an hour but was probably more like ten minutes, she paced back and forth from the fountain at one end of the large court-yard to the bench at the other end, where she had left her belongings. The scent of freshly baked cookies permeated the air, even though the baked goods in the Tea Room were separated by a set of double French doors.

She returned to the bench, and looked at her email. The rival CEO had already sent her a quick note, thanking her for lunch and affirming that she'd be a good fit for their team. Part of her wanted to write back immediately. Yes! Take me right away! But she also knew it wasn't the right job. The competitor was a much larger and more established company. That certainly had advantages, but Amber liked being at a start-up and knew that her next role needed to be at a nascent enterprise too. For her next job, she wanted to be running to something, not away.

As her fingers drummed against the teak wood, she realized she'd sat on this very bench as her grandmother had given her a biography of one of their female senators, discussing the "Year of the Woman" that Amber vaguely remembered from elementary school, when a record number of women had swept congressional victories. Amber still remembered unwrapping the silver paper; she could picture the book sitting on the bench where she'd put it down to give her grandma a thank-you hug.

She had relished that book, not just in the one sitting during which she'd finished reading it that evening, but upon several reread-ings that summer. Her grandma had passed several years ago, but Amber imagined what the conversation would look like if they were to talk about her job today. "Why would you leave such a great job?" her grandmother would probably say. "I know it's frustrating to be passed over for the CPO position, but it sounds like this Leland guy won't last long anyway. The fact that you have as much responsibility as you have would have been unheard of when I was your age."

Maybe that was the critical generational difference, Amber mused. Her grandma couldn't have fathomed having that much responsibility in her own career. Amber's mother could, but had fought overtly, day after day to achieve it. They were both so grateful over how much things had changed.

Amber and her friends had been raised at a different time. She knew there would be challenges, knew there was still discrimination. But fundamentally, the overriding narrative she'd heard throughout her childhood was: *things are so much better now. As a woman, you can do everything men can do. Look at the Year of the Woman—look at how far we've come!* She'd not expected that her gender would still make it so hard. She'd not realized how many barriers still remained—something that was becoming more clear the more she advanced in the workplace. Her generation's expectations were set high—and so the crash into reality as they'd moved up the ladder into more senior positions had been especially hard.[32]

That evening, Amber attended a BBQ held by one of her neighbors.

"Did you see that thread on Twitter, asking women what we would do differently if men had a curfew?"

"Not hold our keys between our knuckles in case we need a weapon?"

"Does that even work?"

"I have pepper spray."

"Not decide which streets to walk down when running at night based on the right traffic and lighting to reduce the possibility of assault."

"Leave your drink on the table while going to the bathroom at a party without worrying about what someone might slip into it."

"Turn my music up when running on a trail without cars so I wouldn't have to worry about being 100% alert all the time."

The men all exchanged awkward glances with one another, in between sympathetic or worried glances with their significant others. Amber watched Phil, who lived next door to her, open his mouth partway and then close it, clearly deciding whether to say something. She'd seen that expression before. It was the expression of a man who wanted to participate, knew maybe he shouldn't, and in the end would succumb to his desire to correct what he believed to be a fatal knowledge gap among the group.

"I totally understand what you're all going through," he said. "I felt that way when hiking in Yosemite, worried about bears."

Um, WTF? Most of the women at the table looked too tired to argue. What was the point anyway? Still, they had a silent conversation with their expressions. One of them had to say something, right?

One of the women, an attorney who lived across the street from Amber, accepted her position as their spokesperson. "I've been hiking in Yosemite too," she said. "I have to say that being afraid that a bear might feel threatened and attack you, in a rare setting that you don't enter every day is different from knowing that in your day-to-day life, there are people who actually have the malicious intention of raping you."

"I don't think it's that different," Phil persisted. "Aren't most sexual assaults by someone you know? So the chance of something happening on the street with a stranger is pretty low."

All the tips Amber had learned in self-defense class ran through her head: *be careful walking by cars where someone could emerge from under to grab you; if a stranger comes near you hold your hands up in defensive position and, by God, don't ever let a threat come behind you. Keep turning your body around if you need to so that your back is never facing the threat. If you do get assaulted, do anything—even bite—so you don't get thrown into a car. Remember these rules. Repeat these to yourself.*

These were part of her daily reality, but not Phil's.

Amber never heard the older generations of women complain about these things. They passed down advice and held their handbags to their side.

Her generation didn't want to accept the state of the world, like the fact that you had to hold your handbags that way in the first place.

In the workplace, you didn't have to worry about whether someone was going to slip something in your coffee or if a potential perpetrator was hiding behind a corner (most of the time, anyway). But you still had to be constantly on your guard. Wondering if you'd couched an assertive statement in the right amount of bubble wrap niceness (so that you weren't considered aggressive or bitchy). Wondering how to handle being treated differently by people, including women, who swore up and down that they didn't see gender.

That defensive posture—whether at work, or while walking down the street—was simply exhausting. Amber wondered how much of women's mental energy was expended responding to (or avoiding) these day-to-day challenges and how much happier (and even more productive) they'd be if they weren't so occupied. Work came with challenges for everybody, but women, and other historically marginalized groups, had an extra layer of challenges, large and small.

The group moved onto discussing a movie they had all recently seen, but Amber's mind went back to her job and whether or not it was time to leave. "Don't let Leland drive you out," she imagined her grandmother saying.

It wasn't just Leland though. She thought about the metaphor of mosquito bites, which was often used to describe the challenge of micro-aggressions. The idea is that one single mosquito bite isn't a big deal. So maybe you feel frustrated because someone says an innocuous comment about women, or someone made you take notes at a meeting even as a senior leader. None of that is harmful on its own. Like one mosquito bite, it's a vague irritation—maybe you want to scratch at it, maybe it leaves a scar, maybe not—you just wish it weren't there. But over time, imagine those mosquito bites accumulating. It's gone from vague irritation to something more harmful.

The thousand everyday cuts added up.

CHAPTER TWENTY-FOUR

Kyle

Kyle hadn't expected his parents to get into an argument about Leland over dinner—after all, they had never even met the CPO—and yet the evening meal turned particularly heated as Kyle talked about the harm that his boss's boss was doing to the business.

"How terrible," said Kyle's mom. "Are you going to talk to HR? If so many of you are considering quitting and he's having a negative impact on the business, they really need to know."

That hadn't ever really occurred to Kyle. Before he could reply, his father's loud voice stopped his thoughts. "That's an absurd idea," he said. "Best thing to do is just keep your head down and do your work." Kyle's father was a successful pharmaceutical executive and took pride in being able to explain the business world to his son. Even just hearing the keep-your-head-down refrain made Kyle feel lighter: it provided something to ground him rather than worrying about workplace drama. He found himself gripping his fork less tightly.

Then he glanced at Nicole. By contrast, she was cutting the green beans on her plate with an edge. He sensed that she was probably seething, as she often was when she felt disgusted by how Kyle's dad spoke to his mom.

Nicole had tried to talk to Kyle's mom about it, exactly once. Kyle's mom simply laughed. "Have you seen *My Big Fat Greek Wedding*? Remember that line about how the man is the head, but the woman is the neck, and she can turn the neck anyway she wants. When it matters, he turns the way I want, he just doesn't know it."

Nicole had tried to laugh politely along with his mom.

This time though, his mom wasn't laughing. She closed her eyes for a few seconds. Counting to three probably. "Just because it's not what you would do, it doesn't mean it's a bad idea," she said.

"It's different in the corporate world," his dad said, looking down at the tablecloth, his voice more conciliatory.

It was a half-hearted, back-handed way of apologizing. They all knew he thought less of Kyle's mom's work in the non-profit sector. Correction: she didn't just work in the non-profit sector. She now ran one of the state's fastest growing advocacy organizations. During Kyle's childhood, she'd worked part-time in a number of different jobs, mostly grant writing and event planning. While he was in high school, she had completed a UCLA Extension certificate in Advanced Leadership. As soon as he had gone to college, she had returned to full-time work and quickly risen up the ladder.

"The non-profit sector isn't as different as you think," his mom said.

His dad ignored her, speaking directly to Kyle, "If you raise problems, they'll just think you want out of the boat—it'll start impacting the kinds of assignments you get, your chances of promotion, and so on. Leland is the team captain, and you have to respect that, help him do his job better."

"You don't just have to go along with a bad captain," his mom said.

His dad continued to ignore his mom. "Remember you had a few captains you hated in high school and college. It didn't matter—you were loyal to the team, and you did what the captain told you."

His mom looked at Nicole, who had opted to stay out of Kyle's parents' bickering ever since the woman-is-the-neck conversation.

"Nicole, you're an organizational psychologist, I'm sure the poor effect of bad leaders is something you study."

Nicole didn't answer her question at first. Then she hesitantly spoke: "I've been reading a bit on the difference between how boys and girls typically play as children," she said. "Organized sports are about following the team captain, and you're taught to follow the captain's instructions: there's a belief in hierarchy due to position. Girls grow up playing things like house or school, where it's more about practicing relationships: who does what, and how they get along."[33]

Kyle had never thought about it that way, but it made sense. It connected to the points and assists basketball metaphor he'd contemplated the previous week.

Kyle's mom pushed again. Apparently, there was a limit to her tolerance for being the neck. "Right, so men have been socialized more to follow the captain," she said. "But I'd think it'd harm everyone in the organization if the captain is bad."

"Well, yeah, if the captain is making decisions that are wrong for the organization," Nicole said. She was carefully speaking in vocabulary that Kyle's dad would understand, "If the captain is pursuing strategies that are less likely to grow revenues or decrease costs, even from a basic bottom-line standpoint, that's not good." Kyle suspected she wanted to roll her eyes at having to make that obvious point. "And leaders who don't have the trust—earned authentically, not just because of title or position—aren't effective. Even if their teams comply with their instructions, they won't work as hard or show as much initiative, and they're more likely to leave."

Kyle's dad's reply was gruff. "You millennials and all this feel-good fuzziness. Don't get me started."

"The younger people view work differently," his mom said. "They're interested in the authenticity of their leaders."

Kyle opened his mouth to say something. After all, it was rare for him to go this long without making a contribution. He thought about how much more he liked work because of his connections to the people there, and how much he enjoyed having a boss like Meg that he respected and trusted. But what was the point? He knew his father was friendly with people at work, but the feeling of connection seemed less important than what he thought of the job itself.

His dad's face was starting to turn red. "No offense, but if I have to sit through another HR workshop on what kind of culture millennials want at work, I'm going to stop hiring them. We keep hearing about how we have to create a 'high-trust' culture, show 'interest in them as people,' and that they care about 'meaning' and 'inclusiveness.' These empty words are just HR speak. We owe people a salary and good benefits for work well done, none of this other stuff. Young people need to just put their heads down, shut up, and do their work."

Kyle pretended to be intently focused on cutting his steak so that his dad didn't see him flinch.

Nicole just looked amused. "Um, I don't think you can stop hiring millennials. We're the largest share of the workforce now. And I don't know if some of these attributes are unique to millennials. Older generations wanted to trust their leaders too and to feel included at work—they maybe just weren't as likely to expect or demand it. And since previous generations were more likely to stick with one employer for a long time—especially without the lure of internet recruiting making it easier to leave—employers didn't need to be as focused on what types of leadership their staff expected."

Before the argument could continue, Kyle's father's cell phone rang. "I have to take this," he said.

He went into his office, the room next to the dining area. Not that the distance mattered. They could hear every single word. It was his boss at the pharmaceutical company, calling on a Friday night, saying they were moving up a deadline to Monday.

He came back into the room. Instead of sitting down though, he picked up his plate, fork, and knife. "Sorry, I've got to make some calls," he said, carrying his meal back to his office. "My team is going to need to come in this weekend, and I've got a list of people to let know."

"What happened?" Kyle's mother asked.

"Oh, you know how it goes. The big boss has decided he wants to meet Monday morning to discuss our current project, rather than Thursday as originally planned. I'm sure I'll hear all kinds of whining from the millennials and Generation Z. When I was your age, I worked whenever I was needed, no matter the sacrifice."

Yeah, Kyle thought, remembering being a small child when his father was his age. How many games did he miss? How often was he there for dinner? He couldn't help but look at his mom then. She gave him a half-smile as Kyle's dad left the room.

His mom took her spoon and swirled it around the mashed potatoes. "I hope your generation pushes all of us in the workplace to stop with this 'always on' culture."

"Really?" Kyle was surprised. "But aren't we the generation that is literally always on?" He pointed to his Apple watch as an example. Perfectly on cue, a text message alert went off at that very moment on his phone.

He tapped the screen. It was a friend confirming that he could play tennis the next morning as they'd planned.

One more tap to send a thumbs-up.

"Yes and no," his mom said. "I think technology can make it harder to achieve balance, but it also allows you all the flexibility to integrate balance in your lives that we didn't have before. What time did you leave work every day this week?"

"Well, mostly 6:00 pm," said Kyle. "But I left at 3:00 pm on Wednesday to get into a class that I liked at the gym before doing a few hours of emails in the evening. And I didn't work Tuesday because Nicole and I took her niece to Disneyland on a less crowded day; I went into the office last Sunday instead."

"I know it's not exactly the same thing since I'm in school right now," said Nicole. "But I operate the same way when it comes to student emails for the classes where I'm a TA. I tell my students I'll reply within forty-eight hours, but that doesn't mean right away. Sometimes

I turn email off on my phone in the evenings or on weekends because I don't want my life to be interrupted by it. Sometimes I respond immediately so it's not hanging over my head. If it's a week before a big paper deadline or an exam, I make sure to be accessible and then I do reply right away if I can."

As Kyle thought about what he and Nicole had said, he realized that it was a different kind of "always on" from what he had seen of his dad growing up. He and Nicole worked hard, but they appreciated being able to do so on schedules that made sense with whatever else was going on in their lives. That was true of their friends with kids as well as their friends without kids. Of course, they bent over backwards when they needed to—they weren't immune to the occasional trade-offs his father had mentioned. But the goal was to try to achieve balance, whereas Kyle sometimes felt his father wore the "always on" mentality—along with as much "face time" in the office as possible—as a badge of honor.

"Many women in the workplace have never been able to be 'always on' due to how often they're also acting as lead parent or have other familiar responsibilities," Nicole observed, "But masculine business culture has often been about constant work as a point of pride."

"Exactly," said Kyle's mom. "I think that's changing though in a few different ways. First, as offices pay more attention to challenges for women in leadership, that inherently means looking at how to create work environments that are more balanced. Second, I think that your generation of men views work differently—some of that is taking on greater childcare responsibilities, but a lot of it seems to be a broader cultural shift. You have more female and male millennials valuing things other than just compensation, like the stuff my husband dismissed earlier—inclusive culture and leadership, finding a sense of personal meaning in your work."

They spent the rest of dinner discussing what seemed to be an interesting overlap in the things that women historically valued at work more highly than men did, and the things that younger generations (both male or female) valued at work more highly than older generations. In the middle of the Venn diagram lay authenticity in leadership and work/life balance. As Kyle listened to the sounds of his dad making calls in the next room, he felt sad about the fact that the interesting conversation they were having wouldn't have been possible if his dad were still sitting at the table.

He wondered if his dad would be able to change as his workforce changed around him.

PART NINE

Intent versus Impact

CHAPTER TWENTY-FIVE

Cassandra

The elevator was overall a strangely revealing place, Cassandra thought as she stepped into the doors to head to the café for lunch with Debra. She often thought if you really wanted to hear the gossip or really understand an organization's culture, all you had to do was ride the elevator up and down.

Entering right after Cassandra was a young woman in her mid-twenties, who she recognized as the executive assistant to one of the vice presidents, along with one of the senior directors, a man in his mid-forties. In the typical way people who don't really know each other don't know what to do in an elevator, they all stared silently at the small TV screen to the right of the doors. As in many office buildings, the screens in every elevator displayed tweet-length news snippets, random trivia questions, and fortune-cookie type motivational quotes overlaying panoramic landscape shots. At that moment, it was displaying the weather, allergy index, and a line that said Hair Frizz index, presumably tracking humidity.

The elevator button dinged pleasantly as they reached the sixth floor. The man pointed at the screen with his index finger and then shifted the same finger to point at the young woman's head. "Frizz! Frizz!" he said, laughing. Then without another word, he exited, still audibly beside himself at his own cleverness, his chin in the air as if proud of himself.

The woman turned to Cassandra. "You know, I know who he is, but we've never actually met," she said.

Bizarrely, the woman's straight blond hair wasn't even near frizzy—not that this made the encounter less odd.

"They say that women can be catty about each other's appearances, and maybe we can. But that kind of behavior, that men think is cute, really isn't."

"Yeah," said Cassandra. It seemed a given that he wouldn't have shouted "Frizz" to a male colleague. She wondered whether he would have said the same thing to an older woman or one more senior than he was: someone who had more power. She knew the answer was probably no.

Another man entered the elevator. "Hey Trish," he said to Cassandra's elevator friend. "I heard your last report really impressed the executives. Nice job."

"Thanks, Will!" she said. For a brief second, Cassandra was glad that Trish had had a positive elevator interaction after the Frizz dude.

Until Will spoke again. "Is that a new outfit? Hot date or job interview?"

Cassandra hadn't paid attention to Trish's outfit before—a dark gray wrap dress with sensible thick-strapped sandals. She felt puzzled. It didn't look like either a job interview or a hot date outfit.

Trish just laughed awkwardly.

Will got out of the elevator, and again Trish turned to Cassandra. "Dressing for work is like trying to solve a riddle," she said. "People read something into everything you do."

The elevator door almost closed when a man and a woman that Cassandra didn't know entered. "Did you hear Quinn got a job offer at Apple? Wonder who she's been screwing there."

A few minutes later, Cassandra and Debra were standing in line behind Haley and Tom at the café ordering line. They were both looking over the list of the specials of the day, and in their silence couldn't help but overhear the conversation of their colleagues—one that didn't surprise Cassandra but that shocked Debra.

Haley and Tom were discussing a few of Haley's current projects. Cassandra could tell that Debra was listening carefully—after all, Debra had been wondering about what Tom was like as a manager to women after hearing the discrepancy between how he had described Haley and Chad. She suspected this conversation was putting Debra at ease. Tom was being supportive, and he and Haley had an easy banter.

Then the conversation took an odd turn. "I'm a little nervous about my presentation tomorrow," said Haley. Cassandra knew that her friend was speaking at a conference session for industry executives that they were hosting in their offices the next day. Haley was, as always, more than prepared, but understandably worried about the high-pressure event.

"You have nothing to worry about," Tom said. Cassandra saw Debra smile at his encouraging tone.

Then, he added:

"Everyone in the audience either wants to marry or adopt you. No matter what you do it'll be great."

His tone wasn't flirtatious. It wasn't overtly condescending. It was simply a straightforward comment, as if he were simply delivering an indisputable fact that he thought should make her feel better. From what Tom had said earlier in the conversation, it seemed he believed in Haley's work and had confidence in what she had to say. But his comment made it seem like the quality wouldn't matter: the audience would simply value her by thinking of her as a daughter (someone to care for and protect) or a potential romantic partner (someone to sexualize).

Haley managed a wry smile, and then added lightly, "Marry or adopt? That's a bit odd. But thanks for the vote of confidence." Then she shot Cassandra a look, as if to say, *Did you hear that? What am I supposed to say?*

Meanwhile, as Tom reached the front of the line, he went to order his food. He and Haley proceeded to their table, while Cassandra and Debra went to theirs.

As they sat down, Cassandra told the CEO about her elevator experience—the comment that Trish had received about the frizz in her hair, the "hot date or job interview" remark, and the "who is she screwing" assumption about the women who had received a great job offer.

The conversation then turned to what they'd just overheard with Haley and Tom. Cassandra talked about an idea that she'd read about that some men can only conceptualize women as a mother, wife, mistress, or daughter, and treat them accordingly.

"Can you elaborate?" said Debra.

"Well, think of it this way," Cassandra started to explain, "When we're kids, a young girl is more likely to play with a group of boys than the other way around. What this means is that some men—not all, of course—don't necessarily know how to interact with the opposite sex except for the frameworks they have in their head for how men interact with women. There's the daughter that men take care of professionally but don't think of as equals—that benevolent sexism we've discussed before really comes into play. The wife is someone who might be seen more as an equal, but sometimes is treated in the same problematic ways the man might treat his wife at home, whether that's shutting her down if frustrated or expecting her to do office housework. The mother is someone who understands all the office rules and takes care of everyone. The mistress is a bit like the wife but with sexual tension."[34]

"Huh," said Debra. "I'm not sure I think that's always true, but I can think of a lot of examples in my head where it is." Then she paused, long enough that Cassandra suspected she wouldn't like what Debra would say next, and that Debra knew it. "What Tom said to Haley, and those statements you mentioned in the elevator—clearly a lot of questionable comments, and we need to educate people better. But I admit that a lot of this #MeToo discussion lately makes me nervous. It's already hard enough for women to get as much mentoring as men—both because of the boy's club and silly things like men being afraid women will cry. I worry about men shying away from professional relationships with women at work because they're afraid they'll say the wrong thing."

As they finished their meal, Cassandra thought about this. She knew that what Tom had said wasn't overt sexual harassment, but it was clearly in a gray area that was more common, less dramatic, and less like *Mad Men,* so it didn't really get any attention. Questionable, but not actionable. Organizations were focused on rooting out Weinstein-type behaviors, ignoring the fact that it was the day-to-day gray areas that undermined a larger number of female colleagues more frequently.

She also wondered whether Debra's generation had had to deal with so many men whose *intent* was truly heinous—the ones who consciously and purposefully demeaned women, often through exhibiting sexual power—that they were less focused on those whose *intentions* were good, but where the *impact* was not.

Later that afternoon, it hit Cassandra how the idea of intent versus impact went far beyond issues related to remarks about women's appearance or relationships with men.

She looked around the conference room as Bart barreled through his presentation of how the HR business partners that reported to him (a group of ten or so staff who were assigned to help each division in the company with employee recruitment, performance assessment, and retention) would work more closely together with learning and development (Cassandra's much smaller team of three people). Bart was an associate vice president who also reported to Terry, and even though he did not manage Cassandra, she enjoyed working with him and always found him a supportive mentor.

The meeting invitation had been titled "Plan Walkthrough," with Bart's ten PowerPoint slides attached. For most leaders, a "walk-through" meant a combination of presentation and conversation, allowing people to ask questions and give feedback throughout. Like a purposeful stroll. With Bart, it was a high-volume, high-speed, high-word-count, breathless assault through each page. You were expected to sit silently and listen.

Everyone was sitting silently, but it was unclear to Cassandra if they were listening. As far as she could tell, several people seemed to be texting one another under the table. You could tell because you'd see someone tap something on their phone, put it down, another person would surreptitiously pick up their phone, and then the two would exchange a glance. She knew this should bother her—after all, she'd worked hard with Bart to create the plan, and the room full of people needed to execute on it. But it didn't really matter. She'd resigned herself to the fact that she'd need to do follow-up conversations with the business partners, individually or in smaller groups without Bart, so that they could go through the same material and actually discuss it and answer questions.

Cassandra's mind wandered to what she was going to eat for lunch. She'd brought an avocado, some chicken breast, and mixed greens to make a salad. But they had really good garlic fries in the company café. Maybe she could convince Haley to split an order with her.

Her internal menu debate was interrupted by Jack suddenly inserting himself into Bart's monologue. Cassandra hadn't realized Jack was even there. He must have snuck in late. It seemed like the more the business was in trouble, the more Jack and Debra were appearing at all kinds of meetings. She wasn't sure whether this was deliberate or whether they were procrastinating, avoiding more important, but difficult, work.

"This makes total sense, Bart," said Jack. "I did have one question though. I thought we were also looking specifically at different criteria we want to use to evaluate managers."

Bart replied with a bristle that seemed inappropriate to use when talking to the CFO. "We decided to look at all employees, not just managers." Then, even more aggressively, he added, "We're not revisiting that. Period."

It was a silly response. Jack outranked Bart and could revisit it as much as he wanted. And Jack hadn't asked Bart to *only* look at managers. It wasn't an either/or. Cassandra watched Jack look thoughtfully at Bart, probably deciding whether to keep discussing this or override him later anyway.

He chose the former. "I agree that we should be discussing all employees," he said. "But hadn't we discussed a specific effort related to manager evaluation and corresponding training sessions? Isn't that right, Cassandra?"

This was a bit awkward for her. "Yes, that's right," she said, trying to keep her tone light so that the junior folks in the room wouldn't leave gossiping about those in charge openly disagreeing. "There are a few manager-specific initiatives we'll be incorporating in addition to focusing on all our employees more broadly."

"NO!" The word came out of Bart's mouth—fast, loud, and with a pout. He banged his pen against the table, but luckily it was too soft to make much of a sound.

"Yes," she replied. It was a reflex she regretted immediately. She really didn't want to stoop to the kind of infancy that didn't belong in a conference room. She started to recover, "We've had to weigh a lot of different factors here." It was a bland statement, but it would buy time while she figured out what to say next.

But he continued, now moving from the infant pout to a chastising tone: "Cassandra, we discussed this."

This is what it feels like to be patronized in public, Cassandra thought. She saw the women in the room look at her sympathetically. She had to recover for them.

"You can see that we've been debating this a bit," she said with what she hoped seemed like an authentic chuckle. "We wanted to make sure to consider every angle. Let me tell you what we debated, and then we would love your feedback."

After the meeting ended, everyone filed out until only she and Jack were left. "Bart's EQ is really something, isn't it?" he said.

"As a woman, I felt really patronized by that," Cassandra said. She wouldn't usually speak so frankly about gender issues to someone like Jack, especially after how clueless he'd been when she'd tried to discuss him thinking that Shannon needed coaching but not Dan. But she felt a little shaken by the experience with Bart now that she could take off the performance face she'd needed to wear for the junior staff. And Debra kept telling her not to bite her tongue, right?

"I don't think it has anything to do with gender," said Jack. "He was rather hostile to me too. And you know that Bart has always been one of your greatest advocates. Like I said, his EQ just isn't good."

Cassandra didn't feel like explaining the situation to Jack. That would take too much energy.

Bart had been hostile and unprofessional to both of them. But there were major differences. His tone and words with Jack were aggressive; his tone and words with Cassandra were chastising and undermining. That difference mattered even more when you considered their relative positions. Jack was the CFO, above Bart on the corporate hierarchy. Cassandra was a senior woman, sure, but she was a director and Bart, as an associate vice president, outranked her by several levels. When Bart, as a senior man, was aggressive to Jack, it made him look petulant and foolish. With Cassandra, it was a more senior man chastising a less senior woman. What signal did that send—whether unconsciously or consciously—to the others in the room?

Jack was right that Bart was a mentor of hers. His intention surely hadn't been to undermine her in the meeting. He just believed strongly that his opinion was right.

But, beyond intentions, there was a greater impact when the others in the room listened to the tone and heard the words a senior male leader said to a less senior female leader in a public setting, without knowing the full context.

Jack's intent was positive too. He didn't want Cassandra to feel that she had been undermined due to gender. He thus emphasized how he'd been treated himself, and noted Bart's EQ—probably so that Cassandra wouldn't take the situation too personally.

What he didn't understand was that the impact on her was personal. And he didn't understand the impact of his dismissiveness. In not being willing to entertain that there could be something especially hard in that situation for a female leader, the impact was that she felt he wasn't willing to look past his own point of view, and that he was fine with making excuses for Bart's bad behavior as "low EQ" rather than consider the impact on Cassandra.

CHAPTER TWENTY-SIX

Debra

I t was rare for Debra to attend a company social event for more than the first twenty minutes. Except for the occasional celebratory or leadership team dinner, she tended to think that the staff should have the opportunity to let loose without the CEO present. Her typical M.O. for most events was to stop by, say hello, deliver any necessary thanks or congratulations, and then leave before most people had even finished their first drink. But Cassandra had stopped by her office that morning and encouraged her to stay for at least two hours at a happy hour at the bar next door, an informal celebration for the team after the conference they'd hosted that day—the conference where Haley delivered the speech that they had overheard Tom discussing with her that morning.

She had got to know Cassandra well enough to assume that the younger woman probably had something specific that she wanted Debra to see. It seemed a little odd—how would Cassandra be able to predict what would happen at the event? But Cassandra seemed prescient enough about all the organizational and interpersonal dynamics at the office that Debra knew not to question her.

As she moved around the bar area they'd reserved, she noticed that several of the staff definitely registered her presence. A few she didn't know personally came up to introduce themselves. Other times she noticed that conversations halted as she entered hearing range.

What was surprising was that some of the staff didn't even seem to notice she was there. It must have been the alcohol lowering their inhibitions and sense. While she and Cassandra ordered her drink at the bar, she heard one of her male employees greeting another loudly, "How's that BSD?"

Perhaps she shouldn't admit that she was eavesdropping, but she couldn't help but ask. "What's a BSD?"

Both men looked appalled, unsure of how to respond. The first man uttered something under his breath as they both excused themselves from the area.

"Was that intrusive of me?" Debra laughed to Cassandra. "I had no idea I'd clear the room."

Cassandra gave her a half-smile. "BSD stands for big swinging dick. It's slang often used in finance to mean an executive who is really good at bringing in the dollars, but some of the senior men here like to use it too."

This was the language that people used at a company event?

As she circulated around the room, the most unexpected behavior to Debra was Tom's. Perhaps she shouldn't have been surprised given his comments to Haley in the cafeteria the day before. Even before an hour had passed, he had already gone past the one or maybe two polite drinks that many of their colleagues were still nursing. She wondered if this was what Cassandra had wanted her to see.

Debra was a few feet away from a conversation that one of the managers in Tom's group, Vicky, was having with one of their vendor partners, when Tom approached them. Vicky had made a presentation to the conference that day too, right before Haley. The vendor partners and Vicky were having a lively discussion about social media.

As soon as he opened his mouth, Debra noticed his tone was different from what she normally heard in her day-to-day professional conversations with him. He took on the quaintly belligerent persona true of some when they drink—a combination of vociferously argumentative and pouty as if he thought he were being "cute."

"The key to social media is thinking about content that generates discussion, not just likes," one of the vendor partners was saying.

"You're wrong!" Tom was strident and delighted. Odd given that what the vendor had said was fairly innocuous. "You need to hear the hard truth," he continued in a stern voice, like someone talking to a small child. No actual hard truth followed, only what could be best described as a loud pout: "Wrong, wrong, wrong!"

Vicky looked resigned and slipped into what Debra could only describe as a good cop/bad cop routine. After each of Tom's negative and confrontational statements, she said something positive. The vendor partner was good-natured—presumably he knew that Tom was drunk or perhaps thought he was just socially awkward. But it was hard for Debra not to wonder whether this would impact their business with him.

Debra was about to step in when Haley, who had been listening from a few feet away, came over and went up to the vendor partner. "Chuck, I wanted to get your ideas on something." She guided him away. Debra made a mental note to check on the situation later, but for now was curious to see how the continued interaction between Vicky and Tom would unfold.

It only got worse when the vendor partner left.

"He's definitely going to renew the contract," Tom said, "He loves you." This could have been an entirely normal comment, except that he said the word "loved" in a teasing, sing-song voice, as if they were teenagers, and then added an inarticulate drunken slur, "We totally bonded as middle-aged men who wanted to talk to you as we watched you deliver your presentation."

Okay, that was enough. Debra went over to the table. "Tom, I think you need to go home now." She or Terry would talk to him about his behavior the next day.

He looked belligerent. "Why do you want me to go home?" Then a switch turned on and he transitioned to being weepy. "Vicky and Haley are much stronger at the job than I am. I'm sure all our vendor partners are going to poach them after seeing them speak at this conference, and then what I am going to do?"

At that point, his upper body collapsed onto the table, knocking over a glass of wine to the floor. It shattered.

"I don't think he can get home on his own," Vicky said to her quietly, brushing a glass shard off her foot as if that were an everyday occurrence. "The team has taken him home a few times. We know where he lives. It's Chad's turn this time. I can go get him."

They took turns taking their drunk boss home? Debra had to take a deep breath. She didn't want to misdirect her anger at Vicky. But what in the world was going on? Not that it would have been any better if Tom had been younger; he was their manager, no matter how old he was. But he was at least two decades older than most of his team, making this type of frat-party behavior seem even more inexcusable.

Debra temporarily ignored the question of Tom's transportation. "Are you okay?"

Vicky looked down. There didn't seem to be any glass on her, but the wine stains on her cream silk shirt would be impossible to remove. "Honestly, it's not that bad. Last time this happened, Haley twisted her ankle trying to help him get up, and Chad dropped his phone and had to buy a new one." She looked immediately remorseful as soon as she realized she'd said this to the CEO, as if she'd broken a code.

At that moment, Jack walked by. Debra flagged him over.

Jack looked over at Tom. He shook his head. "He really can't hold his liquor."

Debra took a deep breath and squinted at Jack. He then seemed to realize that the frequency of Tom's drunkenness was news to her and he physically took a step back, looking sheepish. "I'll take him home," he said.

Jack prodded Tom awake and then led him out of the room.

"I'm very sorry about that," said Debra. "You should know that is not acceptable behavior."

Vicky shrugged. "I know how it goes. Everyone looks the other way. When I first started working here, a few people pulled me aside and said that Tom was a good manager overall, but to leave events after he's had his second drink unless you wanted to be stuck with a mess. I usually do, but this time I was in the conversation with our vendor partner so I couldn't."

"It's not just the drunkenness that's unacceptable," said Debra, "But what he said to you also."

"I hate the implication that my presentation only impressed people because I'm young and female," Vicky said. "But I know it's worse most places. I have friends at other companies who have been harassed and assaulted in the workplace. This is nothing in comparison. I know Tom means well."

"We're not aspiring to be better than most places," said Debra. "And meaning well isn't enough."

Debra realized Vicky didn't seem to be listening. Instead, she was glancing down at her hand. She had just cut herself on a piece of the wine glass that neither she nor Debra had seen on the table in front of her.

After Debra made sure that Vicky's cut was tended to and checked on the situation with Haley and the vendor, she went outside to get some air. She thought about Jack's reaction. Apparently, Tom's behavior was the worst kept secret in the company—with Debra being the only one who didn't know. Did they all really think this was okay because "it wasn't as bad as other places?"

When the #MeToo movement had first broken, Debra and Jack had had a long conversation about how they were glad to see these serious issues being dealt with, but that they were worried about potential unintended consequences too. Would men be less likely to mentor women, for fear it would be taken the wrong way? Would it be harder for cross-gender working relationships and friendships to form in the workplace, like hers and Jack's over the years? She'd read the articles about the generational divide—how many in her generation, women and men, worried #MeToo would go too far. But tonight she wondered if maybe it wasn't going far enough. The national conversation around overt harassment and assault was critical, but it ignored the "gray area" behavior like Tom's that wasn't illegal, but that made women feel less comfortable and less valued at work. Behavior where it seemed like the whole company was "looking the other way."

She thought about what she and Cassandra had discussed and observed over just the last few days—Cassandra's elevator ride, Tom's comments to Haley in the cafeteria, the tequila shots and "BSD." Cassandra had also told Debra about her encounter with Bart—a different type of "bad" behavior but similar in a few key ways: Bart clearly meant well, but still the impact was very different from the intent. What other ways had Debra and the other leaders of the company been "looking the other way," always trusting in good reasons and motivations? Was looking the other way on Tom's questionable comments to female employees any different from looking the other way on Leland's performance issues or Frank's undeserved salary increase?

She realized she'd been muttering to herself as she paced on the sidewalk in front of the bar. Her jacket was still inside. All she wanted to do was head to her car and get it tomorrow. She looked up at the sky and then headed back inside.

PART TEN

Breaking Point

CHAPTER TWENTY-SEVEN

Jack

Jack didn't actually have restless leg syndrome. He could have stopped shaking his left leg—by moving his left foot, currently perched on his right knee, to the floor of Debra's conference room—at any time. But the shaking leg was a type of power pose he'd adopted years ago, a way of showing impatience when his co-workers (or, worse, employees) were wasting his time.

He looked at his watch. 4:10. Leland was ten minutes late to the meeting—and counting. Normally, Debra would have insisted they start on the hour, perhaps one or two minutes past. But this meeting had been called explicitly to review the results of Leland's product relaunch work. In theory, he needed to be there.

In reality, as Jack looked around the room at the members of Leland's senior team present, he knew that Leland would likely detract more than he added.

Was Debra looking at Jack accusingly, or was he imagining it? He envisioned what the voice in her head was saying: *"Where's that joker you convinced me to hire and then betrayed me for by telling George to not let me fire him?"*

He thought about the engagement survey results; that gender gap that he'd chosen to ignore. He imagined the voices in the head of Amber, Meg, and the other women in the room: *"Where's that man you hired over a more competent woman? Have you let Leland stay longer than he should have because you're buddies on the racquetball court? Would you have excused this level of incompetence from a woman?"*

Hell, it probably wasn't just the women thinking these things. Leland's incompetence wasn't making things better for the men on his team either.

The voice in Jack's head didn't know how to reply.

He looked around the room. It was funny how most of the room didn't even seem to notice that approximately 17% of the time allocated to the meeting had already gone by. They were all busy on their iPads, laptops, and phones—and often two of the three aforementioned devices at the same time. Emailing and messaging away. If anything, they seemed perfectly happy to have the extra time on their devices.

Of course, Jack looked at his phone between meetings too. He wasn't a complete Luddite. But it wasn't to fill the void. It wasn't to exhibit extreme multitasking, the endurance sport of the corporate world. It was a purely functional act, to check whether something required his immediate attention.

He glanced down at his phone. Ten unattended emails in his box at the moment, but none requiring an immediate response. He had already texted his brother back about their plans to meet for golf the next day. All that was left for him to do was to look around the room at everyone else on their devices, or to look at Debra and feel the quiet sting of her resentment: his closest professional relationship had degenerated into the pursed smile he recognized as the one she gave those she had dismissed in her mind.

Not knowing what to do with himself, Jack got up from his seat to fill his mug with the pitcher of water on Debra's console. He took his time and even used the silk handkerchief in his jacket pocket to wipe some of the condensation that the pitcher had left on the wood. He had never done that before. He didn't know how else to say he was sorry for what he had done.

He sipped some water from his mug and pretended to stand by the console in case he wanted more water. He didn't want to return back to his seat next to Debra until absolutely necessary.

"Can someone dial Leland's office?" Debra asked.

Meg was sitting closest to the phone at the center of the conference room table. "Does anyone know Leland's extension?"

She was met with blank stares. Had none of them memorized it after all this time?

"It's 7986," Jack said. He knew that the younger generation didn't use the office phones as much—they were more likely to text or use instant messaging. So maybe he couldn't read too much into their not knowing Leland's line. Then again, as they collectively listened to the phone ringing, it occurred to Jack that nobody had volunteered to text or instant message Leland either, as usually happened when someone was missing from a room. Jack realized that he'd never heard anyone ever mentioning texting Leland. Did they even have his cell phone number?

The speaker phone played Leland's office voice mail recording. "The person at this number is not available," said the robotic, pre-recorded voice. He hadn't even replaced the automatically generated message that came with each extension with his own recording.

Meg hung up. 4:13 now. Jack poured a little more water into his mug and went back to his seat. This was getting ridiculous. He looked at his watch, exaggerating the flick of his wrist. "This meeting was supposed to start thirteen minutes ago. Can we just get started?"

Debra sighed. "Yes, I think we've waited long enough."

"I think Leland owned the agenda," said Meg.

Jack noticed she didn't even try to hide her mocking tone. Next to her, Amber started coughing, poorly hiding the laugh she'd nearly let escape. At the other end of the table, he saw Shannon whisper something to Kyle. A few others were rolling their eyes. With every passing month since Leland's arrival, Jack had noticed that these adult professionals were acting more and more like high school students. If things continued this way, he wouldn't be surprised if they were soon passing notes via paper airplane, probably flown behind Leland's head. This group had been consummate professionals under Natalie; now, they were exhibiting juvenile behavior worse than anything he'd seem among managers in his entire career.

He looked around the room. Everyone was staring down at the table. Either they didn't want to be called on, or they didn't want to be caught exchanging glances with their colleagues and friends.

"Let's start with Kyle," said Debra. "Can you give us an update on the two app relaunches that your team is working on?"

Kyle looked amused. "Well, my team hasn't had a chance to get started on either of the two relaunches yet. Leland asked instead that we focus on developing a procedure manual for what needs to get done internally in a relaunch."

"Wait," said Debra. "I thought your team was going to start with customer interviews. Have you actually started the market research we need in order to figure out how the products need to shift?"

Kyle and Shannon exchanged a glance. So did Meg and Amber.

Jack didn't even bother hiding his sigh. Theoretically Debra should have been checking with Leland to gauge his team's progress. She was his manager after all. She was the one who needed to get in front of the Board in two months with a plan. But George had told Debra that he personally was going to hold Leland accountable and told her not to interfere.

"Well, at our department meeting last month, each team came with ideas for new features and positioning for their products," said Shannon. "We had also started scheduling focus groups and customer calls to test those new features and positioning."

"That's sounds great," said Debra, "And yet I'm hearing a 'but' coming."

The group exchanged glances with one another once again. "Leland told us that the priority was to write a procedure manual for how to do product relaunches before we could get started on the relaunches themselves," said Shannon, putting emphasis on the CPO's name.

"What's in the procedure manual?" Jack asked, though he wasn't sure if he really wanted to know.

"We've developed fifty pages of checklists and instructions," said Amber. "Things like what are the different roles involved in a product launch, how to develop an interview guide to ask the right questions of customers, how to select vendors to contract with for market research...things like that."

Debra looked befuddled. "But you have all been doing those things for years. Why would you need a procedure manual? Tell me this thing is finished and we can get started on the actual relaunch work now."

"Well, everyone finished their pages last week," said Amber, "But Leland thought we needed to convert what we'd created from Word to PowerPoint. He spent a day himself converting a few pages from Word to PowerPoint to give everyone an example of the design aesthetic he was going for and how he wanted them to format each page. He thought our teams would be more likely to use the manuals if they were designed a bit prettier, with graphics and such."

She said it all with a straight face, but her lack of expression said everything.

Jack felt like burying his head in his hands, but knew that he'd have to wait until he got back to his office to do that. Time spent bureaucracy building was perfectly fine, even a good idea, when the company was doing well. It wasn't the kind of thing you did when sales were down and jobs were at risk. And it certainly wasn't the job of a CPO to convert a document from Word to PowerPoint.

"It'll take a while to make the formatting changes he requested," added Meg. "But I think everyone will be done in a week."

"So what have we actually done on the relaunches?" asked Debra.

The group was silent for a few beats. Jack knew that nobody was surprised that it was Amber who finally spoke up. "Kyle and Shannon, why don't you share some of the ideas that you brought to the meeting last month before we all started working on the procedure manuals instead?"

"Love that idea," said Debra. "Shannon, why don't you start?"

As Shannon began talking, Jack thought about what the meeting would have been like if Leland had actually arrived. He imagined Leland defending the creation of the procedure manuals by comparing it to the process of sap moving up a tree or something equally absurd. Just last week, Leland had spent four minutes—Jack had secretly been watching the second hand on his watch—on an extended analogy about how all the different kinds of trees were analogous to the different kinds of customer personas. "There are ash trees, and cedar trees, and palm trees, and magnolia trees..."

Was it terrible that as he had watched the second hand on his watch, the image that came to mind was Forrest Gump describing the contents of that box of chocolate?

Leland's old boss had given him such a glowing reference, Jack mused. Maybe he had just tired of the metaphors and wanted to send him away.

The remainder of the meeting was fairly lively. Amber was right. The others did have great ideas, which they spent the rest of their time discussing and debating. By the end of the meeting, they'd come to greater clarity about some interesting new product features they'd be able to add and ideas to discuss with the marketing department for testing new positioning. Debra's voice was cheery but her eyebrows seemed slightly raised in resignation. Jack knew what she was thinking: this was the discussion Leland should have had with his team months ago—instead of assigning and then giving them multiple edits on procedure manuals. And if Leland hadn't been there, it seemed like the team would have done the right things sooner.

What had Jack done?

CHAPTER TWENTY-EIGHT

Debra

At the end of the product meeting, one thing was clear to Debra. As she suspected, they'd have to rely on Amber's new products if they were going to turn the numbers around. Debra remembered the anger she'd felt earlier in her career whenever she felt she had to work extra hard to clean up a mess that her bosses had somehow let a man create unchecked. Now she was that boss. There was no option— saving the business came first.

As the group filed out of her conference room, Debra asked Amber to stay for a few minutes. "I appreciate how fast you've been moving with new products," said Debra, "So I don't want to put any more work on you. But if you have any ideas for what else we should launch next, even just initial brainstorms, I'd love to discuss them."

Jack had lingered as well. "I would too," he said. He and Debra may have been barely speaking at the moment, but they didn't need to look at one another to realize they were thinking the same thing. They were too far behind on Leland's product relaunches to count on them for turning sales around. It was time to put all their resources and time around increasing Amber's launches.

Amber gave Debra and Jack a half-smile—one that said, *I was in the same meeting as you just now, I get it.*

She was more polite than Debra would have been in her situation.

"Sure," Amber said. "I actually have a few ideas I've been writing up. It's a bit unpolished right now, but I can clean it up and give it to you Monday."

"If you have anything written down already, it's totally fine if not yet polished," said Debra, "I have some time free on Saturday and would love to read what you've got. Also that way you don't have to work on it over the weekend."

Jack nodded in agreement.

"Got it," Amber said, "I'll run downstairs and bring them back up to your offices."

"I'll walk down with you," Jack said. "Need to get my steps in for the day anyway."

Debra knew that Jack didn't care about steps. Amber's office was near Leland's, and Jack wanted to see if there was any sign of him there. Not that Debra wasn't curious too. Leland wasn't the kind of person to just blow off a meeting. If anything, he was the type to attend meetings where he wasn't needed, speaking up even when the moment didn't require it, searching for some opportunity to "add value." But it was a Friday after 5:00 pm, and Debra didn't really want to deal with Leland before the weekend—she could do it on Monday morning.

Debra knew that Jack, on the other hand, didn't have the patience to wait before he read Leland the riot act. He had stuck out his neck for this guy—several times—and likely wanted to yell at him right away: (a) about not attending such an important meeting, and (b) for fucking up the relaunches (Jack probably wouldn't mince words) by focusing on procedure manuals instead of getting the actual work done.

Part of Debra wanted to let Jack chew Leland out alone if he found him; after all, even if she were Leland's supervisor, his continued presence—and the fact that George had taken over trying to manage Leland—was largely Jack's fault. Why ruin her Friday evening? But then morbid curiously overtook her. "I might as well get my steps in too," she said.

"Right," said Amber. Debra wondered why they even bothered trying to fool her. The three of them proceeded together down the five flights of stairs; after all, they had to keep up appearances about their "steps" and not take the elevator. Amber took a few minutes to print the document from her computer, and then the three of them chatted for a few minutes before Jack and Debra headed back into the hallway toward Leland's office, around the corner from Amber's.

As they turned around the corner, she noticed that Leland's office light was on, and the door was open. Given that their lighting was attached to strict movement sensors, that meant that either Leland was in his office or had left within the last two minutes. The latter didn't seem possible—they would have noticed him while they were chatting with Amber for the last five.

Oddly though, Debra couldn't make out a human figure. Of course, sometimes the frosted glass walls made it difficult to see the office's occupant if they were sitting in the corner of the room or at certain angles. That had to be it.

"I don't hear any typing," said Jack.

Debra couldn't tell if it was a harmless observation, designed to fill the silence that had marked all their interactions ever since Jack betrayed her to George, or a mocking remark about how Leland's general modus operandi (when he wasn't staring at his index cards) was tapping furiously at his laptop, likely working on those procedure manuals.

Debra resented Jack for it either way—he was responsible for allowing Leland to still be there, so he had lost the right to mock him.

But not as much as she resented herself for not having a stronger backbone.

As Debra walked into Leland's office, with Jack right behind her, she heard a humming sound. If she had been forced to describe it, she would have said it was reminiscent of the barely noticeable buzzing of an old refrigerator.

After the humming, the first thing she noticed was that Leland's black leather laptop messenger bag was still on the small conference table in the center of the room. The second thing she noticed was that the office was much neater than its typical state. Papers were usually strewn about in uneven piles on his desk, floor, and conference table, but they had been neatly stacked and placed on a bookshelf that had previously been bare. The third thing she noticed was the source of the humming sound, but she had to blink her eyes and then look at Jack to make sure she wasn't imagining the sight.

It was Leland. Under his desk. Curled back, his arms wrapped around his legs, like a child who had tried to make himself as small as possible so he wouldn't be found in a game of hide and seek. Rocking. Humming.

Jack's mouth was gaped open. Debra realized that hers was too. She wasn't sure whether Leland had noticed them or not. His eyes seemed fixated on a spot on the ground in front of him.

Then he looked up, made eye contact with Debra, and started laughing.

A nervous twitter at first, high-pitched and halting. That migrated into a full-bodied but silent laugh: shoulders shaking, no sound.

It was Jack who broke the silence: "What the fuck?"

"Jack!" Debra said. Not that she wasn't thinking the same thing, but that's not what you said to someone who had clearly lost it.

Not that she had any idea what you were supposed to say.

Leland had stopped laughing but continued rocking. The humming sound returned.

"Get Terry," Debra said quietly to Jack.

Relieved to have an excuse to leave, Jack didn't even bother to look at Leland or Debra as he left the room. Debra knew that she couldn't simply wait until Terry got there though. The human thing to do was say something, not stare at him as if it were pure spectacle.

She kicked off her heels and crouched down to the floor. A few feet away, as if he were a stray animal that might pounce at any minute if threatened. "Hi Leland," she said, drawing out the words. "Is there anything you want to talk about?"

He made eye contact again briefly. Suddenly, he stopped rocking. He crawled out from under the table.

"I'm sorry I missed the meeting, Debra," he said, an octave lower than he usually spoke. He pulled himself up to standing position, lifted his eyes to look around the room, and blinked several times.

She took a beat too long to reply, and her voice trailed. "That's okay. Do you want to talk?" She realized she was still sitting on the floor, but getting up suddenly seemed unfathomable. Was it contagious?

"No, thank you," Leland said. "Not right now." He grabbed his messenger bag and, before she could say something else, strolled out of the office.

Five minutes later, Jack returned with Terry. Debra was still dumbfounded, heels off, on the ground. Jack offered his arm to help her up. She didn't take it, even though it took her some effort to get up. Debra told Terry she'd call her over the weekend, and the two women left the room.

Jack remained, sitting at the conference table, watching the sunset with an empty gaze outside the window.

CHAPTER TWENTY-NINE

Debra

Debra spent the weekend on the phone with Terry and their general counsel, Sara, a woman in her early forties who they had just hired in the last few years as they expanded their partnerships with other companies and needed more legal support. As Debra let off steam on the elliptical in her garage, wireless headset affixed tightly around her head, the three women discussed over a conference call whether they had enough of a record of Leland's performance problems to lay him off without potential legal recourse.

"It's a little dicey," Sara said. "He could claim mental health issues given how you found him."

"I've wanted to lay him off for the last six months," said Debra. "And have had good reason to do so."

"Why didn't you?" Sara asked.

Debra hesitated before answering her question. She hadn't told anyone, even Terry, about how Jack had gone behind her back to George, and the Board Chair's threat that if she didn't figure out to make things work with Leland, he'd question her performance as CEO. She didn't want to admit she'd lost control over hiring and firing—one of the most important things for any leader to be able to do. She didn't want to seem weak.

But she knew they needed more information in order to advise her well.

She told them what had happened. She thought she'd be able to do so dispassionately—after all, that was a skill she'd mastered over the years—but felt the welling in her chest as she admitted what had happened for the first time.

Terry spoke first. "Oh." Debra could hear the wheels turning in her head. Debra wondered whether Terry had thought of her as weak for not firing Leland earlier. She was weak, just not in the way that Terry had thought.

"Fucking patriarchy," said Sara.

It was the kind of phrase always at the top of the tongues of the younger generations. That always made Debra feel a little uncomfortable. The cause of women didn't need to alienate men, did it? But she'd come to realize that "fuck the patriarchy" wasn't a sentiment about women versus men. It was about all the different decisions and actions that go on in an organization—many of them seemingly innocuous on their own—that disadvantaged or diminished women, especially when taken cumulatively.

She'd been part of the patriarchy too.

"Fucking patriarchy indeed," Debra said. She sped up on the elliptical.

Terry wasn't the type to swear, but she sounded sad. "Yeah, I hate to say it, but it's hard to imagine that would have happened if Leland was a woman." She paused; Debra could almost picture Terry's thinking expression through the phone. "You have an email trail of when you've given Leland tough feedback, right? Plus, you have his last mid-year performance review."

"Yes," said Debra.

"I think that would all hold up," said Terry. "Just start putting together the file."

The file didn't turn out to be necessary. When she arrived at 8:30 am on Monday morning, Leland was waiting outside her office door.

Her first reaction was annoyance. After all, she'd planned to have her assistant schedule time with him the next day so that she could fire him then, after she had a chance to touch base with Terry and Sara one more time that morning. Would she have to listen to him apologize for missing the meeting on Friday? Would they need to have a heart-to-heart about his meltdown?

"Do you have a few minutes?" he asked.

She felt her shoulders relax once she saw the envelope in his hand. "Of course," she said, suddenly feeling generous.

He followed her into the office. At first, she veered to her table, where she usually sat when meeting one-on-one with direct reports. But then she realized the greater courtesy would be to allow him the formality of sitting at her desk, the block of wood between them providing a safe barrier, erasing the vulnerability of Friday evening.

"I wanted to thank you for the opportunity, but I am tendering my resignation," Leland said, handing her the envelope. "I had thought about leaving in two weeks, but if you need extra time, I am willing to be flexible."

Usually, even with employees that were clearly lacking, Debra tried to get the requisite notice period (at least a month at Leland's level) to make the transition as easy as possible. Even underperformers could usually get some tasks done that otherwise would go to someone else.

"I think two weeks sounds fine," she said. "You don't need to come to the office during that time, and I don't even think we'd need you to work full-time. But would love to be able to call on you for any transition stuff during that period if needed." She wondered if he understood her implicit message: she'd rather pay him to do nothing than to continue to cause problems at her company. The two weeks—rather than showing him the door right away—were in part corporate politeness, and in part insurance in the unlikely case there was something she wanted to ask him or a simple task to assign before they halted his paychecks.

He looked relieved. They didn't even try to make any small talk before he gave her a perfunctory thank you and then bolted out the room.

If only her day had ended after Leland left her office. The second resignation Debra received that day was much, much less welcome.

Amber already had a scheduled meeting with Debra that afternoon. In the ten minutes before the younger woman arrived, Debra had printed out the offer letter, including salary details, which she had planned to discuss with Amber in asking her to be the CPO. She was sitting at her desk, reviewing the sheet and thinking about what she'd say to talk up the role, when Amber walked in. This will be easy, Debra tried to convince herself—after all, Amber had always wanted the CPO job.

She should have known that something was wrong right away when Amber, upon entering her office, didn't go to the small table and wait for Debra to get up from her desk to join her, as was usually the case. Instead, Amber sat down in the less comfortable chair in front of Debra's desk, the same place where Leland had been.

"I know Leland's my manager and I should be having this conversation with him," said Amber. "But you and I already had this time scheduled, and frankly, I wanted to let you know directly first. I've decided to go work for Natalie's new company. Just so you know, Natalie didn't try to poach me. We happened to meet up for drinks a few weeks ago, and I asked her if she had any openings. She said yes and described a role that's a good fit for me. I've had time to think about it over the last few weeks and feel certain that even though I'll miss the team here, it's the right decision for me."

The déjà vu was painful. But this time—unlike when Natalie had quit—Debra had a pretty good sense of what had gone wrong.

"I know you've been really frustrated lately," said Debra. There was no graceful way to transition to the next part of the conversation. She wasn't going to try to message Amber. "Leland will be leaving the firm in a few weeks, and what I'd hope to do with our time together today was offer you the CPO position."

It felt empty even as she said it. She might as well have said, *Our first choice was a disaster, but hope you'll forgive me for making you second.* Debra still felt hope though, as she took the offer letter out of its folder and slid it across the desk. There was no way Natalie would have given Amber a salary figure even approaching this in a new firm. And Jack hadn't even hesitated when Debra mentioned they needed to figure out a generous equity package for Amber, more than Leland had received. Amber could be a millionaire in a few years if the company went public as they hoped.

Perhaps this would be enough to make Amber rethink her decision. Sleep on it. Continue the discussion. Maybe she would be able to persuade Amber if they just had a little bit of time. After all, the frustration of dealing with Leland every day, not to mention the insult of his existence, that was all gone now.

Even as she tried to be optimistic, Debra knew that it was futile. This wasn't just about Leland. It was never just one thing. There was an entire system, one that Debra had helmed and that had allowed the existence of Leland. The system was the problem, not the former CPO enabled by it.

Amber raised her eyebrows as Debra read the dollar amounts on the page out loud. She took a visible breath, took the hair tie off her wrist, and put her hair into a ponytail before speaking.

"This is really generous, and I'm very flattered and honored by the offer—" Amber began.

Debra interrupted her, knowing where the conversation was going, "Why don't you take some time to consider it? I know it's a big decision."

Amber handed the offer letter back to Debra. "It is a big decision, and I've already accepted the job with Natalie. But thank you again."

It took every ounce of her self-control for Debra not to burst out laughing when her assistant called her and told her that George was sitting in the reception area. Now he didn't even call first? She fantasized about taking a Sharpie and writing his name over hers on the nameplate outside her door.

Instead, she welcomed him into her office.

"I got an email from Leland saying that he's given notice," he said as soon as they closed the door behind him.

"That's right," said Debra. Was he going to tell her to pay him more to get him back? Give him her job? If only anything didn't seem possible. She looked him in the eye, as if daring him.

"I'm glad," George said. "You know I noticed in my meetings with him that he didn't seem like he was really up to the job. You really should have gotten rid of him much sooner rather than waiting for him to quit."

She couldn't help it. She laughed. Loudly.

PART ELEVEN

"Fix It" Culture

CHAPTER THIRTY

Leland

Leland stood in front of the fridge. His mom's voice was loud in his head, telling him that he was wasting electricity. He should stop staring, close the fridge door. But choosing what snacks to bring to that Sunday afternoon's study group with the guys was a strangely paralyzing decision.

Study group. Really, it was a book club, but they didn't want to call it that. Too girly, according to some of the guys. "We're not going to read romance novels as an excuse to gossip over face masks and wine," Leland's childhood friend Ryan had said when Leland suggested they begin the club ten years ago. Leland had just been excited by the idea of getting together monthly with a group of their friends to talk about a book or film. What did it matter what they called it?

Still, he was proud to have come up with the name "study group." It recalled those days decades ago of sitting on the floor in the dorm hallway all night, leaning against the chipped-paint walls amid the scent of pizza, talking about ideas they'd discovered in class or musings about how they'd either get rich or change the world.

His wife Grace thought the name was more ridiculous than clever. "Just call it a book club," she said once, "Study group isn't exactly a

super masculine name either. Or go for super manly and call your-
selves the Lion Hunters." She cracked up at her own joke. After all,
they did meet at Ryan's bachelor pad, a giant stereotypical man cave
of sorts. Grace had only been to Ryan's place once, and Leland had
caught her texting her friends about it mid-visit. The pool table in the
middle of the living room. Every room floored in ceramic tile—easier
to clean than carpet or hardwood. She took a stealth picture on her
phone of the assorted clump of electronic parts stored in a bucket,
nestled in the second kitchen sink.

Each month they alternated who picked the book or film and who
brought the snacks. Leland scanned the possible refreshment candidates on their refrigerator shelves, packed so tight with Tupperware
that it would be like a game of Tetris if he wanted to add even the
smallest additional item. Since he'd left his job few months ago, he'd
spent a lot of time baking. Exercising twice a day made up for the
extra calories consumed.

Slowly, he was starting to feel like a person again.

His eyes lingered over the container of spanakopita that he knew
his friend Michael, who had spent a year in college in Greece, would
especially appreciate. He went so far as to pick up, then put back
down, the macarons that had taken several days and three different
recipes to perfect. He closed the fridge briefly and walked over to the
pantry, glancing at the kale chips he'd made last night. A lot of the
guys were trying to eat healthier, he thought, his fingers grazing the
freezer bag filled with the green, garlicky snack before pulling his
hand away and closing the pantry door.

He knew some of his buddies would appreciate, and even envy,
the time he'd been spending cultivating his culinary skills. But a few
would rib him, or silently, perhaps unconsciously, judge him. He had
been a C-suite executive and now he was baking for their non-book-
club book club?

He hoped Grace didn't ask him later what he'd decided to bring.

An hour later, Leland arrived at Ryan's house with the loaf of banana bread that he'd grabbed at the supermarket on his way. He took it to the kitchen to slice up and sampled a small piece. If he had been a celebrity chef judging a cooking show, he'd have spat it out. It was too dry and would have benefited from another pinch or two of cinnamon. For a few seconds, he contemplated driving back home to get the macarons.

Instead, he crossed the kitchen to look inside Ryan's freezer. A frozen box of taquitos. Two bags of broccoli. And the winner: a tub of chocolate ice cream. Perfect to offset the dryness of the bread. The flavors would complement one another nicely. Leland felt a little rebellious, bringing the ice cream into the family room with his banana bread without asking Ryan first.

An hour later, not only was the ice cream gone, but only crumbs were left on the banana bread plate. Had his friends actually enjoyed the banana bread, or was it the default response for any gathering of people to simply consume whatever was placed in front of you? Leland had reached for a piece himself a few times when he felt like he should be contributing to a particular point of discussion but wasn't sure exactly what to say.

His mind wandered again to the macarons sitting in his fridge. His family would never be able to finish them.

By this point, the group had stopped discussing the book and had largely broken up into side conversations. Even though he'd known most of these guys for a few decades, Leland still felt awkward whenever they convened in a group. Two or three people at a time was so much easier. You didn't have to worry about whether you were interrupting a conversation or leaving someone nearby out.

The glass of water Leland was holding was three-quarters full, and he wasn't particularly thirsty, but he gulped it down as an excuse to go refill it.

As he entered the kitchen, he found Ryan's dad fiddling with the espresso machine. Jim had been staying with his son while he recovered from a knee surgery after retiring recently from his role as CEO of a small insurance company. When Leland and Ryan had been growing up, Leland didn't think he'd ever seen Jim not wearing a suit. Today though, he was wearing a Special Olympics t-shirt and track pants. It occurred to Leland that in recent years, every time he saw Jim, he had been in a t-shirt or sweatshirt related to an organization where he volunteered or was on the Board. It wasn't for show or as a conversation starter. These were simply the only casual clothes that Jim owned.

After Leland had left his job, Jim had been one of the first people— or, more accurately, one of the only people—that Leland had called for advice and another pair of eyes on his resume. Leland's parents didn't come from the corporate world, and Jim had been a source of advice throughout his career. It had been a long time since Leland had really spent time on resume bullets, talking points, his LinkedIn profile, and all that. When he'd applied for the CPO position with Debra and Jack, he'd been assured he'd be a sure thing and hadn't needed to put a lot of effort into the typical job materials. At his company before that, he'd worked hard to establish a strong reputation, leading to several promotions. Resumes and interviews were just boxes to check in an HR process.

Jim handed Leland the espresso he'd been making for himself, then proceeded to make another one. "How's the job search going?" he asked.

"Pretty good," said Leland, hoping Jim wouldn't suspect the overstatement. Leland was spending a lot more time baking than looking for a job. He opened the fridge door and took out the filtered water pitcher, taking his time to think about what to say next. As he refilled his glass, looking down at the water, he added, "There aren't a ton of CPO jobs open."

"Are you sure that's what you want to do?" asked Jim.

Leland busied himself with sipping the espresso. He couldn't figure out if Jim's mostly curious tone included a hint of judgment.

Did Jim think Leland was too incompetent to be a CPO again?

Not that Jim could have any idea what had really happened. Leland hadn't told anyone about his breakdown. He couldn't get rid of the memory of looking up at the bottom of his desk, and then at Debra's concerned expression as she knelt down. The sudden realization that his IT bands and calves were sore from the crouched position on the floor before he got up. No, that image, and the corresponding sense memory, would stay in his head alone. Even to Grace, he'd simply said that he hadn't been able to turn around the business fast enough and needed to leave before they showed him the door. Having seen how stressed he'd been in the job, she didn't question the decision.

Before Leland could reply, Jim spoke again, "Tell me about a few times over the last year where you've felt most proud in your job. Moments you truly enjoyed, where you felt most you. Things that were truly meaningful to you, not because they received praise from others or look good on a resume."

Would it be rude to make up an excuse to leave the room? Leland glanced at the door and then busied himself taking in the scent of the espresso. Usually, he'd prefer Jim's company to most people's. But right now? He had wanted water and coffee, not career coaching or to face Jim's kind but knowing smile.

But he wouldn't leave the room. And he wouldn't crawl under the kitchen table either. It's not that he hadn't thought about Jim's question before. He was embarrassed by how few moments he could recall.

Jim regarded Leland for a beat, then added, "Don't overthink it, just say what comes to your mind right away."

"One time we were up against a tight deadline, and I helped the team with some pretty difficult coding that nobody else could figure out," Leland said. "If I hadn't, we wouldn't have met the deadline. I think I'm really good at solving thorny technical problems, and the team seemed to really appreciate my being in the trenches with them."

Leland smiled at the memory—the engineers sitting around him at his computer, asking him questions and listening as he explained how he'd solved the problem. One had written him a thoughtful thank-you email the next day.

Jim nodded. "Okay, that's a good one. How about another example?"

"We had a junior analyst that was really struggling with coming up with a business plan, and her manager wasn't really up for coaching her," said Leland, thinking about Erica and Calvin. "I really enjoyed teaching her."

"Hmmm," said Jim. "And what do you see as the most important activities for a CPO to be successful in the role?"

"I guess leading vision and direction for the team, being able to drive decisions, knowing how to manage the chessboard, you know who does what on the team, things like that..." Leland trailed off without finishing the list. He didn't need Jim to point out to him that those weren't the types of accomplishments he'd listed off.

He didn't want to think about whether those CPO activities were ones he even enjoyed doing or was likely to excel at.

Jim put both their espresso cups in the dishwasher. "I've known you for a while, Leland. I've wondered sometimes if you aspired to be a CPO because it was the next rung on the ladder and fit with your definition of success. Rather than being what you really wanted to do, and where you can best contribute to an organization. I don't know the answers, but I think it's something you should think more about."

"I'll think about that." Leland felt embarrassed. He knew that getting deep in code with the engineering team and teaching a junior analyst to write a business plan weren't the kinds of things a CPO should list first as top successes. No doubt, these were important tasks that needed to happen. But they were also ones that he could have delegated while he focused on other elements of the job. Or perhaps these would have been fine activities for Leland if he'd also had a slate of other accomplishments to name that only the CPO could—and needed—to do. You could get in the trenches, but only if you were also doing everything you could to ensure the troops as a whole were executing on the right battle strategy.

Leland rubbed the back of his neck. Could he really consider another path? Now that he'd been a CPO, anything else—short of being CEO—would feel like a step back. Maybe a VP position at a larger company with similar responsibilities would seem equivalent. But the other jobs that might be a better fit for his strengths—coaching, teaching, maybe running a smaller team of engineers? He'd mused that those might be things he did as he was getting closer to retirement, or perhaps after the big party with the gold watch. How would he explain taking that kind of shift in direction now to Grace? How would he explain it to his friends? What would his former co-workers say when they saw anything else on his LinkedIn profile? They'd all think he'd failed at his original path and had had to step off.

"Why don't we grab lunch next week and we can talk more about it," said Jim.

"I'd enjoy that, thanks," said Leland—even though "enjoy" didn't feel like the right word. He wasn't sure he actually wanted to consider the things Jim would prod him to think about.

They walked back into the living room. The guys were discussing the next month's study group selection and whose turn it would be to bring the snack.

"I'll bring it again," Leland said suddenly, surprising himself. "I've been baking a lot and have a few recipes I think you guys will like."

CHAPTER THIRTY-ONE

Jack

J ack looked through his office window at the sky and thought it might be mocking him. That shade of blue that looked too perfect to be real. Bright white clouds that actually did appear happy. Where was the smog layer when you wanted the outside to match your mood?

It was only 3:00 pm, but it felt like evening already. The last few days had been unbearably long, since he'd taken it upon himself to personally sit down with each of the twenty-three staff whose roles were being eliminated.

It was twenty-three for now. In six months, Jack himself would be number twenty-four. Only Debra and Terry knew, so they could quietly start planning how they'd announce the news and begin looking for a replacement. He'd spared Debra the awkwardness of having a "difficult conversation." When they had sat down to start planning layoffs a month ago, he'd told her that he'd leave—a voluntary departure, in HR speak—after helping the company get through this round of budget cuts and restructuring.

Voluntary was a funny word. Like he was going to serve Habitat for Humanity or something. He'd be leaving the company in a difficult spot. It felt wrong, abandoning these people who were in his care. But he knew Debra couldn't trust him anymore, and he didn't blame her. He'd set his fate—their fates—that day he'd betrayed her to George at the Brentwood Racquet Club.

One of the impacted employees, Chad, was the last of his twenty-three meetings. Stacking each and every single meeting into a three-day period had seemed like a good idea when Jack had asked his assistant to set up the self-imposed penance sessions. Now, he felt like he'd been trapped in his office for weeks, not days, as the different employees traipsed in and he struggled to remember the names and backstories of even those he'd worked with closely.

At least he didn't have to break the news himself. That'd happened earlier that week with each employee's HR business partner and department manager.

Chad knocked on the door, a quiet rapping similar to that of someone testing whether a wall was hollow. "Come in," said Jack.

Chad was an athlete—a marathoner, Jack recalled—but his movements were slow and jerky as he walked in and sat down.

"I know you're working out a lot of the logistical details with your manager and HR," said Jack, "But I wanted to thank you for everything you've contributed to the company and offer my support personally as you transition and search for a new job."

"I appreciate that," said Chad. "I won't lie that it's pretty stressful, and that I was caught off guard."

Jack felt the thickness in his throat. Even after three days of doing this, it didn't get any easier. Chad had started as an assistant right out of college and been at the company for eleven years, since near its beginning. Jack still remembered him as a twenty-two-year-old go-getter, introducing himself to Jack in the elevator and talking his ear off about a book he was reading that he thought Jack would like. Over the years, he'd been responsible for some of their most influential marketing campaigns.

But the numbers were clear. Debra, Jack, and the Board had decided they needed to sell a good number of their legacy apps. Between that decision and identifying a few areas where they could save money through automation, they simply needed fewer marketing staff.

Even though Jack had written the talking points for the staff presenting these layoffs as an inevitability—the competitive landscape and business needs had shifted, etcetera, etcetera—he couldn't ignore the truth.

This didn't have to happen.

"I've identified a few companies where I'm interested in applying for opportunities," said Chad. "Could I send you a list and see if you would be able to make an introduction?"

"Please do so," said Jack, grateful to have a way to be helpful. But he still struggled as he tried to swallow.

Jack's last meeting of the day was a different form of penance. Cassandra had emailed him, asking if she could have some time to discuss the company's DEI—diversity, equity, and inclusion—efforts. He recalled that Terry and Debra had tasked her with leading the creation of a strategic DEI plan. Part of him wanted to put the meeting off; after all, he was exhausted and a secret lame duck. But he still had six months to do right by this company he'd co-founded.

Cassandra sat down across him, clipboard in hand.

"I'm glad you set up this time," he said. "I've been thinking about the day when the ELT first saw the gender gap on the engagement survey. That was over a year ago now. I'm guessing it's not any better."

After he closed his mouth, he realized that she had probably come in with questions and that he should have let her start the conversation. But could anyone blame his bad manners, when he was so emotionally spent from all the layoff conversations?

Cassandra looked at him for a few seconds before answering. "As you might guess, a lot of the women across the office are buzzing about Amber's departure," she said.

He had suspected that might happen. In the months after Natalie had left, the executive team had mentioned that the staff were vibrating, their favorite term for talking about undefined stress. He'd joined everyone around the table lamenting the company's misfortune before moving onto the next item on their packed agenda. This time, he was determined to help come up with solutions. "What if we promote Meg to CPO?" he asked Cassandra. He felt a little less tired as he said it and proud for proactively coming up with an action step they'd be able to take quickly. "That'll calm folks down, right?"

Cassandra laughed. Not what he had expected. He'd thought she'd cheer.

He lowered his brow. He had thought she was too deferential a person to laugh at the CFO.

She didn't exactly roll her eyes—in fact, her eye contact was quite steady—but her tone of voice sounded like an eye roll. "Driving one woman out and then replacing her with another one won't really be seen as a win."

"That wasn't what I—" he started to say, letting out a loud breath before he tried to speak again. "I mean—"

He didn't even realize he'd raised his voice until noticing she'd raised hers to interrupt him.

"Women aren't interchangeable, Jack," she said.

Ouch.

He jerked back in his seat. He hadn't thought of that.

"And if you do hire a woman as the new CPO, you should know that doesn't erase the gender challenges," she added. "Having women in leadership isn't enough. It's also about what their experiences are like in leadership and on their way up the ladder to get there."

A year ago, he wouldn't have understood her statement. Now, for the second time that afternoon, he couldn't ignore the painful memory of not backing up Debra's decision to fire Leland. That hadn't *just* been about gender. Hiring and firing were two of the most complex activities any leader did and were rarely about one single thing. But it wasn't *not* about gender either. Would George have undermined a male CEO? Would George have defended a female CPO with the same deficiencies as Leland?

Would Jack have?

Nobody could really know the answer to those questions. But, in the past, Jack had always been able to ignore the questions—after all, George's intentions had been good. So had Jack's.

The road to hell and all that.

His throat was dry, but his water glass was empty.

"You should encourage Meg to apply. I have a feeling she'll do very well in the interview process," said Cassandra. "But also make sure that you're looking at a diverse set of candidates, beyond just Meg. Research shows that if there's just one woman or minority candidate in a finalist pool, statistically that person is unlikely to be hired. The person is seen as different—as 'the woman' or 'the minority' and not assessed fairly according to their own strengths. Even just having two minority candidates increases the odds of one of them being hired dramatically."[35]

"Okay, I understand we may be a little behind on ensuring that our hiring processes take into account the latest research," said Jack. "But, when it comes to Meg, if there's a good chance we'd end up hiring her anyway, why create such a labored process?"

He felt a little calmer at having an intellectual question to think through. He made a mental note that he'd want to see the research she mentioned.

Cassandra wasn't holding back today. "A lot of the women think of our company as a boy's club," she said.

It seemed like a non-sequitur, since they were talking about Meg, not about hiring a man. And he hated that phrase. Boy's club. He remembered his first job, when client meetings had sometimes been held at strip clubs. That really had been a boy's club. She had no idea. He opened his mouth, about to say something, but then stopped himself.

He should hear her out.

"The boy's club can mean a lot of different things. It can mean that men get more access to those in power because they're invited to play golf or to sporting events when women aren't, or male leaders are more likely to stop by their desk to make small talk," she said.

Jack took that in. He'd never golfed with junior colleagues—even though he knew that Dan did, and exclusively with men.

But Jack himself definitely made small talk more often with Kyle and Chad than with Cassandra or other women at the same level.

Why was that? Was Jack more likely to stop by Kyle and Chad's cubicles on his way back from lunch or to the copy room? He stopped by the women's cubicles too—when he needed something, not for informal chitchat.

And Kyle and Chad stopped by Jack's office much more often than any of the women.

"The boy's club is much bigger than the issue of male employees having more access and exposure," she continued. "Think of the boy's club as any action that automatically favors someone who is 'in the network' or decisions made according to 'the way we've always done things,'" said Cassandra. "Maybe eight out of ten times, those decisions end up favoring men—because more men statistically are 'in the network' at senior levels, and because the way organizations have always done things have historically been defined by male norms rather than female ones."

"So hiring anyone—including a woman, like Meg—because they're in the network, is something you'd consider a boy's club action."

"That's right," said Cassandra. "The goal is to take the time to assess the needs of the role and who is the right fit for it."

"Hiring Meg is the faster solution," he said, not so much for Cassandra's reaction as because he often thought aloud. He'd always believed that being an executive—maybe even being a man—was about being decisive, certain, and quick. That's what was necessary when you were responsible for others, whether it was your family or your company.

Cassandra's next statement was half-question, half-assertion. "You hired Leland pretty fast when Natalie departed, right?"

Jack flinched.

She was right to question the decision. The hurry to replace Natalie had made hiring Leland seem like a no-brainer. He hadn't thought they had any time to wait.

But how much had the business ultimately been slowed down by the wrong hire?

Years ago, Natalie had told Jack that she liked to ask job candidates for an example of a time they had to change a long-cherished belief they held about management or work. He'd told her it was a smart question.

But had he thought about how he'd answer that question himself? Jack saw himself as someone who'd done a decent job evolving with the times. Unlike a lot of people his age, he used text messages frequently and had a LinkedIn account. He loved his hard copy of the Sunday paper, but during the week used his iPad to learn what was going on in the world. He'd learned that the working mothers in the office often needed more advance notice if they were going to have evening events.

But these were all examples of changing habits and activities, not changing beliefs, especially long-cherished ones.

Avoiding eye contact with Cassandra, he found himself looking into the bright glare of the LED light panels on one of his side walls.

He returned his gaze back to her. "I know you're just getting started on our DEI plan," he said, trying to put the focus back on her. "What are you most worried about?"

"It's pretty impossible to boil down to one thing," she said. "Everything is interconnected. But if I had to pick one thing, it's the problem of the urgent overtaking the important."

"Well, sure, that's always a problem," said Jack. He sat up a little straighter. Maybe he hadn't quite thought through all the dynamics of the boy's club or known about the research on equity in hiring. But this was familiar territory.

This was a problem he could fix.

The phrase "urgent versus important" was a common one among leadership teams everywhere. When he talked to his fellow executives—it didn't matter where, whether companies, non-profits, universities, hospitals, or government—they all said how they always felt like they were in crisis mode, constantly putting out fires instead of doing the things they wanted to focus on.

"I know it's hard for organizations to focus on anything that doesn't get us another dollar tomorrow, especially organizations like this one facing some financial challenges," he said, hoping that he was using his most reassuring and mentorly voice. "But it's a solvable problem. We'll put deadlines and KPIs—key performance indicators—on your strategic diversity plan and make sure that there's time on the agenda of the executive team's meeting monthly for you to come and discuss it."

Did she look like she was going to laugh again?

"Those are all important steps," Cassandra said. "But when I say I worry that the urgent will overtake the important, I don't just mean that it'd be easy to ignore DEI and spend time instead on more immediate revenue challenges. Even in how we determine what solutions are needed to address DEI challenges, we can pick the quick fixes, or the ones that will be harder and take longer, but ultimately be better in the end. And think about what the company did when Natalie left. Hiring Leland seemed like a quick solution, and the simplest one. Anything else would have taken more time and creativity, because if you'd made Amber CPO, you'd then have another vacant position. But that decision, which seemed to have the advantages of speed at the beginning, has now slowed the company down."

He was about to argue with her, but stopped himself.

He hoped she wasn't job-hunting. Often when employees were this direct, they no longer had any fucks to give.

She wasn't wrong though. His gut reaction to Amber's departure had been to put Meg into the position—the fastest solution. Maybe it was also the right solution, maybe it wasn't, but he hadn't given it a second thought.

He'd always thought his quick decision-making was one of the most important characteristics he'd brought to the company. After all, the leadership team was constantly toggling back and forth across so many different challenges at once. Someone like Cassandra had no idea how much they were balancing at any given time. Any person at her level maybe saw a sliver of it, 1% or less. When you had to grapple with the full chessboard, you had to move fast on as many things as you could.

"I'll send you a few books that might be helpful," said Cassandra.

He thanked her for the suggestion, hoping she didn't notice the insincerity in his words. Did he really have time to read a whole book when there was so much going on?

Jack couldn't remember the last time he'd even started a book. What a luxury. She had started naming the books she'd email him about later, but his mind had wandered to his to-do list. Oh, how great it would be to be Cassandra's age and level, and to have time to read.

Wait. Jack suddenly felt a dull pain in his stomach. Since when had expanding his perspective and learning new things become a luxury?

Even if he was planning to leave this job, he wasn't ready to retire. He didn't want to be a dinosaur.

It wasn't until Cassandra left the room that he realized he'd taken a blank piece of paper that had been sitting on his desk and torn it into a few dozen little pieces.

CHAPTER THIRTY-TWO

Amber

Amber stopped by the farmer's market at lunch only intending to pick up three items. Tomatoes. Red peppers. Corn. If only those free samples of Honeycrisp apples hadn't beckoned her away from her path to the parking lot. Just a quick stop to grab a tooth-picked slice on her way to her car. Only a few seconds detour in theory—except that, right behind her, reaching for a Fuji apple in the next bowl, was Jack.

They exchanged a side hug, perhaps the most awkward of embraces. Amber tried not to stare at Jack's outfit. She'd never seen the CFO in jeans before, even in their casual office.

"Good to see you, Amber," Jack said tentatively, as if knowing she might not feel quite the same way. Had Jack aged several years in the last six months or was that Amber's imagination? She inspected him to see if she could glean any signs of stress. From the updates that Amber had been getting from Meg, she knew her old CFO had plenty to keep him awake at night. She knew about the layoffs and that the company would be in far worse shape if it hadn't been for her former team's new launches.

"I was just picking up some fresh tamales," Jack said. "My grand-daughter really likes the chicken ones."

What Amber should have done next was agreed with Jack. After all, she enjoyed the chicken tamales too. She'd even come to know the purveyor over the years, enough to go beyond pleasantries about the weather and ask about her grandchildren.

Instead, she did what she always did when confronted with an awkward conversation.

"We should grab coffee to catch up some time," she blurted out. As soon as she said it, she regretted it. But no matter, it was the kind of thing people said all the time but never had any intention of fulfilling.

He looked surprised. "Do you have a few minutes now?"

Damn. Should she make an excuse?

Curiosity got the better of her. She glanced at the time on her cell phone. "I've got until 1:00," she said. That wasn't quite true, as her next meeting wasn't until 2:00. But it only gave them a twenty-five-minute window.

Boundaries, boundaries, boundaries, her friends were constantly reminding her.

As soon as they sat down at the coffee shop, he spoke without hesitation. "I realize that if you had been CPO, we'd be in a much better spot right now."

She'd been wanting to hear those words for over a year and had never expected them to actually come.

She felt the welling in her chest and didn't trust herself to speak.

Jack should have stopped talking, but Amber's silence clearly unnerved him. He let out a self-deprecating laugh. His previous tone—wistful, but unhesitant—turned to stammering. "I just didn't know what else to do when Natalie left," he said. "If I could have cloned you, I would have. I just didn't see how you could be CPO, because I couldn't imagine anyone doing your senior director job but you."

The heaviness in her chest disappeared.

Maybe Jack was further along in his understanding, but he

still had a lot to learn. "Can you *imagine* now what you would have done differently?" she asked. If he noticed her emphasis on the word "imagine"—which he'd used himself first—he didn't let on.

"I know we shouldn't have hired Leland," said Jack. He didn't make eye contact, gazing up at a spot behind her, then down at his coffee, then up again. "But I still feel like we were trapped. We needed a CPO fast. We needed the job that you were doing to still get done without missing a beat."

"Did you consider splitting up my old job into two? Or hiring a contractor to take on some of the CPO responsibilities for a period of time, so I could have done most of the job while still having time to train a successor in my old role? Or even hiring a consultant or asking members of the team to figure out how we could restructure to get everything done?"

She paused to take a breath, but he interrupted her.

"Well, no, that's not how we do things, and—"

Amber couldn't stop herself from interrupting him. "There's rarely a perfect solution when it comes to how to organize staff. But you said you *couldn't imagine* any alternatives. *That's* the problem."

She felt emboldened as she thought more about the conversations she'd been having with her new co-workers at Natalie's company, about how they wanted to approach the organization differently compared to their previous jobs.

Her new co-workers came from a wide variety of former employers, from a small non-profit focused on promoting music in the elementary education curriculum to one of the largest law firms in the world. They all said the same things: they felt their former organizations had been stuck in so many ruts that it was hard to imagine a way out. Policies, or processes, or just unquestioned ways of doing things that made everyone's lives difficult, but which leaders saw as too complex or risky or not worth the time to address.

Despite her frustration with Jack, Amber felt a sudden burst of empathy. "This isn't just you," she said. "It's true of a lot of leaders at a lot of places. People often aren't willing, or don't take the time, to imagine whether there are alternatives that could work, especially if those alternatives are contrary to the way they've always done things."

She paused to take a breath. "I'm not saying any of the ideas I've just mentioned would have been the right one. Every idea I mentioned would have had advantages and disadvantages, but so does every plan. But even now, you immediately wrote these ideas off because they felt less familiar to you, not how you'd normally solve a problem."

To her surprise, he didn't argue.

Instead, he slumped down a little in his chair. "You're right," Jack said. "My wife tells me that I always want to kill the problem as quickly as I can." Then he added, "I've started reading this book about how white men can be diversity partners, and it talks a lot about white male culture in the U.S."

She raised her eyebrows.

On the one hand, she was pleasantly surprised that he was reading a book on diversity.

On the other hand, reading a book about white male culture didn't actually sound that helpful.

He chuckled self-consciously. "I realize how that sounds. Hear me out. Before I read this book, I don't think I could have identified a white male culture. Or I would have said something superficial like football and beer. But the book uses the phrase 'fix it culture' and talks about things like rugged individualism, low tolerance of uncertainty, action over reflection.[36] I always thought of those as things you needed to do succeed in business, and not considered that there could be other, equally valid approaches."

Wow. She had never thought she'd hear that kind of self-reflection from Jack. He was voicing exactly what she and her new colleagues had often discussed as the type of culture that had kept their old employers in those ruts.

"It's white male culture, and it's also the dominant organizational culture—how businesses in particular operate, but also many other types of organizations," she said.

She remembered an article that she'd come across months ago that she'd wished Debra, Jack, Leland and other senior execs at the company would read. She and Meg had joked about sending it to one of the printers near their offices in the hope they'd accidentally pick it up. Of course, it was easier to fantasize about passive-aggressive printer use than to actually do it.

"There's an article I'll send you later," said Amber. "I've seen hundreds of definitions of management as opposed to leadership, but this one really stood out."[37] She studied his expression. In the past, she'd found that Jack was always polite whenever she or her peers brought up any leadership reading they'd done, but couldn't hide his vague disinterest. He might have talked the talk at company meetings about an open-door policy or mentioned that he'd hired staff who were smarter than he was so that he could learn from them. The real message was received from his facial expression and body language: he clearly had felt that even relatively senior employees with less age and experience couldn't possibly have much to teach him.

Today though, he was leaning forward in his chair. His head was tilted slightly to the side.

"It talks about how management is about creating and enforcing predictable systems for the here and now," Amber began. "You need management operations to ensure the survival of what currently exists. However, with how much everything is changing right now, we also need leadership—and that's about preparing for futures that weren't previously imagined. That requires openness to novel ideas and bringing others along to new visions."

She wondered if he'd be insulted. She'd just described leadership in a way that was antithetical to what Jack had just listed as the white male cultural attributes he'd read about and said that he'd identified with. Preparing for different-in-kind futures required not going it alone, a high tolerance of uncertainty, and reflection before action.

But he seemed to be taking it in. "I'd love to see the article," he said. His next words were hesitant, "You mentioned you have a hard stop. I know you're busy, but I'd be interested in getting more of your thoughts another time. I'm not sure what I'll do next, but I want to better understand these issues. I'll buy you lunch."

Interesting—what did he mean by not being sure what he'd do next? She wondered if he planned to leave the company.

"Of course," she said, figuring there was probably a 50% chance that he'd take her up on it. She realized it didn't matter to her either way, but she smiled as she walked to her car knowing that she'd finally said many of the things she'd wished she had said when she still worked at his and Debra's company.

A few hours later, Amber let out a full-bodied laugh as she crumpled a piece of paper and threw it into the trash can. A perfect shot.

She'd never done that before—usually she missed by at least half a foot.

Around the conference table, the team let out a cheer. Zane, her co-chair for the meeting, gave a loud "Niiice." He'd started at Natalie's company on the same day as Amber and they'd quickly become friends.

Someone called out for her to do it again. She shook her head with a grin. "I know better than to expect lightning to strike twice. But let's take a fifteen-minute break."

Amber had been surprised a few weeks ago when Natalie asked if she'd be willing to co-chair a six-person strike force alongside Zane, their Chief Talent Officer. The group would be charged with designing a new process for hiring and onboarding new staff.

"Really? You want me to co-chair a talent strike force?" she had asked. Even after several months in her new role as Natalie's Chief Strategy Officer, Amber was still taken aback when her boss took an approach so markedly different from how things had worked at their old firm. Despite Amber's interest in talent issues, she'd always been given the signal from Debra and Jack that her time would be better spent elsewhere; that she should leave talent to the HR team.

"There's nothing more strategic than talent," said Natalie. "And we'd benefit from your creative mindset."

Even the conference room itself was a contrast to their previous company. Amber reflected on how Debra and Jack had brought in a design firm to explain to the employees how each decision was important for representing an element of their culture. They were told that modular seating represented the agility and flexibility of a tech company; that having both square and round tables in the central spaces would create a sense of "flow" (whatever that meant), and that the carefully chosen photos framed on the walls (such as one of three people in suits jumping in the air in front of a fountain) would remind people that work could be fun.

That design firm probably wouldn't have approved of Natalie's company's main conference room, she mused as she looked around. The room was bookended by two gallery walls holding thirty different pieces of framed artwork in total, in a range of styles, sizes, shapes, and frames. All had been created by employees or their family members. In the center of one wall, there was a beautiful oil landscape of Mt. Fuji by an executive assistant who attended art school in the evenings. Next to it, a black and white stylized photo of a busy New York City street taken by Natalie, who had grown up there. On the other wall, the largest piece: a crayon drawing of a dog by someone's five-year-old daughter. In its expensive frame, picked up at an estate sale for seventeen dollars, the drawing had been mistaken for a piece by a famous abstract artist by more than one visitor to their office.

As the rest of the group left the room for the break, Zane came up to Amber. "Nice job getting folks to talk who normally don't," he said to her. "I learned a few things from your techniques."

"Thanks, I really like how you teed up that exercise," said Amber.

Part of Natalie's pitch to her about the company had included how much she wanted to create a culture of peer-to-peer collaboration, hiring individuals that not only played well with others superficially, but that had a humility and receptiveness to new ideas from unlikely sources and that enjoyed helping one another. Zane had never worked in product strategy, but he'd become one of her best thought partners during their weekly lunches. Moreover, he'd been eager to co-chair the talent strike force with her, sharing power over outcomes that would primarily impact his team.

Before the break, Amber and Zane had led the group in brainstorming all the different assumptions they all came in with about how interviewing processes had to work. "Some people use the phrase *sacred cow*," Zane had said to get the group started, "Basically anything about the interview processes that you've always thought had to be that way."

After twenty minutes, they'd filled a page on the easel pad—the page that later became the object in Amber's trash can basketball victory. Amber herself had put down her assumption that the primary input into job hiring is a series of one-on-one thirty- or sixty-minute interviews. She'd had passing experience with other options—panel interviews, homework assignments—but the series of interviews had been by far the most important activity everywhere she'd worked.

After the break, the group got right into brainstorming how they might make a better hiring process.

"Have you all heard of the blind audition?" asked their lead accountant. "Orchestras wanted to make sure they weren't biased toward graduates of certain schools, so they started having them play behind a screen. This led to an increase in women being hired. Interestingly, they had to tell the musicians to remove their shoes before entering the stage for it to be a truly blind audition, because the sound of high heels could give away when it was a female musician."

"That's really neat," said their main recruiter. "A lot of organizations train people on unconscious bias or implement competency-based rubrics to help interviews assess candidates fairly and evenly. We're developing a lot of those processes here. But the next step is what's called discretion elimination, or making sure that identity-related cues that could unintentionally trigger bias are wholly out of the way. It wouldn't necessarily make sense to do that for every single part of the candidate selection process; for instance, we wouldn't be able to ensure diverse pools in a totally blind process. But we're looking at things like removing names from writing samples."[38]

Amber noticed one of the team members writing down ideas and looking up in thought. He was one of the quieter members of the group, but when he spoke, he always had something to say that really contributed to the discussion. She waited until he seemed to be done jotting down his thoughts, then called on him.

"Maybe we could consider adding an instant chat session to the interview line-up," he said. "A friend of mine works for a start-up where the CEO does that with every single potential employee to ensure cultural fit."[39]

"That's cool," said Zane. "I'd love to see more about that. So much of our work internally and externally is through instant chat or email, so it's interesting to think about incorporating that into the interview process."

"While we're on the topic, can we talk about how to assess 'cultural fit' generally?" one group member said.

"Yes! How horrible is it that so many organizations use the so-called airport test," said another.

Half the room groaned. The other half looked puzzled. "What's that?"

"It's probably most used in jobs that require a lot of travel," said a woman who'd previously worked at a big consulting firm. "Not an actual test, but basically every interviewer has in the back of their mind the question: 'If I were trapped at an airport with this person for three hours, would I enjoy it?' At my old firm, after we interviewed candidates, folks would always discuss how the person did on the airport test." She gave a half-sigh/half-laugh before continuing. "The obvious problem is that it can lead organizations to hire people they like most, rather than ones who are the best fit for the job."

"That's pretty silly," said the accountant, one of the people who hadn't heard of the airport test before. "If you were stranded at an airport with someone and didn't have enough in common to chat for three hours, there are plenty of other things you could do to pass the time. You could each read a different book on your phones, or watch separate TV shows on your laptops, or go your own ways and reunite on the flight."

Everyone laughed. Perhaps the airport test had been invented before devices.

The former consultant had stopped laughing before the rest of them and put her finger up in the air. "You know, one thing I learned from being stuck in a lot of airports with colleagues at my old job, is that what actually matters most is who can figure out how to deal with the unexpected challenge of being stuck at the airport. Who got on their laptop right away and started looking for alternative flights that would still allow us to get to the destination in time? Who asked the service desk if there's conference space rentable in case we needed to videoconference into a meeting? You also learned a lot while traveling about how people treat people, like airport or airline staff."

"So that's the *real* airport test," said Amber. "Not can I sit next to this person for hours and make small talk, but how do they handle the practical challenge of being stranded? Can they help come up with creative solutions?"

"Yes, exactly!" said the former consultant, "You get a sense of how someone thinks, works, and contributes to the team under pressure."

The recruiter got up from her chair and went to the whiteboard, writing THE REAL AIRPORT TEST in blue dry-erase marker. Amber loved the fact that any member of the team felt free to write on the board or grab the marker at any time.

"Some companies use simulation interviewing," said the recruiter. "They design activities for candidates to go through that mimic real activities. So like sorting through emails if it's an executive assistant job, or designing a branding campaign if you were joining our marketing department."

"Oooh, so we simulate an airport!" someone called out.

"I have an idea," said the usually quiet employee, this time not even needing to be drawn out. "We could turn a conference room into a mock airport, or at least like a high school play set for one. A service desk, a waiting area, a food area."

"That's genius!" another team member said, leading the usually quiet employee to blush. "We'd give the interview a scenario. What time is it now, where they have to be and when, who are the colleagues with them in the airport."

"Really interesting," said Zane. "There wouldn't be one single right answer. But we'd really see how people think through it."

"I could see it working for any job role," said another team member who had several years' experience managing large groups of people. "I've hired a lot of people in the past who have had good technical skills but are unable to work with others, or they can't respond flexibly when hitting a roadblock. This airport test simulation could test how people did on those competencies in a way that interview questions, which are so easy for the person to script in advance, don't always do."

"We could give the person a few minutes to brainstorm quietly at the beginning to ensure that more introverted personalities have a little bit of time to reflect," said the former consultant.

Amber loved the way the team followed the rules of improv whenever they engaged in creative brainstorming. She'd seen at previous workplaces how often group brainstorming sessions quickly shut down any innovative ideas as soon as the naysaying starts—put smart people in a room together, and their brains often couldn't stop going through the dozens of reasons something wouldn't work (especially if the folks in the room knew they'd have to implement the new ideas later). By contrast, Natalie had mandated that all ideation sessions follow the motto "yes, and" often used by improvisational actors. They even had an improv coach come to work with the team every other month. The former consultant who had just spoken could have started with an objection ("But this could unintentionally disadvantage more introverted personalities.") Instead, she provided an "and." In other words, she assumed they were going to go with the idea and gave a suggestion for how to make it stronger.

To be sure, there'd be plenty of time for weighing the actual implementation risks and advantages. But they always started with a spirit of curiosity and exploration.

Amber looked at the clock. They always tried to end longer meetings a little early when they could. She made eye contact with Zane and then glanced at the clock. He nodded.

"Amber and I will circle back with the group by the end of the week on next steps," Zane said. "It'll probably involve breaking you all up into pairs to run down a few ideas further."

"Thanks, everyone, for a really energizing session," said Amber. "I know Zane and I are really looking forward to the next time we meet."

As Amber returned to her office to get her handbag and leave for the day, she opened up the photos app on her phone. She scrolled through the photos she'd taken of the whiteboard from today's brainstorming session, thinking about how much they'd accomplished that day. Even though she worked fewer hours now, she probably got more done in an afternoon than she sometimes had in an entire week in her old job—where it had often felt like she was spending half her time dreading meetings and the other half in the meetings she had been dreading.

Out of habit, she picked up her laptop and was about to place it in her handbag, as she'd done for much of her professional life. Even after several months of time in her new job, the muscle memory was so ingrained. She laughed out loud to herself as she put the laptop back on her desk, grabbed the faux suede jacket from off her chair, and turned off the light for the evening.

CHAPTER THIRTY-THREE

Kyle

"**A**re you planning to leave too?" Kyle asked Meg.

He'd meant to work up to the question to his manager in their weekly one-on-one. Instead, he blurted it out. He'd seen the research saying that one of the best predictors of whether you were engaged in your job was if you had a best friend at work. His first thought after hearing the good news/bad news several months ago— Leland out, but Amber too—had been: "Oh, shit, how long before Meg leaves too?"

He'd been sitting on the question for a while, but now it was on his mind. He'd started considering applying for other jobs. If Meg left, he'd likely update his resume a little faster.

"I don't have plans to," she said.

Kyle shifted in his chair. He'd noticed the strain in her voice. He didn't even know what to ask next.

He wanted to tell her that he saw more than she realized: the challenges that the women faced. But is that something you could say to your boss? He could imagine what she'd probably think: did he really see, or was he just parroting what he'd heard his female friends say?

He thought about how many times Jack or another executive had asked for Kyle's perspective on something, when a woman might have been more qualified to make a contribution. He knew Jack had stopped by his cubicle much more than that of all the women at his level combined. But what had really blown his mind was when Shannon had recently pointed out to him that this wasn't just true when it came to Kyle's female peers, but that his voice might sometimes carry even further than women senior to him, like Meg and (when she was still at the firm) Amber.

Was that true? Did Meg know it? Did she resent him for it?

He hadn't planned to say more. But those extra beats of silence were hard not to fill. The words came out before he had time to think about them. "I'd told my mom about Leland, months ago. How much he was hurting the business. How Amber should have had that job. How we all told Terry we had concerns when she asked shortly after he started but didn't say anything after that. She said that I should say something again. I never did."

Meg took a few seconds longer to respond than she normally would.

"What were the reasons that you decided not to?" she asked.

A clinical question. No hint of judgment.

But Kyle couldn't help but wonder: was she secretly wishing he had said something?

"I guess I didn't see any benefit," he said. "I thought I'd just be seen as a troublemaker." He paused. "Did you and Amber ever say anything?"

He realized he'd probably put her in an awkward position of having to share more than she wanted to with a direct report. They'd worked together too long for Meg to spin him. If she did, he'd see through it, and she knew it.

"We did a few times," Meg said. "But I'm not sure that we were considered the most credible sources."

She didn't elaborate. His mind quickly went through what she might mean by that. Of course. Amber would have been seen as a sore loser since it was widely believed that Leland's job should have been hers. And everyone knew that Meg was Amber's friend.

But the two women had been in the best position to know how Leland's performance was hurting the business. Between them, they had been managing the majority of the product portfolio. And yet it would have been too easy for the executives to write them off as having an agenda.

Maybe Kyle himself couldn't have single-handedly done anything. But Shannon told him time and again he had the ear of Jack and other executives in a way that the women didn't. There were other men at Kyle's level who enjoyed the same kind of access. What if just a few of them had spoken up? If they had spoken up, would that have enabled Shannon and others to also share their perspectives more easily?

It hadn't seemed like his problem at the time. Fast forward to having recently needed to let someone great on his team go due to the budget cuts. Not only had this been one of the hardest conversations in his professional life, but he'd also be dealing with the aftermath for a while. There'd be the extra work and a morale hit for the rest of the team. The justified fear that any of them could be next. Raises and bonuses seemed unlikely, or likely at best to be paltry.

And if Meg quit next? That wouldn't be good. Kyle's father would probably tell him that could be his opportunity: perhaps he could have Meg's job. But Kyle didn't actually think he'd be good at Meg's job, at least not for a few years.

"It's all so fucked up," he said. He didn't know what else to say.

"Don't blame yourself for not saying anything," Meg said, as if reading his mind. "One thing I've been thinking a lot about is how often leadership books and articles give advice about managing upward, leading from behind or below. There are good things about that advice. It empowers staff, no matter how junior or senior, to share perspectives that might be beyond the line of sight of the folks at the top, and to take ownership in the organization's success. Leadership isn't just top-down."

He nodded. Her inclusive style was part of what he liked about working for Meg.

She continued, "I hope you feel comfortable talking about problems that you see, and if you don't, that we can have a conversation about it. But there are also bad things about all the talk about upward management. It lets decision-makers off the hook. It means staff end up blaming themselves over decisions they didn't make or actions that weren't their responsibility. What Leland did or didn't do isn't your fault."

Kyle had taken a class on business ethics in school. It focused on big topics like environmental sustainability, corporate social responsibility, and whistleblowing. But in truth there were hundreds, maybe thousands, of mundane day-to-day decisions where it was unclear what the right thing to do was. In his personal life, one of his friends had organized a bystander intervention training for their friend group. They talked about what to do if your uncle said something racist at the Thanksgiving table, or if you saw someone being harassed at the grocery store. How to safely intervene, whether by directly confronting the harasser, showing support to the victim, or getting help. Kyle liked to think he'd both know what to do, and actually do it, if he saw someone getting harassed while in line buying potato chips. That he wouldn't succumb to bystander apathy.

But what was the calculus at work? When you saw something wrong, when should you say something, and when should you let it play out?

His eyes moved to Meg's desk. She always had a stack of manila folders in the corner, representing her current projects. Today there were probably five times as many as usual. Leland's and Amber's responsibilities had been split up among a handful of different leaders, but he suspected Meg had borne the bulk of it. A row of empty Diet Coke cans sat on her window sill, something he'd never seen before; either she was caffeinating more or didn't have the time to take them to the recycling can in the pantry.

"I know you've got a lot on your plate," he said. "Is there anything I can do to help you?"

She looked surprised. He realized it was the first time he'd asked in the three years he'd worked at the company. Points versus the assist again.

"Not right now, but I appreciate it," said Meg.

He stood up and was about to leave, but then turned around. He pointed at the manila folder at the top of her pile. From the label, he could tell it was on a topic that he knew a lot about, and that he'd heard that she was working on. "Could I help you with that?" he asked. "I can read the file and give you an executive summary by the end of the week."

"That'd be great," she said.

The rooftop garden was typically too crowded during lunch hour, so Kyle and his friends often took a late lunch at 1:30 pm so they could have the space to themselves. He was the first to arrive and sat on the edge of one of the brick herb planters, taking in the scent of mint.

"How was your check-in with Meg?" Shannon asked after she, Cassandra, Haley, and Rita had also arrived. He had mentioned on their group text that morning that he'd been thinking about asking her directly if she was planning to quit. It was rare that their entire group was able to make it to lunch: usually someone had a meeting at the same time or a deadline to meet. But with the current chaos, they all needed the mutual support.

He told them about his conversation with Meg.

"We didn't talk specifically about gender," he said when the group asked. "I felt weird asking." He paused. "Do you think she's raised the gender problems with Debra?"

"Probably a little," said Cassandra. "But my guess is that a lot of the more senior women bite their tongues."

"I mean women already take on all kinds of extra emotional labor and office housekeeping," said Haley. "Being the person to speak up on behalf of women feels yet like another 'extra task' on the list."

"Yup, another task unevenly done by women as if gender equity were just a women's problem, not an everyone problem," Rita said.

"Plus, who wants to be seen as *that person?*" said Haley. "The woman who brings up all the gender issues. It hurts your career if you're defined as the woman ringing the diversity bell, not the woman who is awesome at the same types of activities men are judged by, and the same kinds of accomplishments you'd attribute to a man."

"I read an article about that," said Cassandra. "Basically, this study looked at the performance ratings of executives who demonstrated what the authors called diversity-valuing behaviors. So, those behaviors could include valuing cultural, religious, gender, and racial differences, or feeling comfortable managing people from different backgrounds. Turns out that when white men exhibit these behaviors, there is no impact on how their bosses rate their competence or performance. But when non-white men or women exhibit these behaviors, their evaluations overall are much worse by their bosses. Additionally, a white male can hire someone non-white or a woman without being judged any differently as far as competence goes, but when a non-white or female manager does it, they are seen as less effective."[40]

"So basically, it says that women and people of color get penalized for helping one another?" asked Kyle. His gut reaction was that he wanted to look at the study. He didn't question the fact that these gaps existed. But correlation didn't always equal causation. Maybe there were other factors involved.

Wait. His mental narrative was sounding a lot like his dad. He'd noticed that his dad started to come up with intellectual arguments whenever he felt defensive. That was always the case when Kyle and his dad fought about politics. Is that what Kyle was doing? Hearing his female friends talk about these challenges made him feel a lot of things. Sad and frustrated on their behalf. Ashamed to be part of the dominant group, but also resentful that he was made to feel shame for something that wasn't his fault; a system that he hadn't created. Worried and angry that, the more discussions like this happened, the more Kyle's own competence and well-earned accomplishments would be called into question. Besides, he was one of the good ones. He had female friends and close female direct reports. He wasn't old-fashioned like Jack, or a jerk like Dan, or clueless like Tom.

"You can't be serious?" Shannon was saying to something that Rita had said.

Rita nodded, and Cassandra and Haley both made proper facial expressions and grunts of incredulity.

Kyle did the same. He realized that he'd stopped paying attention and hoped they hadn't noticed.

The group soon dispersed, but Kyle didn't have another meeting for thirty minutes, so he went to the café. There was no line, but as he ordered his coffee, he noticed Debra was still waiting for hers. He debated whether or not to go over and say hello.

"I'd been meaning to get time with you," said Debra. "We're looking for a few folks at your level to create a small tiger team to examine the wearables market. The exec team was discussing it, and Jack and Saul both sung your praises."

"Thanks, that sounds exciting," he said. Usually, he would have stopped there, excited to be have been called out by the CEO and that two other executives had recognized his contributions. But then he wondered who wasn't getting this tap on the shoulder. "Who else will be involved?" he asked.

"So far you and Haley," she said. "If there ends up being more work than makes sense for the two of you to do, we can bring in others."

"Great," he said. As the two of them returned to silence while waiting for their coffee, he thought about the fact that it had been Jack and Saul who recommended him. He knew that he had more access to both of them than the women at his level.

Then he channeled his father in his head. Kyle wasn't the only one who had been hand selected. Haley had been too. One woman. One man. Totally equal.

But why wasn't Rita on the list? She was passionate about the topic. In her free time, she was volunteer consulting with a friend to figure out if wearables distribution could be used to solve health disparity issues. She'd even taken a few PTO days to go to a big conference on forecasting the wearables market.

Her volunteer work had been highlighted in the company newsletter. But would Debra have seen it? Who would have spoken up for Rita when the executive team met to nominate candidates? If any of the executives had run into Rita in the coffee line, they'd likely struggle to remember her name. This wasn't speculation. He'd seen it happen a few times.

By contrast, Haley was well-known as a rising star in the company. She'd presented her work at several high-profile events and even received several company awards. Haley was one of the few directors whose name was known by Debra and the other senior-most executives. They didn't just remember her name when they saw Haley in the coffee line, but might even proactively go out of their way to say hello to her. Haley's reputation had been earned. You'd want her on your team, no matter what the topic and her level of expertise was. She'd probably be Kyle's first pick in any corporate draft.

If you thought about gender equity as just having an equal number of men and women, then the proposal seemed fair and right. Haley and Kyle. But if you thought about it in terms of making sure that women were as recognized and leveraged for their unique skills and expertise as often as men were, it didn't feel right. Kyle knew that many of his female colleagues struggled to have the access that he had; the mere fact that Haley also had that kind of access did not make up for the fact that many women did not.

It wasn't Kyle's job to amplify Rita's voice and reputation. Her managers should have been doing a better job ensuring that her work and interests were known by those at the top. And there were definitely things Rita could do herself to network more at the company.

But was that just bystander apathy talking?

He impulsively walked over to the table where Debra was sitting with her coffee and a stack of papers. "Debra, what would you think of also including Rita in the work with Haley and me?" he asked. "She's probably the person at the firm who knows the most about the topic—certainly more than I do." He elaborated a little on Rita's accomplishments, suggesting that Debra read more about them in the company newsletter.

"That's a great idea, Kyle, I had no idea," said Debra. "Thanks, I'll give Rita a call, and find some time for the three of you to meet with me so I can talk a little more about the project."

He tried to banish his dad's voice from his head, as it was already questioning his decision. Rita could outshine him in the work. Even if she didn't, would three people getting credit for whatever they did make his role less significant than if it were just two people? What if Debra decided they only needed two people and kicked Kyle off the project?

But the project would go better with Rita on it, and that's what was better for the business—and ultimately for Kyle and his team. He wanted to learn from Rita on the topic.

Kyle got into the stairwell and was about to exit at Rita's floor to tell her about the conversation. But as he was swiping his badge and opening the door to her floor, he paused before walking through it. Telling Rita would get him friend points and ally points. But shouldn't she hear the news from Debra herself?

He closed the door and went back into the stairwell.

PART TWELVE

Resetting

CHAPTER THIRTY-FOUR

Debra

Debra looked around Natalie's office. Framed pictures not only of Natalie's own kids, but also little ones who Debra assumed were nieces and nephews. A pale yellow crocheted blanket tossed over an ottoman. In the corner of her office, several baskets of fruits and vegetables. She remembered that Natalie grew these in her backyard.

Early in her career, Debra had always been told to limit personal items in her office for fear of not being taken seriously. She remembered a female mentor explaining that men got points for putting pictures of kids up, but for women even pets were a stretch if you didn't want the men to primarily see you as a caregiver.

It made Debra feel like a rebel still, just for having framed photos of her dogs on her desk.

She'd given that advice to Natalie too, once upon a time. Natalie had listened to it, when she worked for her.

If Natalie noticed Debra looking around, she didn't say anything. But she was observing Debra in return. "I think this is the first time I've seen you without high heels before 5:00 pm," said Natalie, gesturing toward Debra's black flats.

Debra let out a laugh. "I still love a lot of my pumps and wear them often if I don't have to do a lot of walking. But you can consider me woke now on all the little ways I didn't even realize how much I was going along with how the business world has been defined by men."

Natalie gave a jolt—perhaps at Debra's even using the word "woke." This was the first time the two had reunited since Natalie had left Debra's company. Multiple lifetimes ago.

A caveat felt necessary. "Or at least more woke," Debra said. "I guess I'm woke enough now to realize how much I probably still don't know."

"What's changed for you?" asked Natalie.

Debra hadn't been planning on anything other than small talk when she had realized she'd be a block away from Natalie's office for another meeting and had asked if she could come by. But as she sat with her former mentee, she felt the urge to say more. After all, Natalie's departure had been the initial spark that had eventually led to Debra working with Cassandra to better understand the barriers facing the younger generation of women.

"A little after you left, George gave a speech at a company off-site, where he talked about how women needed to lean in," said Debra. She winced a little at the memory, "I feel embarrassed about it now; all the things I didn't understand. I came up the ladder in a time where the focus was primarily on ensuring women got a seat at the table—we had to tell women to grab their place, to lean in. I get it now—what a slap that advice can feel like when women are so often hindered from leaning in, or not rewarded for doing so."

"Yeah, I never liked the phrase because it emphasized the idea that women were at fault," said Natalie. "It comes with an implication that women need to be more like men. Are we asking men to collaborate or listen as often as we're telling women to be more assertive?"

Debra thought about her visit to Fay's company, and her own realizations about the so-called feminine traits she'd suppressed to be accepted in a man's world. It was that Goldilocks dilemma—she'd been discouraged from certain ways of being stereotypically feminine and expected to uphold others.

"There's a lot my generation of women felt we had no choice about in the workplace," she said, "Your generation is right not to stand for that."

She let out a slow breath, surprised by how free she felt. She'd been told by mentors earlier in her career that, as a leader—especially a female one, who was more prone to being criticized due to her chromosomes—she shouldn't show weakness.

Another thing that she'd been taught that she now needed to unlearn.

"I'm so grateful to have had the opportunity to learn from you," said Natalie. "And I know that I can't begin to imagine what your generation had to go through."

The statement of gratitude meant more to Debra than she'd realized it would.

Natalie canceled her next meeting, and Debra ended up staying another hour. She'd taken furious notes when Amber stopped by and described the innovative work they were doing to mitigate bias in their hiring process. The "airport test" simulation idea that Amber described was fascinating—and also frightening: to even contemplate the risk of implementing something so different from anything they'd ever done.

Past Debra wouldn't have even realized that fear was influencing her response. She would have come up with a dozen reasons why something so different wasn't even possible.

Present Debra made a note in her phone to follow up with Amber to learn more.

After that, it was Natalie taking the notes as she asked Debra for advice on growing a business in these early days. Even when it came to that advice, Debra realized she had to take a different approach than she might have in the past. Natalie wasn't interested in the same types of investors that Debra had been. "I don't want to grow at breakneck speed," said Natalie. "I want to make sure the staff have true work/life balance."

Was that meant to be a jab at Debra?

She had to remind herself that this wasn't about her. It was about Natalie, starting an organization based on a different set of values—ones that didn't actually sound that bad.

As Debra pulled into her parking spot, she saw Chad exiting the revolving glass doors, holding a large cardboard box. He was one of the twenty-three casualties of the budget cuts they'd been forced to impose over the last month. Between working with Jack on the painful list of budget reductions, the good work Amber's team had done, and a few preliminary relaunch successes, Debra had been able to convince the Board into believing they had a plan and that (at least for the time being) she could still steer it.

The air conditioning in the car had never felt better, even when she'd been in the blazing sun in Las Vegas or Palm Springs, the kind where her kids' crayons had melted in the trunk while they parked the car for lunch. She didn't want to open the car door. If she got out of the car right now and started walking up the path to her office building, she'd end up crossing paths with Chad right before he reached the sidewalk.

But she needed to be a leader even, or maybe especially, for those who now had to leave. She forced herself to turn the keys. She grabbed her handbag from the driver's seat. Peeking out of the handbag was the paper bag filled with persimmons that Natalie had given her before Debra had left her office.

A few seconds later, Chad stopped in front of her. He was the first to speak—a graceful move. His words were graceful too. "I really appreciate your leadership and support, Debra. Thank you."

If she had been a better leader, would he be carrying that box?

Her worries about the twenty-three would soon need to turn further to the impact on those left: they'd all have more work to do. They'd be absorbing the work of their departed colleagues and would be worried about whether more layoffs were coming. It wasn't just Debra's job at stake.

Don't be maudlin, she chided herself.

"If there's anything I can do for you, please let me know," she said. They exchanged a few more pleasantries. Five minutes later, as she entered the building, she couldn't remember what else she had said to Chad, except that she'd handed him the bag of persimmons. A ridiculous act, but one that had made sense in the moment.

She looked at her watch. She had a few interviews for senior candidates today. They had decided that they'd take their time in hiring replacements for Leland and Amber. Jack had offered to stay until they stabilized the product leadership team but had said he'd leave after that. It was one of the saddest parts of this whole thing—a long friendship shattered by their bad business decisions.

At least in recent weeks, the Jack that had once been her best ally had returned. He'd been quietly talking to investors and Board members about how George had undermined Debra's abilities to do her job. He'd admitted his own faults and told them he was planning to leave, making sure they'd see it as a positive when he did so, rather than a further indictment on Debra's leadership. He was determined to leave the company and Debra in the best possible position when he left.

He'd also started reading more and they'd had a few conversations about DEI. She knew she'd just started scratching the surface on the challenges. She'd been so focused on the gender gap, where they had a lot of data, admittedly because there were fewer people of color at the company, especially at senior levels. That had to change too. They had to look at how to create a more equitable workplace for all sub-groups, not just the biggest one.

The business challenges would only further intensify their DEI challenges. They were facing more competition, which could lead to an increased belief that speed and proven methods were more important than taking that quick pause to test their assumptions or allow for other perspectives. Potential future budget cuts could mean continued difficult decisions about who stayed or who went.

She was jolted out of her reflections by a voice. She realized someone was standing in front of her.

No, two someones: Kyle and Rita.

"We can't wait for our meeting with you at the end of the week," said Rita, "You'll love the wearables partnerships proposal that we've been working on."

"And wait until you hear how Rita has engaged staff at all levels in the project through some mini-hackathons," Kyle said.

Debra had realized a few months ago that they'd need new ideas to survive, and that these couldn't be derived top-down. She'd asked Kyle, Haley, and, belatedly, Rita to put together some ideas. They'd not only done it, but they'd engaged the entire company in the process.

In addition to being the undisputed expert on the wearables market at their firm, Rita was also gifted at creative ways of communicating with the staff and getting feedback, ranging from mini-hackathons to use of internal social media. Debra had asked her for a reverse-mentorship on these new types of staff engagement efforts. Just that morning, Debra had put up her first post on the company's internal social network, building on a few discussions she'd had with Rita about how to get more frequent staff input across levels and departments.

When she got back to her desk, Debra opened her inbox. Fifty unread messages. A light afternoon, but still overwhelming. She closed her inbox and opened her internet browser instead to go to her personal email account. She sent a note to her financial advisor, with a link to Natalie's website and one sentence: *I visited this company today and want to invest.*

Tonight, she'd look through her Rolodex and figure out which other friends and colleagues might be interested in Natalie's work.

Looking around her office, she suddenly felt a little cold. Did it always smell a little bit like lemon Pledge in here? She reached into her handbag and pulled out her wallet, finding the photograph of her kids on the boardwalk when they were little, a bit faded after she'd been carrying it around for twenty years. She rested it against the frame with her dog on her desk, making a mental note to bring in more photos and a frame.

CHAPTER THIRTY-FIVE

Cassandra

When Cassandra was bored, she doodled in curlicues. When she was nervous, dark angular lines covered the margins of her notebook. Looking at the empty seat next to her at the front of the room, she pressed her pen hard on the paper while tracing a pattern of triangles and squares with as much force as she could without breaking the paper.

There was no logical reason for feeling this level of anxiety. The meeting wasn't scheduled to start for eight minutes. Her former classmate Bree, who worked at a DEI consulting firm nearby, was the type of person who set her watch a few minutes late so that she always arrived on time. Debra had given Cassandra forty-five minutes on the Senior Management Council monthly agenda. The goal was to tee up the larger development of a DEI strategic plan that Cassandra would be leading for the company, introducing Bree as a consultant they'd be working with, and doing some preliminary listening to see what was on the senior group's mind (to be followed up later with smaller group and one-on-one conversations, where they'd expect more honesty).

Even if Bree were late, Cassandra could easily start without her. They'd gone over the plan for today over a working lunch the day before. Still, Bree's presence would make Cassandra feel less like the interloper at the SMC meeting—the lowly director allowed to crash the monthly session comprised of senior directors and above. Not that Cassandra hadn't been reassured multiple times by Terry and Debra that she'd soon be promoted and officially join the SMC. But she knew not to get her hopes up given the budget situation. She had had to draw on Bree's friendship and goodwill to do this session at a discount.

She tugged at the edge of her sleeve. Knowing she'd be in front of a few dozen people, she'd taken extra care with her outfit today: her best jeans with a button-down, light peach silk blouse. She wondered if Debra would be judging her for the pastel color. Too feminine; not in the right place on the Goldilocks spectrum. Or maybe that was the old Debra. She'd noticed the CEO had recently added framed photos to her office. And it went beyond that. Both Debra and Jack seemed like different people now. Others had noticed too. Jack had read the books that Cassandra had told him about, and he'd started incorporating concepts from them into his daily conversations. More than that, even though they were probably working harder than ever these days, they also seemed less hurried.

As promised, Bree arrived a few minutes before they needed to start. "I'm going to start with something that's going to feel a little uncomfortable," she said once everyone was in their seats and Debra had introduced Bree, Cassandra, and the session. "Cassandra and I sent a survey to your employee resource groups and asked for their candid feedback on their experiences working here from a DEI perspective. I want to read a few of the comments we received."

She nodded at Cassandra to tee up the slides. Cassandra found herself fumbling with the laptop as she connected it to the projector, hoping nobody saw her hand shaking. She bit her lip. Knowing what was coming, how could she not feel nervous? She took a few seconds longer than she needed to then open up the file, which would display the exact quotes they'd received from staff on the screen as Bree read them aloud. As she looked around the room, she saw a group of people that, for the most part, prided themselves in valuing DEI. Many of them would be shocked at what they heard. Would they believe it? "I've done this at dozens of organizations," Bree had reassured her, saying that while the comments (sadly similar at most places) were hard to hear, it was a necessary conversation.

And so she began. Cassandra flipped through the slides as Bree read aloud:

> "A male colleague told me that I look great for a pregnant woman, and then started to ask me detailed and intrusive questions about my pregnancy."
>
> "My male colleague and I were recruited at the same time and both asked about promotion timeline—even though I have more work experience and education than he does, he was told a year and I was told two."
>
> "At a company party, a group of men were joking about getting the date rape drug."
>
> "Co-workers have made fun of me for including pronouns on my signature file."
>
> "A man on my team towered over me at my desk and yelled at me, and when I mentioned this to our manager, I was told to toughen up."
>
> "I've been told that I speak good English, I guess because I'm Asian American. I was born in New York and have a master's in literature."
>
> "My manager keeps pressuring me to wear a dress, which I haven't done since I was seven."
>
> "I'm a gay male and have been asked who is the man in the relationship with my partner."
>
> "I've had colleagues express surprise that, as a Latina woman, I'm an engineer."

*"There have been three high-profile special project opportunities
in my group in the last year, and they all went to men without
women being given the opportunity to even indicate interest."
"A Black colleague on our team is often referred to as articulate by
other colleagues, as if it's a surprise."
"I've heard my co-workers make fun of our clients' accents—
it's not funny."*

Even Cassandra, who had read the comments multiple times
before this, felt the weight of them. She looked around the room.
Bree had told her to expect potential disbelief, a crossed-arms vibe
she'd seen many times before, especially in audiences like this one
that didn't yet have a culture of open conversation around these types
of topics. "At the beginning of the DEI journey" was how Bree put
it. The room was silent, but there were no crossed arms. Everyone
seemed frozen.

"This is the real, unfiltered experience of many of your colleagues
and team members," said Bree. A few people in the room started at
the sound of her voice. She spoke at a lower volume than she usually
did, but anything louder than a whisper would have felt jolting.

Tentatively, a few people started sharing their reactions. Shock.
Horror. Sadness. Not wanting to believe it but knowing it was true.
That if even one person felt this way, they needed to be better. Bree had
told Cassandra the difficult thing about this part of the session was
the balance of letting people process their reactions without turning
the entire session into people from less marginalized groups talking
about how hard it was to hear the truth, how guilty they felt, how
unsure they were of the path to becoming better allies. "Ideally, we'd
have a whole week for a session like this, so we weren't rushed," Bree
had said during their planning session, "Not just forty-five minutes.
But I know it's hard for organizations who are still at the beginning of
the DEI journey to know this won't ultimately work without commit-
ting the time. Consider this baby steps."

As the next baby step, Bree signaled at Cassandra to shift the graphic on the screen. It was a version of a graphic frequently used by DEI consultants called the "Diversity Wheel," showing a few dozen elements of diversity. The wheel included elements like age, gender, sexual orientation/identity, physical ability, race, and ethnicity. It also included elements like education, work experience, political beliefs, family influences, recreational and personal habits, military status, religion, role in the organization, management status, and more.

The tension in the room seemed to drop as people started reading the graphic, letting their analytical brains kick in.

"I like this a lot," said a woman who Cassandra didn't know. "It's a useful way of understanding all the different factors that make up who someone is. I could see using this as a way to talk to members of my team about what they think is important for me to know about them."

"The part about personal habits really resonated with me," said Saul, the COO. "Recently I planned a wine tasting as a team event, and hadn't realized I had a team member who doesn't drink."

Dan raised his hand and jumped in, "Yeah, I worry too that we have too many alcohol-related events, and how much that might alienate our employees who don't drink."

Suddenly, the room seemed to wake up. There were five more comments in a row about discriminating against non-drinkers. All the tension had disappeared. A few folks looked as ready to jump out of their seats with enthusiasm as one could while sitting around a huge conference room.

"Let's crowdsource a list of non-drinking-related events and email them to all the managers to consider," said Bart. "I can ask my assistant to take that on."

"I've got a few people on my team who have great ideas," said Dan.

A few additional topics came up during the rest of the session, but the conversation about drinking dominated.

"This is the most productive DEI session I've ever been to," Saul said to Cassandra as the group was filing out of the room. "I love the fact that we left with that concrete action item around non-alcohol-related team events."

"Loved it too," said Jack. "So great to see a quick win right away."

Cassandra wasn't sure how she felt.

After everyone else had left and she had said goodbye to Bree, Cassandra decided to stay in the empty conference room and reflect on what she'd just seen. She walked to the far end of the room. All the windows were locked so that you could only open them a few inches. You weren't really supposed to do even that, so as to not screw with the HVAC. But it was okay to break the rules for just a few minutes, right?

She opened the window and took in the cool breeze, watching the leaves of the palm trees outside sway slightly.

On the one hand, agreeing to develop a list of team events that weren't alcohol-centric was an important task: one that needed to be done and that would hopefully create a more inclusive culture.

On the other hand, the alcohol discussion seemed like a deflection. Talking about other topics on the wheel—for instance, gender, race and ethnicity, sexual orientation—was a lot more emotionally loaded and uncomfortable. The room had briefly sat in that discomfort and even processed it—Cassandra was proud of them for that—but only to a point, before they jumped at the opportunity to engage with the DEI content in a less threatening way.

On the one hand, she knew how important it was for any DEI discussion to have an action item that could be a "quick win" of sorts, so that leaders and employees feel that there's forward momentum.

On the other hand, an overfocus on "quick wins" was what led to whack-a-mole solutions, and that could keep the organization from properly addressing the thornier problems.

She'd been talking to Bree about the DEI trainings and policies that her firm usually developed with other organizations, but that didn't seem like enough. Luckily, they were open to working with different groups in different ways.

What would it look like to get beyond whack-a-mole—to truly transform their organization? Cassandra didn't have another meeting on her calendar for a few hours, and she knew this conference room wasn't booked for the rest of the morning. She took her wireless earphones out of her handbag along with her journal and pen.

A few times, she wrote a sentence and crossed it out, thinking that something wasn't realistic, that it would never happen here. Earlier that week, when she'd had coffee with Amber, at Debra's suggestion, and learned about the culture Amber and Natalie were building at their company, Cassandra couldn't help but feel sad. That was so much easier to do when you were starting from scratch.

As a German minor in college, she'd loved the language's multi-syllabic words that expressed emotions that didn't quite have a corresponding word in English. *Sehnsucht* described thoughts and feelings about parts of life that were unfinished and imperfect, alongside a yearning for the ideal alternative experiences. That's the emotion she felt as she got deeper into trying to solve the DEI challenges. Looking at the number of things she'd already crossed out on the page as unrealistic, she let out a slow sigh.

Then she remembered what Amber had said about the rules of improv, always going with "yes, and." That was a good way to ensure voices and ideas were heard—and to foster creativity—in a group session, but why not apply it to her solo brainstorming session as well?

Stop censoring yourself, she thought. She ripped out the piece of paper with all her scratched-out sentences and started with a fresh page. In big letters, she printed at the top: "WHAT WOULD A TRANSCENDENT DEI STRATEGIC PLAN LOOK LIKE?"

She started to write.

Where Do We Go from Here?

How much discomfort are we willing to withstand to close equity gaps? The answer is less than we want to admit. An October 2020 *Saturday Night Live* sketch, "5-hour Empathy," dramatizes this point through a scene in a manicured living room, reminiscent of a thousand commercials you've seen before. Actor and comedian Beck Bennett looks sorrowfully at the camera as he reflects on recent protests and civil unrest. "It's clear that people are hurting," he says. "How can I help when I don't even understand what some people in this country go through every day? I wish there were an easy way."

Cue the solution. Kenan Thompson's voiceover states that there is indeed an easy way: the 5-hour Empathy drink. The bright little red bottle will give imbibers a "complete intimate understanding of years of systemic oppression and ever-present racism." "That's great," says Bennett's character before his expression shifts to fear with a tinge of shame. Grabbing a magazine, he leans back on the couch but continues to be chided by the voiceover until he pretends to drink the bottle so that he'll be left alone. Heidi Gardner, playing his partner, briefly makes an appearance and then slinks out of the room when she realizes what is going on.

Bennett tries to reason with the voiceover that there's no need for him to partake: they fired Uncle Ben, he says, alluding to Mars Incorporated's decision to change the name of its rice brand because of its racist origins. Eventually, Bennett jumps out the open window. "That makes sense," says Thompson's voiceover, representing the Black man who has seen this scene play out too many times before: the ally whose support is contingent upon convenience.

The SNL sketch is focused on race, a topic that Americans are even less comfortable talking about than gender. But the same lessons apply. The idea that one could fully understand any kind of –ism in five hours is laughable, but even the discomfort of that mere five hours is something that Bennett's character is willing to dive through a glass window to avoid. The sad fact is that, in the workplace, it is even easier for organizations to avoid—or at least deeply shortcut—the real work needed to understand the equity challenges their employees face. When organizations refuse the 5-hour Empathy drink, their time does not go to reading a magazine while leaning back on the couch. It goes to the many activities required to keep a workforce productive and paid, making it feel right and fair not to expend the time. Bennett's plea that he doesn't need the drink because "they fired Uncle Ben" mirrors the way that organizations point to a few—often mainly symbolic—DEI actions as evidence they've done enough and can now move on to other things.

For those who admit their organizations are too tentative when it comes to race but don't think they have many problems left when it comes to gender, I hope this book has made you think again. Conversations about gender inequity are only comfortable as long as they stay on the surface level. That's what's so convenient about the simplified "lean in" narrative: it's much easier to tell women to raise their hands than to tackle deep-seated, systemic, and cultural challenges. For all DEI issues, it's easier to think the problem comes down to a few bad actors than to realize how those with good intentions are complicit. It's easier to feel compassion for the roadblocks our colleagues face from afar than to take the 5-hour Empathy drink.

Most of all, it's easier to overfocus on a few discrete immediate solutions than to grapple with the complexity of the machine. If you've ever felt that solving an organizational problem is like a game of whack-a-mole—as soon as you think you've dealt with one thing, it emerges somewhere else—you're not alone. Workplaces are complex systems, with a dizzying amount of interdependent relationships, processes, policies, and cultural norms. You may think you've whacked one mole down, but there's a lot going on under the surface, and before you know it, the mole has popped up somewhere else. The more entrenched and complex a problem—as is the case with DEI— the more this is true.

I wish I could say that organizations could solve their equity gaps with the right set of trainings; revised hiring, performance evaluation, and promotion policies; a salary review; and a dashboard of quantifiable goals (for instance what percentage of women you'd like to see at each level). These are all necessary and important tactics, but alone they will always fall short. The saying is that you can't fight city hall, but the real challenge is that our brains will act against even changes we think we want if they require sustained shifts in mindset and behavior. This is not out of malice. Millennials talk about "adulting," and it's an easy meme to mock, but the truth is that most people, no matter their age or job, feel at least a little overwhelmed by how much they have to get done at work and in life, and how much the goal posts keep changing. Faced with the pressures of adult jobs and lives, our brains protect us. The ultimate mental auto-complete is the defense mechanism that keeps us from entertaining different ways of doing or thinking about things (unless it's something easy—a policy we can just send around over email) because we can't actually make more space in our brains, much less our inboxes or calendars.

Transcending Our Limits:
Four Pathological Thought Patterns

When we last left Cassandra, she was contemplating what a transcendent DEI strategic plan would look like. To *transcend* is to rise above limits, and I think of these limits as all the ways that human beings, with our minds on auto-complete and our schedules overwhelmed by #adulting, unintentionally get in the way of our own best intentions. Across this book, our characters have had to battle a number of what I'll call pathological thought patterns, or ways of thinking that are so deeply ingrained that we can't fully appreciate the harm that they cause.

At the fictional company we just visited, Kyle had to reconsider his view of assists rather than just points; Jack had to examine whether his approach to fast decisions actually slowed things down; and Debra had to look at whether the advice she'd been giving younger women about navigating the Goldilocks dilemma served them or the business well. In each case, we saw the characters start to overcome **the first pathological thought pattern: clinging to cherished beliefs**. If something is a cherished belief, it's because it has served us well in the past, and, to varying extents, may still serve us today. What makes cherished beliefs have such a strong grip on us is that they are not wholly bad, and revising them brings discomfort and new challenges to overcome. But our workplaces will not become more equitable unless both individuals and organizations are willing to admit that some things we've previously considered to be unequivocal truths are now sabotaging our intended outcomes.

The second pathological thought pattern is organizational impatience, or the tendency to overfocus on short-term gratification and easy wins. This is an understandable pathology. Most professionals find themselves staring down to-do lists that never end, a challenge that only intensifies as they climb the ladder: quick and easy wins allow us to file away problems as solved in our brains so that we can move on to the next item. As Jack reflects, much of corporate culture is built on a "fix it" mentality that values action over reflection. At many organizations, the incentive structures—both financial and in terms of informal recognition—are built around short-term gain. Plus, if our society's desire for instant gratification was not clear before, the COVID-19 pandemic has certainly illuminated it. These factors combined all lead to whack-a-mole actions intended to kill the problem but that merely injure it for a brief period, potentially to come back stronger or in a different form. They also lead to an unwillingness to commit sufficient organizational resources to initiatives, such as those related to DEI, where the bottom line benefit may be longer term and less certain. In our story, the problems created by organizational impatience were most obvious in Debra and Jack's hiring of Leland, as well as their decision to not seriously address their gender engagement and retention gap much sooner.

The third pathological thought pattern is underestimating just how persistent mental auto-completes, or unconscious biases, are in our culture. Our programming starts young, whether through differing representations of male versus female characters in children's books or unequal treatment of boys and girls in elementary school.[41] One University of Illinois study showed internalized gender bias taking root as early as age six.[42] The problems continue throughout childhood and into adulthood. Growing up and seeing more male politicians or doctors or CEOs on TV than females in the same professions has fed into our programming, whether or not we realized it. And while media representation has been improving across the last few decades, it remains far from perfect. Additionally, we continue to unconsciously absorb biased messages in our day-to-day lives: in the workplace, when we hear the Chads of the world getting recognized for their technical skills and the Haleys getting recognized for being the glue of the office, that's feeding into the programming behind our mental auto-completes. Many organizations now implement bias trainings, which are a necessary first step—so long as we recognize that an afternoon or two of training is no match for a lifetime of (continued) faulty programming.

The fourth pathological thought pattern is an identity-blind approach to DEI that avoids the fact that different marginalized groups face separate and distinct challenges. In our last chapter, we saw how eagerly the characters shifted from uneasy topics—such as hearing the negative experiences their staff faced based on gender, race, or sexual orientation—to discussing whether they had enough events for non-drinkers, a more comfortable topic. The organizational default is to discuss DEI in the broadest possible terms, focused on generic efforts toward kinder and more fair workplaces (i.e., creating better managers, more accessible social events, or greater transparency around promotion decisions). These are important initiatives, but do not come close to acknowledging the distinct challenges faced by historically marginalized groups. The same type and level of effort needed to help non-drinkers feel more included at work cannot be used to ensure that, for example, female or Black or transgender colleagues (not to mention those with intersecting identities) overcome systemic and cultural barriers. Furthermore, while these barriers overlap across different marginalized groups, they are also not identical. Many employers took a first step toward transcending this pathological thought pattern by making public statements in support of Black Lives Matter after the killings of Ahmaud Arbery, Breonna Taylor, and George Floyd in 2020. What remains to be seen is whether this willingness to discuss anti-Black racism will lead to sustained reflection and action, and whether employers are willing to speak and act boldly in response to the distinct challenges confronting a range of historically underrepresented and marginalized groups (i.e., women, LGBTQ, other racial and ethnic groups) without collapsing them back into one generic DEI umbrella.

Embracing Three Sets of Habits

We can transcend these pathological thought patterns by creating new habits, or learned behaviors that require practice at first, but that with time become involuntary.

First, to overcome all four pathological thought patterns, organizations must prioritize the full range of EQ competencies; this requires destigmatizing inner work. Since Daniel Goleman first published *Emotional Intelligence* in 1995, the titular phrase (and its shorthand EQ) has become a part of the popular lexicon. Goleman's definition includes both social competencies (i.e., empathy, influence, conflict management) and what I'll refer to here as inner competencies (self-awareness, emotional self-control).[43] As we've seen across this book, many EQ competencies are seen as "feminine," meaning men are more often excused from displaying them than women are, and women are forced to walk a complicated tightrope. That needs to change. But what also needs to change is that workplace discussions of EQ tend to be lopsided toward the social: after all, whether one can relate well to others or not has obvious implications if a salesperson can't figure out what will sway a potential customer or a supervisor alienates their entire team. By contrast, inner competencies are harder to tie directly to the bottom line.

Ultimately, getting past our pathological thought patterns requires inner work: it is our emotions that get in the way of any attempt to question cherished beliefs, and we cannot transcend mental auto-completes without self-awareness. Additionally, DEI work requires we engage in conversations that might be awkward and uncomfortable at first, and that requires not only empathy for others and relational skills, but also the ability to manage our own discomfort. Due to the rising popularity of mindfulness, some workplaces are starting to focus more on the inner competencies, recognizing that meditation can keep us from being unwittingly controlled by our thoughts and emotions. However, words like "self-awareness" and "mindfulness" still seem fuzzy to many, even though mindfulness is anything but: its practice ultimately results in mental discipline, by which we become aware of our unconscious reactions and auto-completes, allowing for more reasoned and deliberate thinking and decisions.[44]

The second set of habits that organizations need to cultivate is to continuously evolve their DEI practices with the same rigor that a business would use for a new product in a competitive market. One mistake that organizations often make is to invest upfront in rolling out new trainings, policies, or processes, and then to assume that "the boxes are now checked" and these can run on autopilot. This ignores the fact that any newly implemented practices (DEI or otherwise) might have unintended consequences—and need to be revised in much the same way that a product or service is adjusted based on how real-life consumers react after an initial launch. For instance, employers may implement performance evaluation policies designed to mitigate bias by focusing only on their employees' measurable, concrete outcomes, only to then find that these policies make things worse by not accounting for an unequal playing field to begin with. When rolling out new products, businesses value the voices of customers who have opted for competitor offerings instead, wanting to understand why. As employers evolve their DEI plans, they similarly need to create a habit of getting candid viewpoints from employees who will tell them what might be uncomfortable to hear. Furthermore, DEI needs are not static, but are likely to shift alongside what's going on in the world and within the organization itself. As Debra reflects, as her company faces more competition, that could lead to an increased belief that speed and proven methods are more important than taking the momentary pause to test assumptions or allow for other perspectives. A transcendent DEI strategic plan must examine, both upfront and continuously, how other shifts in the organization's strategic objectives and challenges will lead to future DEI roadblocks, as well as opportunities.

Third, organizations must be more expansive and explicit about the values that are guiding different decisions, as well as when those values need to be prioritized differently. Organizations that do not develop a habit of examining the criteria they use to make decisions end up in the trap of "the way we've always done things" (or, the favorite phrase of Debra and Jack, "this is just how business works"). For some decisions, speed may matter more than for other decisions. Different decisions may require a different place on the spectrum of optimizing for short-term versus long-term revenues. Talking about criteria more explicitly can help organizations be honest with themselves about their DEI commitment; for example, what other initiatives they're willing to delay or stop to adequately resource DEI. At the end of the day, we'll need to see decision-making criteria that favors DEI goals coming from the top: Boards and investors that are willing to see, for example, 20% growth while meeting certain DEI goals as more desirable than 30% while not; shareholders that demand not only diverse representation on executive teams, but to see retention rates as well; performance reviews and compensation/promotion decisions that expect specific, DEI-advancing behaviors by managers and staff, and that hold the line on not looking the other way or making excuses for an employee or leader who is otherwise well-liked or brings in the money.

Why We Need Fiction

My goal with *Beyond Leaning In* was to help readers put themselves in the shoes of multiple, disparate characters, all with the intention of examining how they're interconnected and what barriers are getting in their way. Studies show that fiction can help build empathy, the first step for any individual or organization's DEI journey.[45] We tend to think of empathy as related to understanding individuals better, but I hope this book helps us empathize with the challenge of organizations too.

The next step is to make the shift from empathy to action. Fiction can be used for another purpose too: to imagine possible futures that might previously have been inconceivable. That's why organizations like Boeing, Nike, Lowe's and others have hired science fiction writers to support future visioning and strategic planning.[46] Unlocking the imagination allows us to envision bold and creative possibilities that our minds might not have otherwise entertained.

When it seems inconceivable to solve today's problems and to make bigger changes than feels realistic, the tools that speculative fiction writers and other purveyors of the imaginative arts use can help pave the way.

If you'd like to learn more about next steps for using the imaginative arts to create more equitable workplaces—that transcend unproductive thought patterns and build the new habits we need—please visit www.beyondleaningin.com

On my website, you'll also find information about:

- The *Beyond Leaning In* podcast , where you can learn more about the research that informed this book and listen to the reactions of readers across genders and generations
- Dozens of comics I've drawn based on scenes in this book (a few representative examples are included in the pages that follow)
- Presentations and workshops
- Resources for educators

Dear Reader,

I need your help. For independent authors like myself, it's not easy to get the word out compared to books that have the backing and resources of traditional publishers. The success of *Beyond Leaning In* will rely on thoughtful and honest endorsements from people who enjoyed reading it and want to encourage others to do the same.

I have two main hopes for this novel. First, to help as many women as possible make sense of their own experiences. Second, to inspire a new type of dialogue among professionals across genders and generations.

To fulfill these hopes, I'd be grateful for your help with any or all of the below:

- Reviewing this book online—wherever you bought it, or at Goodreads.
- Talking about it on social media, or sending a personal note to three friends.
- Bringing this book to your workplace, professional group, educational institution, or book club. I've included questions on the next page to facilitate group discussion, and my website includes information about workshops for employers, as well as a free in-depth instructional guide for college and university faculty.

Sign up for my mailing list via the QR code below or at www.melanieho.com/reader for updates on new content and a free reader's guide to go deeper with the major lessons in this book. Each month, I randomly select one subscriber for a free 30-minute virtual coaching or consultation session for themselves or a friend.

I look forward to hearing from many of you! Ideas? Questions? Feel free to contact me on social media or at www.melanieho.com.

Warm regards,
Melanie

Reflection and Discussion Questions

Use these questions as a starting point for journaling about your experience reading *Beyond Leaning In* and/or for discussing the book with fellow readers, whether informally or through book clubs and discussion groups.

1. Were there particular scenes or characters that resonated most with you, and why?
2. What is one new concept that you learned about from reading this book? How is that concept relevant to your personal or professional life?
3. Did reading this book change your mind about anything or make you think differently about a previous belief or habit?
4. What is one thing that you will do differently after reading this book? How will you hold yourself accountable for doing that thing differently?
5. Who in your personal and/or professional life would you like to discuss or debate topics covered in this book with, and why? What specific topics do you think would make for a productive discussion with these individuals?

For more supplementary materials,
please visit www.beyondleaningin.com

Selected Comics

Visit www.melanieho.com or @melanieho13 on Instagram for the complete selection of the author's comics based on scenes and concepts in *Beyond Leaning In*.

Unequal Penalty

"BET WITH" vs. "PROVE IT AGAIN"

"Bet With" vs. "Prove it Again"

Are Men Told to Listen?

The Cupcake Trap

What Leaders Say vs. What Women Hear

Mother-Daughter Movie Night

THE GOLDILOCKS DILEMMA

The Goldilocks Dilema

Endnotes

1. Generational differences are a running theme throughout this book. Discussions of generations tend to solicit enthusiasm from some and groans from others. It can certainly be foolhardy to make sweeping generalizations about people based on the years they were born. But it would be equally foolhardy to think that how people relate to one another and to organizations isn't influenced by what's going on around them at certain stages of their growth and development. To that end, this book was heavily informed by Neil Howe and William Strauss's extensive research on generational cycles, as well as Joan C. Williams and Rachel Dempsey's *What Works for Women at Work*, which is written by a mother-daughter duo and adeptly incorporates a cross-generational perspective to examine many of the themes visited throughout this book. For more information: Williams, J.C. & Dempsey, R. (2014). *What works for women at work: Four patterns working women need to know.* NYU Press; Howe, N. & Strauss, W. (1992). *Generations: The history of America's future, 1584–2069.* Quill; Howe, N. & Strauss, W. (2009). *Millennials rising: The next great generation.* Vintage.

2. A few books that I've found useful on the importance of organizational culture include: Coyle, D. (2018). *The culture code: The secrets of highly successful groups.* Bantam; Collins, J. (2001). *Good to great.* Harper Business; Hsieh, T. (2013). *Delivering happiness: A path to profits, passion, and purpose* (Reprint edition). Grand Central Publishing.

3. This is not meant to undermine the harm that destructive leaders cause. Organizations should have a no-tolerance approach to bullies. Period. However, poor leaders shouldn't be excused just because they're nice people. This applies to both men and women, but we'll see across this book the many ways that men, such as Leland, get away with leadership deficiencies in ways that women do not. In leadership, being a "nice guy" compensates for a lot of sins that being a "nice gal" does not—and the bar for what it takes to be considered a nice guy tends to also be much lower. Furthermore, as Amber contemplates, it's not always the most destructive personalities that cause the most long-term harm. For more on the impact of absentee leaders, see Gregory, S. (2018, March 30). The most common type of incompetent leader. *Harvard Business Review*. Retrieved from https://hbr.org/2018/03/the-most-common-type-of-incompetent-leader

4. Lombrozo, T. (2017, May 22). Think your credentials are ignored because you're a woman? It could be. *NPR*. Retrieved from http://www.npr.org/sections/13.7/2017/05/22/529391023/think-your-credentials-are-ignored-because-youre-a-woman-it-could-be

5. Madden, J.S. (2012, January 1). Performance-support bias and the gender pay gap among stockbrokers. *PSC Working Paper Series*. Retrieved from https://repository.upenn.edu/psc_working_papers/35

6. Bohnet, I. (2017, October 3). Tackling the 'thin file' that can prevent a promotion. *The New York Times*. Retrieved from https://www.nytimes.com/2017/10/03/business/women-minority-promotion.html

7. In *Thinking, Fast and Slow*, Daniel Kahneman explains how our brains rely on mental shortcuts—what I'm calling auto-completes—for the majority of the mental processing required of us in day-to-day life. As Kahneman notes, only about 2% of our thinking is slow, deliberate, labored, and conscious. The main operating

system in our brain is actually a fast one, allowing us to draw conclusions based on small amounts of data, so quickly and automatically that we don't know what we're doing. When you drive a car on an empty road, or know what 2+2 is without having to do math in your head, see danger as you're crossing the street and pull a child out of the way, or change your approach to a meeting because you see anger on your boss's face, your brain is taking shortcuts. These shortcuts conserve our mental capacity for the activities that really need slower and more involved thinking, like doing your taxes, parking in a narrow space, or developing a complex argument. We couldn't actually function in the world without these shortcuts that our brains take based on past experiences and intuition. However, like the auto-completes on our phones, the shorcuts in our head can be wrong and even pernicious. For more information: Kahneman, D. (2011). *Thinking, Fast and Slow*. Farrar, Straus, and Giroux.

8. There have been particularly interesting analyses of how women versus men are endorsed in analyses of letters of recommendation. Flaherty, C. (2018, June 19.) Help that hurts women. *Inside Higher Ed*. Retrieved from https://www.insidehighered.com/news/2018/06/19/study-finds-recommendation-letters-inadvertently-signal-doubt-about-female

9. See chapter one in Tulshyan, R. (2015). *The diversity advantage: Fixing gender inequality in the workplace*. Forbes Media. Tulvshan discusses research showing that women are less likely to respond to job listings with words considered more male, like "determined," "assertive," "analytical," and "independent." Meanwhile, women are more attracted to job descriptions with words like "dedicated," "conscientious," and "sociable." Men, by contrast, apply either way.

10. Pells, R. (2017, November 13). Male scientists more likely to share work with other men, study finds. *Times Higher Education*. Retrieved from https://www.timeshighereducation.com/news/male-scientists-more-likely-share-work-other-men-study-finds

11. Internalized bias often leads to what psychologists call stereotype threat, where one performs less well at a specific task due to
awareness that one is in a group that might be considered weaker
at that task due to stereotypes. For example, one study showed
that female performance on a math test is impacted by whether
or not the woman is told that men usually do better on that particular test. When women hear that they aren't likely to do as
well on the test, they perform substantially worse than equally
qualified men. By contrast, there is no difference when women
are told that the test does not produce any differences. For more
information: Spencer, S.J., Steele, C.M., & Quinn, D.M. (1999,
January). Stereotype threat and women's math performance. *Journal of Experimental Social Psychology*. Retrieved from http://www.
sciencedirect.com/science/article/pii/S0022103198913737

12. For example, women often get vague feedback ("Jill, your replies
to partners about client matters are often not on point"), rather
than objective feedback ("Jim, you have missed important opportunities to provide clear and concise information, such as X. I have
some thoughts on how you could prevent that from happening
again, such as Y"). For more information: Cecchi-Dimeglio, P.
(2017, April 12). How gender bias corrupts performance reviews,
and what to do about it. *Harvard Business Review*. Retrieved from:
https://hbr.org/2017/04/how-gender-bias-corrupts-performance-re-
views-and-what-to-do-about-it. Notably, the difference in type of
feedback that males versus females receive begins early. As Pat
Heim, Tammy Hughes, and Susan K. Golant discuss in *Hardball
for Women*, in elementary school, boys get more support in terms
of improving their problem-solving skills, with teachers forcing
boys to work out problems they don't understand but simply telling girls what to do, especially in subjects like math and science,
where the teachers do not expect the girls to be as strong. See:
Heim, P., Hughes, T, & Golant, S.K. (2015). *Hardball for women:
winning at the game of business* (3rd ed.). Plume.

13. See chapter six in Heim, P., Hughes, T., & Golant, S.K. (2015). *Hardball for women: winning at the game of business* (3rd ed.). Plume.

14. In one University of Washington study, when asked to name classmates they considered strong in understanding the classroom material, men consistently rated men much higher than women—even when the study controlled for higher levels of male participation. Female students who were equally outspoken, with equally high grades, received far less recognition from their male peers. For more information: Yong, E. (2016, February 16). XY bias: How male biology students see their female peers. *The Atlantic*. Retrieved from https://www.theatlantic.com/science/archive/2016/02/male-biology-students-underestimate-their-female-peers/462924/

15. For a discussion of benevolent sexism, see chapter one in Kramer, A.S. & Harris, A.B. (2016). *Breaking through bias: Communication techniques for women to succeed at work*. Bibliomotion, Inc.

16. The term "responsibility magnet" is described in chapter ten in Heim, P., Hughes, T., & Golant, S.K. (2015). *Hardball for women: winning at the game of business* (3rd ed.). Plume.

17. The criticism that women face when providing constructive feedback is described in Sheppard, L. & Aquino, K. (2017, August 4). Why women get criticized for being candid at work. *The Atlantic*. Retrieved from https://www.theatlantic.com/business/archive/2017/08/women-work-queen-bee/535797/

18. The most well-known example of this experiment was conducted by Francis Flynn and Cameron Anderson, then at Columbia University and New York University, who provided business school students with a case study about a female entrepreneur named Heidi Roizen. Half the students received a version of the case with "Heidi Roizen" renamed as "Howard Roizen" and different pronouns. Students were then asked to rate "Roizen"

along several dimensions, and were much harsher on Heidi. See chapter three in Sandberg, S. (2013). *Lean in: Women, work, and the will to lead.* Knopf.

19. See chapter fifteen of Williams, J.C. & Dempsey, R. (2014). *What works for women at work: Four patterns working women need to know.* NYU Press.

20. For an extensive discussion of the tightrope phenomenon, see Part II in Williams, J.C. & Dempsey, R. (2014). *What works for women at work: Four patterns working women need to know.* NYU Press.

21. The assertive style is often referred to as "agentic." For one examination of agentic versus communal traits, see: Eagly, A.H. & Carli, L.L. (2007). *Through the labyrinth: The truth about how women become leaders.* Harvard Business Review Press.

22. For an in-depth discussion of the "feminine values" that are especially important in 21st century leadership, see Gerzema, J. & D'Antonio, M. (2013). *The Athena doctrine: How women (and the men who think like them) will rule the future.* Jossey-Bass.

23. Discussing that some traits are "stereotypically feminine" versus "stereotypically masculine" inevitably leads to the question of whether and in what ways men and women might be wired differently from birth. For the purposes of this book's discussion, where you stand on the nature versus nurture debate does not matter. Across the last few chapters, we've looked at what are often seen as feminine traits: empathy, listening, collaboration. These are characteristics that have great benefit to organizations but that are often devalued in the workplace because they are associated more with women than with men. Whether or not biology plays a role, they are also traits that women are socialized to care about from a young age, meaning women are more likely to be practiced at these activities by the time they get into the workplace, only to find that they need to suppress them to seem more like

men. While women do not have a monopoly on these skills—and not all women have them—they are often honed through the way women are socialized. It's also notable that the nature versus nurture debate is itself a gendered one. Research has found that women are more likely to see gender differences as based on societal expectations, whereas more men believe the differences are biological. See: Parker, K., Horowitz, J.M., & Stepler, R. (2017, December 5). On gender differences, no consensus on nature versus nurture. *Pew Research Center.* Retrieved from https://www.pewsocialtrends.org/2017/12/05/on-gender-differences-no-consensus-on-nature-vs-nurture/

24. Debra's story about needing to mute her "social sense" was inspired by Sally Helgesen and Julie Johnson's *The Female Vision: Women's Real Power at Work*, which argues that the way that women are discouraged from sharing—and leveraging—what they notice interpersonally is a detriment to business outcomes and leads women to feel disengaged as their skills are not appreciated or utilized. For more information: Helgesen, S. & Johnson, J. (2010). *The female vision: women's real power at work.* Berrett-Koehler Publishers.

25. The challenge that women face as being dependable "number twos" who never reach the top position is well-articulated in this article: Chira, S. (2017, July 21). Why women aren't C.E.O.s, according to women who almost were. *The New York Times.* Retrieved from https://www.nytimes.com/2017/07/21/sunday-review/women-ceos-glass-ceiling.html

26. For more information: Khazan, O. (2017, January 6). Women know when negotiation isn't worth it. *The Atlantic.* Retrieved from https://www.theatlantic.com/business/archive/2017/01/women-negotiating/512174/; Artz, B., Goodall, A. & Oswald, A.J. (2018, June 25). Research: Women ask for raises as often as men, but are less likely to get them. *Harvard Business Review.* Retrieved from

https://hbr.org/2018/06/research-women-ask-for-raises-as-often-as-men-but-are-less-likely-to-get-them; Bowles, H.R., Babcock, L., & Lai, L. (2007). Social incentives for gender differences in the propensity to initiate negotiations: Sometimes it does hurt to ask. *Organizational Behavior and Human Decision Processes*, 103(1), 84–103.

27. For an extensive discussion of the prove-it-again phenomenon, see Part I in Williams, J.C. & Dempsey, R. (2014). *What works for women at work: Four patterns working women need to know.* NYU Press.

28. Peter, L.J. & Hull, R. (2011). *The Peter principle: Why things always go wrong.* Harper Business.

29. The bulletin board test is discussed in Christensen, C.M., Allworth, J. & Dillon, K. (2012). *How will you measure your life?* Harper Business.

30. For more on the challenges faced by working parents and the need to get beyond traditional gender roles in parenting, see Slaughter, A.M. (2015). *Unfinished business: Women men work family.* Random House. The phrase "lead parent" also gained attention in an *Atlantic* article by Anne-Marie Slaughter's husband, Andrew Moravcsik, describing his role as primary caregiver. Moravcsik, A. (2015, October). Why I put my wife's career first. *The Atlantic.* Retrieved from https://www.theatlantic.com/magazine/archive/2015/10/why-i-put-my-wifes-career-first/403240/

31. Budig, M.J. (2014, September 4). The fatherhood bonus and the motherhood penalty: Parenthood and the gender gap in pay. *Third Way.* Retrieved from https://www.thirdway.org/report/the-fatherhood-bonus-and-the-motherhood-penalty-parenthood-and-the-gender-gap-in-pay

32. As a PricewaterhouseCoopers 2015 study revealed, millennial women entered the workforce aware of the challenges they'll face

and then became even more cognizant over time. The study found 49% of millennial women at the entry level believing they can rise to the senior-most ranks with their current employees, compared to 71% of men, but equally concerning was the fact that this number dropped to 39% for millennial women who were more established in their careers. Simply put, as women advance the ladder, they became even more aware of the barriers they faced in getting to the next rung. Compared to their entry-level counterparts, millennial women with more tenure in the workforce also saw their employers as more biased at attracting employees (20% vs. 31%), promoting from within (36% vs. 52%), developing employees (23% vs. 38%), and retaining employees (26% vs. 39%). PricewaterhouseCoopers. (2015). The female millennial: A new era of talent. Retrieved from https://www.pwc.com/jg/en/publications/the-female-millennial-a-new-era-of-talent.html

33. In *Hardball for women: Winning at the game of business*, authors Pat Helm, Tammy Hughes, and Susan K. Golant talk about how the social codes embedded in the games boys and girls play growing up connect to their differing behavior in later life at work. One notable difference they discuss is the "follow the captain" mentality of organized sports and how it influences male behavior later in the workplace. For more information, see chapter three in Heim, P., Hughes, T., & Golant, S.K. (2015). *Hardball for women: Winning at the game of business* (3rd ed.). Plume.

34. This observation is from chapter two in Evans, G. (2001). *Play like a man, win like a woman: What men know about success that women need to learn.* Currency.

35. Johnson, S.K., Hekman, D.R., & Chan, E.T. (2016, April 26). If there's only one woman in your candidate pool, there's statistically no chance she'll be hired. *Harvard Business Review*. Retrieved from https://hbr.org/2016/04/if-theres-only-one-woman-in-your-candidate-pool-theres-statistically-no-chance-shell-be-hired

36. Jack's revelations to Amber about white male culture are from *Four Days to Change*, by Michael Welp and Bill Proudman. Based on their work as co-founders of a company called White Men as Full Diversity Partners, the book tells the story of four white men who spend four days together understanding what it means to be a white male, with the ultimate goal of being able to advance broader DEI goals. The group discusses the strongest tenets of white male culture in the United States, including rugged individualism, a low tolerance of uncertainty, action over reflection, rationality over emotion, the idea that time is linear and future focused, and status and rank over connection. A key teaching point is that the strengths of white male culture—such as confidence or being analytical—are vulnerable to being overused, both by individuals and by organizations. For more information: Welp, M. & Proudman, B. (2016). *Four days to change: 12 radical habits to overcome bias and thrive in a diverse world.* EqualVoice.

37. Prive, T. (2020, October 30). Where does management stop and leadership start? *Inc.* Retrieved from https://www.inc.com/tanya-prive/where-does-management-stops-leadership-start.html

38. The blind audition in orchestras has been touted as a way to achieve discretion elimination, with employers and researchers looking at how to translate the methodology into other arenas. Others worry that it can be taken too far; for example, one music critic has noted that, while blind auditions diversified orchestras from a gender perspective, they are counterproductive for achieving racial diversity. For a few perspectives of the blind audition: Miller, C.C. (2016, February 25). Is blind hiring the best hiring? *The New York Times Magazine.* Retrieved from https://www.nytimes.com/2016/02/28/magazine/is-blind-hiring-the-best-hiring.html; Rice, C. (2013, October 14). How blind auditions help orchestras to eliminate gender bias. *The Guardian.* Retrieved from https://www.theguardian.com/women-in-leadership/2013/

oct/14/blind-auditions-orchestras-gender-bias; Anthony, T. (2020, July 16). To make orchestras more diverse, end blind auditions. *The New York Times.* Retrieved from https://www.nytimes.com/2020/07/16/arts/music/blind-auditions-orchestras-race.html

39. This was inspired by the unique interview process used at Auttomattic, the company behind WordPress. For more information, see: Mullenweg, M. (2014, April). The CEO of Automattic on holding 'auditions' to build a strong team. *Harvard Business Review.* Retrieved from https://hbr.org/2014/04/the-ceo-of-automattic-on-holding-auditions-to-build-a-strong-team

40. Johnson, S.K. & Hekman, D.R. (2016, March 23). Women and minorities are penalized for promoting diversity. *Harvard Business Review.* Retrieved from https://hbr.org/2016/03/women-and-minorities-are-penalized-for-promoting-diversity

41. Research shows that, as early as elementary school, when girls call out an answer, they're told to raise their hands and are seen as being bossy or show-offs. Boys who do it? They are seen as confident. In children's books, the majority of characters are men. Male characters appear more in illustrations. The female characters are more likely to be nurturers, to be doing indoor activities, and to either have no job or stereotypical ones. The male characters are the leaders, telling female characters what to do. From an early age, we send messages to boys and girls about gender and leadership, even without realizing it. See chapters two and six of Heim, P., Hughes, T., & Golant, S.K. (2015). *Hardball for women: Winning at the game of business* (3rd ed.). Plume.

42. Yong, E. (2017, January 26). 6-year-old girls already have gendered beliefs about intelligence. *The Atlantic.* Retrieved from https://www.theatlantic.com/science/archive/2017/01/six-year-old-girls-already-have-gendered-beliefs-about-intelligence/514340/

43. For a good overview of the varied domains and competencies within Goleman's definition of emotional intelligence, see: Goleman, D. & Boyatzis, R.E. (2017, February 6). Emotional intelligence has 12 elements. Which do you need to work on? *Harvard Business Review*. Retrieved from https://hbr.org/2017/02/emotional-intelligence-has-12-elements-which-do-you-need-to-work-on

44. For a great skeptic's introduction to mindfulness, see Harris, D. (2019). *10% happier: How I tamed the voice in my head, reduced stress without losing my edge, and found self-help that actually works—a true story* (Reprint edition). Dey Street Books. For a discussion of the connection between mindfulness and emotional intelligence, and how mindfulness allows us to upgrade our internal operating systems, see Mager, D. (2019, March 22). Mindfulness and emotional intelligence. *Psychology Today*. Retrieved from https://www.psychologytoday.com/us/blog/some-assembly-required/201903/mindfulness-and-emotional-intelligence

45. Schmidt, M. (2020, August 28). How reading fiction increases empathy and encourages understanding. *Discover Magazine*. Retrieved from https://www.discovermagazine.com/mind/how-reading-fiction-increases-empathy-and-encourages-understanding

46. For an excellent and detailed account of how Lowe's in particular leveraged science fiction writers and comic book artists, see Ramsoy, T.Z., Furr, N. & Nell, K. (2018). *Leading transformation: how to take charge of your company's future*. Harvard Business Review Press. Also see Merchant, B. Nike and Boeing are paying sci-fi writers to predict their futures. *OneZero*. Retrieved from https://onezero.medium.com/nike-and-boeing-are-paying-sci-fi-writers-to-predict-their-futures-fdc4b6165fa4

Acknowledgments

Countless women shared their stories with me across the last decade: on airplanes and in conference hallways, at networking receptions and through online discussion boards, over coffee and cocktails, via phone or videoconference. *Beyond Leaning In* was inspired by their passion and commitment to making better workplaces, along with their candor about the challenges that professional women face and why these feel so hard to overcome.

I started research for this book in 2012 and then began writing the stories of Debra, Jack, and Cassandra during National Novel Writing Month in 2017. Thank you to the NaNoWriMo organizers and community for providing such a great forum for aspiring novelists—especially those with busy day jobs—to build early momentum. My gratitude to book coach Arielle Eckstut for suggesting that I participate in NaNoWriMo, identifying the best parts of what I'd scribbled during that month to build the final project around, and providing expert guidance and cheerleading at key points since. The thoughtful critique that she and David Sterry provided on my first few pages was instrumental for helping me find this book's style. I'm grateful to have attended a weekend writing retreat and taken several online workshops led by Wendy Rohm, whose unique meditation exercises helped me identify key character motivations, and whose insights and edits on early chapters helped me keep going. David Attis, Diane Kelleher, Julianne Helinek, Liz Rothenberg, Megan Adams, and Melanie Bowen were wonderful beta readers and brainstorming partners, providing encouragement while asking the difficult questions. Special thanks to Carla Hickman for her thoughtful advice and support throughout this book's journey, including frequently exchanging ideas about the research on gender and indulging me in discussing the characters as if they were real.

Navigating the process of bringing *Beyond Leaning In* to life was made enjoyable due to the talents of a fantastic group of professionals. Thank you to cover designer Laura Duffy; interior designer Domini Dragoone; editors Hugh Barker and Susan Gaigher; and StudioPod producers Katie Sunku Wood, Julian Lewis, and TJ Bonaventura. I owe much gratitude to Sarah Moore Ferris for helping create workshops and materials to bring the book's concepts to life in classrooms and workplaces. This book is largely about breaking unproductive thought patterns, and I'd be remiss if I didn't thank my therapist Adam, who helped me examine mine and garner the courage to make a career leap; otherwise, this book might still be 80% done and sitting unfinished on my laptop. By the time *Beyond Leaning In* finds its way to your real or virtual bookshelf, dozens of others will no doubt have played a critical role in its launch; I wish I had a time machine so that I could acknowledge these folks now, but instead will settle for expressing my gratitude in advance.

I am lucky to have been surrounded by incredible friends, mentors, and colleagues across my life. My interest in the different forms and purposes of the novel was cultivated during my time as an undergraduate and doctoral student in the UCLA English Department, where I learned from a truly extraordinary set of fellow students and faculty. I am likewise grateful to my former colleagues at the Advisory Board Company and EAB Global for their force of insight and generosity of spirit. Finally, thanks to my mother Ellen Ho, my brother Steven Ho, my sister-in-law Nina Petronzio, and my nephews Oliver and Jonathan Ho (the twinjas) for their love and support. This book is dedicated to the memory of my father, Kie Ho, who explained the word feminism to me when I was a little girl, modeled his dedication to leadership and to the written word, and always encouraged me to do things differently.

About the Author

Melanie Ho is the founder of Strategic Imagination, a firm dedicated to drawing on the unique power of the imaginative arts to help organizations achieve transformational change. She believes that the problems facing our society, including persistent equity gaps, won't be solved unless we find new ways of getting past our trapped mindsets—and that the tools of fiction, theatre, comics, and other imaginative arts are a critical part of the solution. She has worked with organizations ranging from small start-ups to multi-billion-dollar global conglomerates to leading universities.

Across the past twenty years, Melanie has delivered over a thousand presentations to a wide range of audience sizes and types. Her experience includes facilitating retreats for chief executives; addressing 1000+ person audiences; and appearing on NPR, CBS, and NBC. She speaks on a variety of topics, including women in leadership;

diversity, equity, and inclusion; the future of education; and the use of creativity and the arts in business.

Melanie previously served as a senior vice president at EAB Global (formerly part of the Advisory Board Company), an education research, technology, and services firm headquartered in Washington, DC. She led a team of over a hundred researchers that provided strategic, operational, and change management advice to more than 1500 educational institutions worldwide. As one of EAB's primary spokespeople, Melanie has presented to campus leadership teams at dozens of universities including Harvard, Columbia, Cornell, Georgetown, NYU, UCLA, UC Berkeley, McGill, Rutgers, Case Western, Auburn, and Penn State.

Prior to her twelve years at EAB, Melanie taught literature, writing, and leadership courses at UCLA while earning her Ph.D. in English. She received UCLA's Distinguished Teaching Award for her innovative approaches to pedagogy, including incorporating problem-based learning and the use of technology into the literature curriculum. Her research focused on the relationship of early 20th century American novels to education and self-help as a growing set of professionals and managers turned to books to help them navigate the challenges of modern life.

To learn more about Melanie, visit www.melanieho.com

Made in the USA
Middletown, DE
04 March 2023

26035715R00210